WOMEN

AT SEA IN THE

AGE OF SAIL

DONAL BAIRD

NIMBUS

PUBLISHING

Nimbus Publishing Limited
PO Box 9166
Halifax, NS B3K 5M8
(902) 455-4286

Cover and book design: Margaret Issenman
Printed and bound in Canada

Canadian Cataloguing in Publication Data

Baird, Donal M.
Women at sea in the age of sail

Includes bibliographical references and index.
ISBN 1-55109-267-0

1. Women merchant mariners—History—19th century. 2. Seafaring life. I. Title.

VK26.B35 2001 387'.0082'09 C2001-900320-X

Canadä The Canada Council | Le Conseil des Arts
        for the Arts | du Canada

We acknowledge the financial support of the Government of Canada through the Book Publishing Industry Development Program (BPIDP) and the Canada Council for our publishing activities.

DEDICATION

TO ALL THOSE UNDERSTANDING AND COURAGEOUS WOMEN WHO ACCEPTED
AND ADAPTED TO THE DETERMINATION OF THEIR MEN TO GO TO SEA,
AND TO THOSE WHO EVENTUALLY BROKE THE BARRIERS
TO SAILORING CAREERS OF THEIR OWN.

Preface

In the nineteenth century, many women chose to share with their husbands the frequent dangers and hardships of life aboard the square-rigged sailing ship. These women rarely showed any hope or ambition of being part of a ship's working crew—the conventions of Victorian femininity and the customs of the day made such career goals unrealistic. Rather, they went aboard largely to pursue family life and to make a home. They bore children at sea without doctors or midwives, and faced seasickness, loneliness, storms, mutiny, and shipwreck alongside their male shipmates. Some learned to navigate and, on occasion, a captain's wife found herself taking command of the ship and bringing the crew to port.

In writing this book, I have made extensive use of the diaries and letters of women mostly from Nova Scotia and New Brunswick, two Canadian provinces that produced an exceptional number of ocean-going vessels and sailors to sail them. By no means all excitement and adventure, the writings of these Maritime women establish the atmosphere and recount the day-to-day happenings of life lived on that frightening yet fascinating part of the Earth: the sea. The conclusion is that women, like men, sometimes chose to live life under sail and for the most part met its challenges with courage and forbearance. Unlike the stories and histories of men at sea, which have many times been told, the stories of women at sea in the nineteenth century have only begun to be written and shared. I would like to express my gratitude to those who have made this modest contribution to such a history possible: the many professionals and volunteers in archives, museums, and libraries who assisted in gathering archival material, and the descendants of these seafarers who kindly shared their family histories with me.

Contents

INTRODUCTION: EARLIER TIMES

Early nineteenth-century historical and fictional accounts of life at sea portray a rough world of men where brutality and violence are commonplace and casualty rates high. The most famous and influential of the histories is Richard Dana's *Two Years Before the Mast* (1840), which portrays the wretched conditions under which seamen worked in the first half of the nineteenth century. Dana voyaged in 1847 around Cape Horn to California under the command of a brutal captain, experiencing for himself the rough life and cruelty routinely suffered by crew. Popular fiction paints a similar picture of the nineteenth century sea life: a man's world with hard-swearing bully mates swinging belaying pins at cringing sailors, violent storms, dreadful food, and mutiny. Robert Louis Stevenson's *Treasure Island* and Alexander Laing's *Seawitch* are good examples.

But the renowned American writer of sea stories Jack London reveals another side of this hardy, masculine world, one that begins to take shape around the middle of the nineteenth century as women take to sea in increasing numbers. In *The Mutiny of Elsinore* (1914), when London's hero sets sail in a windjammer, it would seem merely a literary device that places the elderly Captain West's attractive daughter Margaret aboard to care for her father and keep him company. But London had been to sea himself, so he knew that it was common for shipmasters to be accompanied by their wives and sometimes their children, and that when wives tired of the sea they were often replaced by older daughters.

London's novel attests to the minor but significant female presence that had become part of life at sea by mid-century, at which time shipmasters were increasingly allowed, even encouraged, to have their wives accompany them on sea voyages. These women had a significant effect on the character of shipboard life, which as the century progressed was less and less marked by the cruelty that Dana describes, and more and more marked by the presence of women as London depicts.

The women in these pages come from the three major sea-faring cultures in nineteenth-century ocean trade: Britain, the United States, and British North America (renamed the Dominion of Canada in 1867). The role of the "Bluenosers" in particular was significant, for out of the small ports of Nova Scotia and New Brunswick there came large numbers of ships, seamen, and captains. There were no female captains and regulations referred to captains only in the masculine. An official break in the assumption that taking ships to sea was entirely a man's job did not come until 1939, when the Canadian Board of Trade amended its regulations to eliminate references to licensed masters in the masculine. Such changes were needed as women began to show an interest in and more actively pursue careers at sea. In that year, Molly Kool, a determined New Brunswick coastal mate, passed her master mariner's examinations. At the time, Kool was reported to be the first female master mariner in North America and the second in the world.

Although it was not entirely in the role of homemaker that women acted before 1939, it had been unthinkable for them to hope for professional seafaring

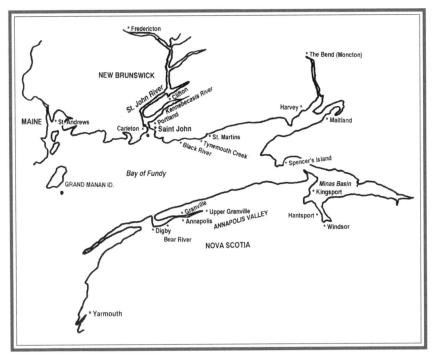

Canada's East Coast Bay of Fundy, whose adjacent New Brunswick and Nova Scotia shores produced prodigious numbers of wooden sailing ships for captains, their wives, and their children to sail aboard in the nineteenth century.

careers of their own. Women were not legally "persons" until the 1880s and did not gain the right to vote until 1918 in Canada and 1920 in the United States. Advances made by women around the turn of the century in fields of work open traditionally only to men, such as medicine, science, and law, contributed to improved perceptions of women's intellectual capabilities. Recognizing and assigning value to women's contributions in the running of a ship was, however, something the world was apparently not ready to do.

But from early in the nineteenth century, widespread resistance to women's participation in sea life did not prevent some women from finding their way onto the seas in various capacities. To serve in naval and merchant ships, they occasionally disguised themselves as men. They sailed alongside men as pirates and worked for men as prostitutes in the free-wheeling eighteenth century. By the mid-nineteenth, a more moral time, they served also as stewardesses and as jacks-of-all-trades on family-operated coastal vessels. They traveled as missionaries and they traveled as passengers.

Women occasionally disguised themselves as men in order to serve as sailors, servants, and marines, notably in the British Royal Navy. During the Napoleonic Wars in the early nineteenth century, when the Royal Navy was reduced to pressing men into service against their will, a number of women passed as sailors and marines, sometimes for years. The most celebrated was Mary Lacy, alias William Chandler, a runaway servant girl who apprenticed to a warship's carpenter, serving seven years on warships and five as a shipwright in a naval dockyard. Lacy's identity was not discovered (at least by official accounts) until she formally retired and was awarded a pension by the Admiralty.

Women went to sea in other navies too. When the French ship-of-the-line *Achille* blew up at the Battle of Aboukir Bay, two of the French seamen fished from the water by the British were discovered to be women, one having lost her clothes. In the War of 1812, when U.S.S. *Constitution* fought H.M.S. *Guerriére*, one of the marines aboard the American ship was Lucy Brewer. She had sailed with them in disguise in order to escape working in a brothel. In the peace after the Napoleonic Wars, the practice of permitting women onto Royal Navy vessels, a consideration previously at the captain's discretion, was assumed by the Admiralty and curbed substantially. Women gradually disappeared from naval vessels, not to reappear as working crew until the mid-twentieth century.

A century and a half before women took a place alongside men to work at sea without drawing much notice or comment, they roamed the seas as pirates. Hsi Chi Sing Yi was admiral of several squadrons of her own pirate vessels in the China seas around 1800. The most famous of the women pirates was the British pair Ann Bonny and Mary Read. A fellow pirate was the common-law husband of Ann Bonny, and Mary Read was raised as a boy and went to sea so disguised. Mary had been both a soldier and a seaman, leading an exciting career at sea and eventually a life ashore that included marriage. After being widowed, Mary Read became a pirate captain and the two women worked together out of Port Royal, Jamaica. Both Bonny and Read were ultimately convicted of piracy. The loose, baggy, effeminate clothing affected by pirates and the practice adopted by young pirates of wearing their hair long helped the women remain inconspicuous. Although many young seamen were still beardless in their early teens, it was not easy for women to conceal their gender living in the confinement of a ship's mess deck or fo'c'stle. Those who worked at sea in the merchant service disguised as men were discovered before long, although Rebecca Ann Johnson served as a seaman on a British collier for seven years before being discovered. Her mother had died in the Napoleonic Wars while serving with a gun crew in a warship. There were inquiries into these cases and the courts tended to suspect immorality was involved—on the part of the women, not the men.

In another case, a thirteen-year-old American, Ann Jane Thornton, signed on as a cabin boy while pursuing a man. It is not recorded whether she caught him or not, but she did spend three years at sea as cabin boy, cook, and, stewardess. At sixteen, she signed on as a seaman aboard the *Sarah* for a voyage from the United States to Britain. She dressed as a sailor, washed herself in her bunk, and refused her grog ration, perhaps for fear of exposure under the influence. She did the work of a seaman, including the dangerous work of handling topgallant sails high aloft in severe weather, and endured a hard trans-Atlantic voyage, taking abuse from the other sailors, who accused her of not working quite so hard as they did. *Sarah* was a few days out of London when Thornton's true gender was discovered. After a formal inquiry in London, she was given passage home to the United States, where she disappeared from the public record. The captain reported afterward that "she had born it all excellently and was a capital seaman." It is likely that the true gender of some of these women was well known to some of the seamen, but that it might suit the sailors not to betray them. They may have enjoyed their company or had sexual liasons with them. In those times seafaring was a man's world, but a few determined women managed to invade it one way or another.

As the nineteenth century progressed, a small number of women, usually the wives of cooks and stewards, were employed as stewardesses in the otherwise all-male crews of merchant vessels. In the passenger vessels, of course, women were employed in the steward's departments. Rarely were they cooks in Canadian deepsea cargo ships; those most frequently employed were Chinese or Philippine men.

Nineteenth-century women usually went aboard sailing ships as passengers or guests, but there was one cargo vessel job for which they formally signed on as official crew: stewardess. (Although on their discharge certificates their name had to be entered in a space marked "name of seaman.") As stewardesses, women took the place of the steward or assisted him, keeping the quarters and serving the table for the officers or "the afterguard." There were not a great many of these stewardesses. In her study of nineteenth-century Canadian sailors *Jack in Port: Sailor Towns of Eastern Canada* (1982), Judith Fingard notes that stewardesses "overwhelmingly shared the same surname as the cook, cook-steward or steward."

Working as a stewardess was a way for women to accompany their husbands to sea. Apparently some masters liked them for the "civilizing effect" they provided and for the companionship they offered other women aboard. Stewardesses were often responsible for midwifery and nursing services as well. Captain Frederick William Wallace, author of the authoritative *Wooden Ships and Iron Men* (1924), explains the benefits of having a stewardess:

> *It was quite a common thing for a man and his wife to look after the cooking and the upkeep of the cabin quarters, either one going in the galley and doing the cooking. A stewardess was much better than a man in many ways. She usually kept the cabin neater, could make more out of the food provided in the way of tasty dishes, and would superintend things pretty much in the manner of a boarding house mistress or housekeeper ashore.*

Seaman's Certificate of Discharge for Maud Lloyd, seventeen-year-old stewardess in the fast Yarmouth ship Tantramar. Lloyd sailed from Halifax to Barry, Wales to Montevideo, Uruguay in 1895. Captain Keay reports her conduct as "very good."

Wallace also notes that masters, often not very clean themselves, were fastidious about cleanliness in the galley and in the serving of meals in the cabin.

Despite the advantages that stewardesses offered, according to figures from the port of Saint John, they were relatively few in number. In the decade 1881 to 1891, a mere twenty-five were on the articles of departing vessels each year compared to three or four thousand seamen. Stewardesses were usually the lowest paid of the crew, making anywhere from five to twenty-five dollars a month; some, however, made as much as a seaman. Occasionally, a token payment of one dollar was given for the trans-Atlantic voyage. Fingard suggests that token payments were offered in situations where the master took on the stewardess as a favour to the husband, but it might also have been used in cases of stranded stewardesses offering to work their way home.

Some stewardesses would sail with their husbands for a voyage or two and then stay home for a while. Fingard suggests that women stayed home when their husbands were unable to find work for their wives. However, there are a number of other equally likely reasons for these women to remain ashore such as maternity leave, the yearning for home, the need for a rest from the sea, or the need for social and feminine companionship. Also, like captain's wives, stewardesses might take one or two voyages and decide to retire from the sea.

A few women going to sea would have their own agendas to pursue, as in the case of two with a missionary spirit. A book entitled *Life in Feejee, or Five Years Among the Cannibals* was published in Boston in 1851, and the author was identified simply as "A Lady." This lady was Mary Wallace, whose husband was Captain Benjamin Wallace, a tough Yankee trader who engaged in the dangerous but lucrative trade of carrying *beche de mer* (seaslugs) from Fiji to Manila in the 1840s and 1850s. Mary was acknowledged to be a pious woman, an opinionated feminist, and tough in her own right. On one long trading expedition of five years to Fiji in her husband's ship *Zotoff*, Mary went along, to the wonderment of the captain's associates and crew, who were certain that she would cramp his free-wheeling, scofflaw style. As it turned out, Mary Wallace exerted considerable influence on her husband; when *Zotoff* was in Fijian trading rounds, Mary made contact with and supported the missionaries who were trying to convert the

Ella Spicer, Captain Edmund Spicer, and daughter aboard the ship George T. Hay, *about 1903. At right is the stewardess, likely Maud Lloyd.*

islanders. She also saw to the *Zotoff* crew's religious observances and, through her husband's authority, was able to influence the major Fijian chiefs. She must have been respected by the common people as well because even today a popular girl's name in Fiji is *Walesi* or *Merewalesi* for "Mary Wallace."

Another vessel to carry missionary messages was the *Day Spring*, built in 1863 by Carmichael at Pictou, Nova Scotia. This little 116-ton brigantine was sponsored by the Presbyterian Church and paid for by the thousands of pennies donated by children from Canada to Australia. Throngs of children saw the white ship and its courageous band of missionaries off from Halifax on their long voyage to the New Hebrides. In a vessel the size of a large tugboat, they would venture halfway around the world to a place where missionaries had been known to be murdered by their parishioners. *Day Spring* was sturdy, the builders having kept in mind the typhoons of the South Pacific, and was equipped with a five-hundred-volume library. Several husband-and-wife teams of missionaries were aboard, as was the wife of William Fraser, the shipmaster. The Frasers sailed nine years among the islands of Fiji and the New Hebrides and south to Sydney and Melbourne, carrying missionaries and supplies before finally leaving the vessel to go home to Nova Scotia. No ordinary seamen, the ship's crew attended regular worship services and followed strict prohibitions on alcohol, tobacco, and swearing.

With the spread of colonialism and emigration to the new colonies established by Europeans in the nineteenth century, women sailed the seas as passengers in increasing numbers. However, the square-rigged sailing ships they travelled in provided a means of transportation whose comfort and reliability were at the whim of the weather. From the makeshift passenger carriers of the Irish emigrant trade to the rough and ready luxury of the cabins in the crack packets, travel conditions differed greatly. Except for a few well-heeled passengers who were reasonably comfortable in cabin class, travellers bunked in crowded dormitories, separate for men and women. While work kept the crew of cargo ships occupied and orderly, accounts of the passenger vessels paint a picture of general chaos, the captain sometimes struggling to keep a frightened, unruly—often drunken—lot of passengers under control. Maintaining order was par-

A group of missionaries and their children, the captain, and his wife set forth confidently on a five-year voyage in the South Pacific during 1864 in the little 116-ton brigantine Day Spring. *The Pictou-built missionary vessel was paid for by the pennies of schoolchildren.*

ticularly difficult in the cut-rate vessels engaged in carrying poor emigrants to North America at the time of the Irish famines in the 1840s and 1850s. Cargo vessels were loaded up with the destitute, who paid extremely cheap fares but had to provide their own food. Disease spread rapidly among the half-starved passengers, crowded below deck with inadequate ventilation. Great numbers did not survive to see the shores of Canada and the United States. Many were buried at sea (hence the popular term "coffin ship"), while many others died in island quarantine stations like Grosse Isle in the St Lawrence River and Partridge Island at Saint John.

The worst conditions, save those of the African slave trade, were for sea-going women and children on the annual summer migrations of Newfoundland fishermen to the Labrador coast. These fishing migrations continued until the early twentieth century. Small fishing schooners carried families crowded into airless cargo holds on this journey and they made the return trip on top of the cargo of fish, with insufficient room to sit up. The willingness of these emigrants to undertake these difficult voyages can only be attributed to their determination to overcome grinding poverty and keep their families together.

The trans-Atlantic packets of the first half of the nineteenth century attempted to provide the first scheduled passages from Britain to North America, a formidable challenge given the vagaries of sailing on this notoriously rough water. By mid-century, steamships with their steadier pace took over the scheduled passenger trade and offered improved comfort and reliability. An apprentice on the sailing packet *Henry Pratt* was taught navigation by the captain's accomplished wife, who later (as a widow) operated a navigation school in London. She may have run the *Henry Pratt*, too. The apprentice, Sam Samuels, described her as handling the lines and the wheel while the mate's wife handled the belaying pin: "It was easy to see who the real captain and mate were," was his comment.

The packet masters were inclined to be hard driving and high spirited, determined to keep to their schedules whatever the weather. American owners favoured having captains' wives sail with their shipmasters, believing that the women's presence had a civilizing effect. Despite being encouraged to have their wives accompany them, few packet captains complied. Samuels took his wife on the ferry service across the rough North Atlantic, and as a result no swearing was allowed on the afterdeck of *Dreadnought*, flags were flown at sea, and prayers were held on Sundays. As to the value of flying flags at sea when there were no other ships nearby, Samuel's wife explained simply: "God sees them."

But the presence of women aboard ship did not necessarily guarantee good behavior and order. A good example of the lack of decorum frequently found aboard the early to mid-century passenger ships is found in the diary of Edwin Bird, who travelled to Australia with a load of emigrants from England in 1855. His trip was made in the renowned Canadian-built *Marco Polo* under the command of the famous and hard-driving Bully Forbes. The passage was characterized by an inordinate amount of parties, drunken fights, and thievery. Among the more raucous was a party of brides-to-be from Ireland on their way to Australia to meet their promised husbands.

Mrs. Forbes, her daughter Maggie, and the wife of the first mate were also on the second of *Marco Polo's* fast voyages to Australia. Music, dancing, singing, drinking, fisticuffs, and dog fights were the standard evening entertainment on the uproarious voyage. The captain kept order of a sort by the power of his personality, a few clouts, and the occasional trial. He put those convicted of theft, drunkenness, and insults to the women in chains. Of the convicted, one had insulted Mrs. Forbes and threatened to shoot the captain. Though life on shore had its own difficulties, it always took courage for the women to leave the familiar comforts of home and friends for shipboard life.

It would be a new era, beginning around mid-century, when the women who came to live upon the seas were the wives of merchant ship captains, assigned the honoured position of homemaker in "the cabin," the officers' quarters in the stern.

Around 1850, at which time cargo vessels were regularly trading all over the globe with voyages frequently lasting a year or two, it became acceptable for women to go to sea with their captain husbands in North American ships. The women aboard ship were now not employees, but the guests of the shipmaster and home-

A woodcut of Marco Polo, *built as a timber carrier in 1850 but demonstrating performance elements of the fast packets and clippers while carrying loads of sometimes unruly immigrants to Australia.*

makers with their own duties and responsibilities. These seafaring women are clear in their own words about why they chose to go with their husbands to sea for long periods rather than stay at home: they often saw the hardships of life at sea as of less a burden than the hardships of separation between husband and wife and father and children. Inevitably, some grew to love the sea, gaining an interest in the running of the ship. Others more accurately withstood the life with a measure of ambivalence, some for as long as thirty years. Still others tried but could not handle the physical rigors and seasickness, and were forced to choose life on land over the company of their husbands. The most common reason women had for quitting the sea, however, was the need for proper schooling for their children. Second to that, a yearning for female companionship and a social life were women's reasons for returning home.

Official documentation of women's forays to sea is sparse; naval records and nautical histories tend to tell the stories of men at sea, and because families of captains were neither on the official crew lists nor recorded as passengers, we often know husbands names, but not the given names of the women themselves. For information about women at sea, then, personal records—diaries and letters—have had to suffice. Unfortunately, some of these writings are incomplete, providing us with only a partial glimpse of what life was like for these women.

Mary Lawrence, an American whaling captain's wife, took kindly to the sea and wrote eloquently about her life in her diary. When water suddenly comes pouring into the cabin from the deck overhead she comments, "I thought the ship was going down, but it was only a broken skylight. For several days past we have been under the necessity of holding our mugs with one hand and our plates with the other and occasionally snatching a mouthful between the rolls." On another occasion, Mary Lawrence remarks: "It sometimes seems impossible that we can live through it, but our gallant ship rides along fearlessly. It is grand beyond anything I have ever witnessed, sublimity itself." Then, when the sea is calm, she writes: "Everything is smiling and serene; one would never suspect the treachery that lurks in his bosom. I do not wonder that so many choose a sailor's life. It is a life of hardship but it is a life full of romance and interest."

Not all wives and daughters who went to sea would be content to stick to the domestic scene or be satisfied with a little navigation practice while aboard. On the small, family-owned coastwise trading vessels, women pitched in with the rest of the family to help the captain in the struggle to make a living. There were numerous such vessels coasting about Britain throughout the nineteenth century, and well into the twentieth century families operated motorized freight vessels called goelettes on the St Lawrence River. As early as 1840, Betsy Miller, an Englishwoman, became involved in running several ships—owned by her father—that operated along the coast and on UK to US trade routes. Betsy Miller served as "ship's husband," attending to ship maintenance and eventually commanding the coaster *Cloetus* in the treacherous waters and weather of the British Isles.

Annie Harding of Appledore found herself at sea when her father became owner-master of the trading smack *Dahlia*. Captain Harding's two sons were a major part of his crew, but they wandered off to work on the more glamorous deep-sea square-rigged ships. The captain was not in good health and the third son was a mere boy, so he could not afford to keep idle ladies aboard; however, Annie was determined to help and to be a sailor—she steered, trimmed sails, learned the coast and tides, and predicted the weather. In addition, the enthusiastic Annie helped pump the leaky vessel and cooked for the crew. Intelligent and hard working, she was soon capable of standing a watch in charge. Nevertheless, her father eventually sent her ashore to work.

But Annie Harding's affinity for the sea won out, and she met and married William Slade, mate of the Pugwash-built *Hawk*, which was also coasting around Britain. Slade was ambitious and a hard worker, but illiterate. Annie taught him to read and calculate and he eventually became a qualified master, taking command of *Francis Beddoe* with his wife as navigator and business manager. She went on shore long enough to give birth to their son, with whom she returned to sea after three months. The Slades bought a quarter share of the small vessel *Alpha*, and, except for occasional visits ashore to give birth to more children, Annie stayed at sea. Once again in the position of contributing to a family vessel, Annie Slade was a hard worker at any task: seamanship, cooking, and the ship's housekeeping. One voyage she elected to stay home for a change, leaving her husband to sail with a substitute, but he did not get far. From a port along the coast he sent his wife a wire asking her to send him a new mate because his crew had quit. Unable to locate a mate, Annie hopped a train and joined the vessel to take the job herself. To her it was all part of the family job. William, who joined the crew at the age of twelve, said of his mother: "She took to the sea like a duck takes to water. She had the right instincts inborn. She was so natural and unperturbed in a man's job at sea." Her sea worthiness was considered surprising not only because she was a woman, but also because she did not come from a traditional seafaring family. Around 1900 Annie retired ashore, but she returned to sea often, to the relief of son William who had great faith in her. In her nineties, Annie Slade made only occasional trips as a passenger. Young ladies were brought along to look after her on these voyages, but they were often seasick and it was in fact she who usually took care of them.

One anecdote about Annie Slade told by William seems apochryphal in that it surfaces in stories about other places and involving other people, including Amelia Holder (though the Annie Slade version is the more detailed and rings truer). As the story goes, Annie Slade was instinctively roused from her sleep and like a good officer went on deck to look at the sails. She decided her husband was carrying too much canvas for the wind and says, "You are driving the ship too heavy. If you don't take in the topsails you will lose the lot." He laughed at her patroniz-ingly, "She'll carry it or drag it and I'll be in Waterford tonight." Annie went below to put the boys back in their bunks and came up on deck again. Just as she came up the topmast, topsail yard, and flying jib all came crashing down in a tangle. She shouted at her husband, "I told you so! Now get up and clear that lot away. I'll take the wheel." "All right, keep her on course, we won't be long" William Slade replied meekly as he set to work while the children peeked from a cabin port, impressed with their mother, as good a seaman as any man.

These anecdotes show women occasionally making their way to sea and hold-ing their ground under difficult conditions. In the historical accounts and in their own private diaries and reminiscences, women rarely voice a desire to join the working crew of ships at sea—women in the nineteenth century were, after all, products of their culture. Only late in the nineteenth century and early in the twentieth century did women (and some men) begin in any organized and effec-tive way to break through barriers restricting women from equal opportunity employment. Today, women are everywhere on ships at sea, though in modest numbers. They are on the bridge in command, in the engine-room, and even climb-ing far aloft in modern versions of the square-rigged sailing ship.

This book tries to provide insight into what life was like for women who ven-tured into the male-dominated world of nineteenth-century nautical life. Whether real or perceived, a domesticating influence accompanied women at sea. More importantly, however, these women had the opportunity to meet the kinds of peo-ple and see the kinds of things that were part of a world not usually open to them as Victorian "angels of the house." As more and more women ventured to sea, they showed others and perhaps even realized for themselves their own strengths and abilities, a realization that contradicted—maybe even helped to destroy—the Vic-torian standards of femininity that held women unequal to men. This book is about how women left the familiarity and security of hometowns, why they stayed on ships or quit them, how they coped with rolling, pitching home-making, how they related to the dominant male society aboard, and how they viewed the exotic far-off ports they visited.

I
WHALING WIVES

EXAMPLES OF THE AMERICAN WOMEN WHO LIVED AT SEA FOR YEARS IN WHALING VESSELS AND THE SOCIAL LIFE IN THE FLEETS. A NOVA SCOTIA WHALING FAMILY ON A LONG CRUISE.

THE NEW ENGLANDERS

The incentive for wives to go to sea with their husbands was particularly strong in the case of whaling ships because of the great length of the voyages. For this reason whaling saw the first substantial number of women going to sea. In other sea trades, the absences from home were seldom so long. Life on land was hard enough in the mid-nineteenth century, but in a little ship that might be at sea for years at a time it was considerably harder. Poor food, a confined, usually all-male community, and lack of medical care made the journeys all the more onerous. Some women, perhaps the more independent and adventurous in spirit, went to sea and enjoyed the life and the chance to be with their husbands while they worked. Others found compromise by seizing opportunities to take time out part of the way through the voyage.

Shipmasters are noteworthy for their brevity, recounting in their logs only the legal and navigational facts required of them. The mention of anyone other than crew was rare. Whaling wives, on the other hand, were often faithful diarists, and some of these personal records have been preserved. Mary Lawrence describes life on a whaling ship from her perspective, "We are, as it were, shut out from our friends in a little kingdom of our own of which Samuel is the prime ruler. I should never have known what a great man he was if I had not accompanied him." She called herself "the captain's best mate." Desire Fisher sat at home in Edgartown on Martha's Vineyard for five long years, reading love poems sent by her husband. Having enough of marriage through poetry, she joined him in 1858 in his ship *Navigator*. One voyage convinced her she was better off alone in Edgartown after all—an aborted mutiny aboard *Navigator* had helped her decide.

Before petroleum was extracted from the ground and broken down into its components, whale oil was the lamp and lubricating oil of choice and the whaling industry was strong. The thick layer of blubber was stripped off alongside the ship at sea and boiled, then the oil was extracted, barrelled, and stored in the hold. When there was a full load of oil, the vessel sailed for home. It was a smelly, messy business and other seamen considered whalers to be of a lower caste. Eventually, kerosene replaced whale oil as fuel for lamps and cook stoves, but by then whales had been hunted to near extinction and the whaling industry was all but dead.

During its heyday in the 1840s, New England ports such as New Bedford and Nantucket were the whaling centres of the United States. By mid-decade, there were 735 New England whaling vessels out of a world fleet of a little less than 1000. Oil and baleen represented a major export for the young United States. Whaling was so lucrative and specialized that the whaling towns depended heavily upon it. While early whale-catching was local and carried out in small boats, it became necessary for whalers to travel farther and farther afield, first to the north and then far down the Atlantic. Eventually, New England and Canadian whalers were pursuing dwindling herds around Cape Horn, up the coast of Chile, and across the Pacific as far as Siberia and the Bering Sea. The voyages necessarily became longer and longer, eventually lasting from two to four years. With a large proportion of the men from these communities away for long periods and many never returning at all from the risky life, the whaling towns became dominated by the women who remained behind. The women looked after their husbands' business interests and became the shopkeepers, balancing job and child rearing like the women of today. The main street of Nantucket became known as "Petticoat Row."

Naturally, the wives of whaling men were not happy to have them away for so long. Lydia Gardner of Nantucket said that she was married for thirty-seven years and her husband was only home for five of them. As owner or part owner of a whaling vessel the master was free to take along on a voyage anyone he liked. Taking a wife to sea eventually caught on and proved beneficial in providing the captain with company in the very limited society aboard. Women provided a home-like atmosphere, and though they had only slight dealings with anyone but the officers, they generally had a civilizing influence on the entire crew. The first American wife to go to sea with her whaling husband was Mary Russell in 1817. When Mary's son was twelve, Captain Russell signed him on as a cabin boy and took him off to sea. On the next voyage, Mary was not to be left behind. She joined her husband and son, and eventually a younger son also joined the seagoing family. As a sea-going wife, Mary Russell found she had some expertise to offer. "I have often had reason, since I left Nantucket, to bless the little knowledge I had of medicine as it has contributed to take a great care off the mind of my husband. He examines the cases and reports them to me. I am happy to say that the medicines I have administered have never failed of their desired effect."

The numerous whaling wives of New England left many accounts of their lives at sea to enlighten future generations. Charity Norton sailed with her husband John frequently, rounding the notorious Cape Horn at the tip of South America six times. She is said to have been actively encouraged by the owners to go in order to keep her husband from tyrannizing his crew. On one occasion, Captain Norton had twelve would-be deserters strung up to the rigging. Charity, reputed to be formidable but warm-hearted, came on deck and asked him what he was doing. He replied, " I'm going to lick them!" "Oh no you're not," she retorted, and the men were released. (So much for the supreme authority of a shipmaster.) One seaman in their vessel said, "I'd kill the old man as soon as a kitten, but I suppose the old lady would feel bad," a comment that reveals the civilizing influence of women aboard and the attitude of the crews towards them. In contrast to the popular notion that seamen considered women aboard ship to be bad luck, it appears women had an effect on the crew that garnered them a certain amount of respect.

Personality conflicts and mood changes were expected on these long voyages. Lucy Smith had low points early on a long voyage, but came home in an upbeat mood. Two weeks out in the whale ship *Nautilus*, she wrote, "Although I have been seasick, I have not yet been homesick nor have I ever for a moment thought I would wish my husband to be here without me." That was in October 1869. But at Christmas she was complaining that it was not a very merry one for her, even saying that there seemed little on earth to live for. She was afraid when all the crew were out in the boats chasing whales, with only the steward, carpenter, and a sick seaman left on board to tend the ship. Later she felt that nothing could be more depressing than life aboard her ship.

In July of 1870, Lucy Smith notes that it was a year since her husband had returned from his last four-year voyage. That long absence no doubt prompted her sailing with him on the present trip and she mentions how glad she is that she can be with him on this voyage instead of being left at home, and how she hopes he will never go on another without her. Theirs would be a four-and-a-half-year voyage. Her last night on board in May of 1874, Lucy says of *Nautilus*, "Although many times life on board has not been particularly pleasant, it is with feelings of pleasure not unmingled with pain that I shall bid her adieu." The ship had been home to her, her husband, and her son Freddie, who went to sea at four and returned to land aged eight. On shore, Lucy reportedly misses having the steward and cabin boy as servants and babysitters.

It may be observed that the image of the Victorian woman as weak and help-less was only an affectation and that the Victorian woman could be very tough when pushed. Women in the male-dominated world at sea varied in their accom-modation to it as any collection of women would to a test of mettle on shore. Caroline Mayhew, a doctor's daughter who became a doctor herself, became the navigator and de facto captain of the whaler *Powhatan* in 1846 when smallpox broke out and laid the officers low. The crew felt no resentment—they were thankful she was there to guide them home. In fact, they gratefully presented her with gifts of their handiwork, such as the popular scrimshaw carvings.

One of the best of the whaling diaries belongs to Eliza Azelia Williams, who not only spent many years on whaling expeditions and survived several wrecks, but was also an articulate journal writer. She learned to "shoot the sun" to determine latitude and acquired a fine appreciation of the mechanics of sailing. Despite her strength of character and accomplishments, Eliza Williams did not become involved in the operation of the vessel. She was diminutive and ladylike and typically supportive of her husband, possibly at the expense of her own chance to acquire new and practical skills.

Eliza Williams went to sea, like others, because it was the lesser of two evils. She was naturally timid and, when left behind, was not happy handling the duties of her husband's business on her own. After seven years of marriage, she decided to accompany him on the voyage commencing September 7, 1858. The trip lasted thirty-eight months. Two sons, Henry and Stancel, were left behind for schooling; the third, William, was born at sea. A daughter, Mary, was born later in the voyage in 1861. William would be three years old before he stopped for any length of time on shore.

When starting out for the first time, Eliza Williams writes of her slight apprehension but generally optimistic feelings about going to sea. She starts off in the pilot boat, going out to join her ship *Florida* at anchor off New Bedford. Whalers like *Florida* were seldom much more than one hundred feet long and three to four hundred tons. Eliza is hoisted over the high side of the ship in an armchair. Before leaving she reflects on this departure from family and friends:

> *Now I am in the place that is to be my home, possibly for three or four years; but I cannot make it appear to me so yet, it all seems so strange, so many men and not one woman beside myself. The little cabin that is to be all my own is quite pretty, as well as I can wish or expect on board of a ship. I have a rose geranium to pet and I see there is a kitten on board.*

In her daily journal she doesn't mention that she starts this adventure five months pregnant. Her husband, certainly conscious of her condition, sails to the Pacific via the Cape of Good Hope to avoid the stormy Cape Horn route. Eliza finds it a strange new world with nothing to see but sky, water, and their little ship. She is seasick at first but gets over it and becomes a keen observer of the whaling business. The weather turns "rugged" with what she calls a gale, though her husband laughs and tells her she has not seen a gale yet. Her journal stops for a month in December while they cross the Pacific Ocean. Upon arriving in Manganui, northern New Zealand, her writing resumes. She speaks of a real storm, and the house she has made for four pigeons that come aboard from another whaler. Then, as a sort of afterthought, she mentions the birth of her son: "We have a fine healthy boy, born on the 12th January, five days before we got into port." The baby arrives after a long and painful delivery, with Captain Williams acting as midwife in the cramped cabin.

Manganui was one of the many recognized whaling-ship rendezvous, a tiny settlement of Europeans among the Maori. Here, Eliza meets other captains' wives. Happy to have some company, the harbour master's wife comes aboard to help with the baby. Both women return to her house ashore where Eliza stays for two weeks. There she meets another whaling wife who stayed ten months to have her baby while her husband was off whaling.

Florida's hunt for whales takes Eliza to the coasts of Japan, Siberia, and Mexico, and to Honolulu in the Sandwich Islands, a popular resting place for whaling crews. They approach San Francisco, but do not go into the harbour for fear too many of the crew will desert to follow the gold rush. Major storms, dark skies, howling winds, seas thundering in over the rail onto the deck, and a confusion of objects flying about on deck and below colour Eliza's diary. Water that leaks into the accommodation has to be bailed from the saloon floor with buckets. Eliza, little Willie, and baby Mary, who is born while the ship is at anchor in Banderas Bay, Mexico, learn to take the difficulties of shipboard life in stride. Eliza learns to appreciate and enjoy the complexity of handling sail when tacking a square-rigged ship, and she becomes all too aware that their lives depend upon the successful execution of this task when they are being blown onto a lee shore.

Eliza Williams went on two long cruises, each time leaving children at home and producing more along the way. Flora, for example, was born on the Sea of Japan. Eliza's husband was prospering and she wanted him to retire, but small-town life would not satisfy him. As women of the pioneer days did when their husbands would not settle, she followed him wherever his career took him. After railway access improved movement across the continent, the New England whaling base was relocated to San Francisco, and the expeditions thus shortened to one season only. Pushing into the Bering Strait and the Arctic Ocean brought perils from the ice pack. Almost the whole fleet (thirty-two whaling ships) was trapped in the ice in 1871. The captains abandoned their vessels, departing for home in the few ships that could move. The Williams family was forced to trek on the ice and crowd onto another ship. The previous year, they had been wrecked in another ship at Point Barrow, Alaska. After the Arctic wreck, Captain Williams, who had been establishing business interests ashore in New England and California, finally gave his long-suffering wife her wish and retired from the sea.

Having adapted completely to a rolling world, children that were born and lived on the sea frequently knew no other life; trying to walk on land terrified them.

Alice Rowe went to sea at eleven months in her father's ship *Village Belle* and first learned to walk on a heaving deck. She was terrified at her first attempt to walk on the stationary floor of a house. She went ashore with her family, but returned to sea at fourteen in 1883 when her father took *Russell* on a four-and-a-half-year voyage. Alice was eager for the sea, enthusing in her diary, "I just want to shout right out and tell everybody I am going on a long sea voyage with father and mother. All the boys and girls I know think I am lucky and want to come too. I wish they could, but they can't. Although I am only a little girl, I will write a book all myself and make pictures, too." And she did. She wasn't quite right, however, about the others not being able to go; Harry Kidd stowed away with them and, when discovered, was made a cabin boy.

Life aboard a whaling vessel could be exciting, but for a youngster it was at times monotonous, especially on a Victorian Sunday. Six-year-old Laura Jernegan writes in her diary, "It is Sunday and a very pleasant day. I have read two story books. This is my journal. Goodbye for today." On other days, she writes of her brother, the dog, pet birds, and the egg production of the hens: "We had two birds, there is one now. One died. There names were Dick and Lulu. Dick died, Lulu is going to. There is a fly on my finger. He has flew off now. We have 135 barrels of oil, 60 of humpback and 75 of sperm." The last news was of most significance aboard a whaling ship. Laura's little brother Prescott was afraid of land, crying when told to get out of a boat onto the shore at Honolulu. Laura was taught in the morning by her mother, Helen, who was happy at sea. A swing installed by the crew and "a small cabin boy" kept Prescott occupied and amused.

One of the more famous American whaling wives was Honor Earle, whose husband was master of the whaler *Charles Morgan*, now enshrined in the Mystic Seaport Museum. A former teacher, Honor had no difficulty with the math of latitude and longitude. Happy to have something constructive to do in the operation of her husband's vessel, she was rated the official navigator of the *Charles Morgan* from 1890 to 1906

A Canadian Whaling Voyage

The large New England fleets dominated the whaling industry of the nineteenth century. Canadian seafaring entrepreneurs did some whaling in the 1840s, sending a few ships out of Maritimes ports like Saint John, Halifax, and Yarmouth. These ships used the same methods and round-the-Horn itinerary as the Americans, with voyages of two to four years. After exhausting the Atlantic, they too embarked on the longer expeditions around the Horn to the Pacific Ocean whaling grounds as far as Japan and, eventually, to the Bering Sea and the Arctic.

James Coffin of Barrington, Nova Scotia, first went to sea at the age of twenty. He writes rapturously in his personal journal about the fair Mary Doane, the girlfriend he left behind. He recalls fondly their childhood friendship and how he had walked out with her on his arm years before. After rising through the ranks, James Coffin returned to Barrington in eager anticipation of what he calls "the company of the fair." Coffin's fifth whaling voyage, projected to last five years, was his first as a master and thus he was able to take his wife, none other than Mary Doane, whom he had married after his third voyage. The whaling ship owners seem not to have been too happy that Mrs. Coffin and Esther, the Coffins' daughter, were aboard for the voyage. James Coffin justifies his impudence in taking his wife and child with him by insisting that his officers enjoy the company of his family. And when the Coffins' son is born at sea, James twits the owners by telling them that his "wife has taken to shipping hands contrary to orders" and that they "have just shipped a very small sailor in a quite unorthodox but quite satisfactory manner."

In the spring of 1845, Captain Coffin, now thirty-one, returned home from a four-year expedition in the Saint John whaler *Margaret Rait*, and went to the port of Saint John to oversee the rigging and fitting of a new whaler. The 398-ton *Athol*, the pride of the Saint John whaling fleet, would be the last of its whalers. Ships were regularly returning from long voyages with declining numbers of full oil barrels to show for their efforts.

Young Benjamin Doane, one of the many seafaring Doanes of Barrington (and unrelated to Mary apparently) had been persuaded by Captain Coffin to sign on with him for the maiden voyage of the *Athol*. Coffin was also fortunate in signing on a young doctor recently apprenticed to a Barrington physician. It would be a luxury to have professional medical care on such a long voyage. Only a young man in search of adventure would agree to such a proposition. Doane had some previous experience on short whaling trips in the North Atlantic. Whaling was tough, but there was potential for good earnings on shares during a long voyage. He and the captain went to Saint John together and Doane found work helping the riggers and carpenters finish the newly launched *Athol*, which lay anchored off Sand Point at the harbour entrance. Mary and Esther arrived from Barrington to embark as well.

Benjamin Doane kept a journal, recording a picture of nineteenth-century whaling life in Canada and, incidentally, the role of women accompanying the fleet. Doane's journal was published in

Mary Doane Coffin spent three years at sea, from the Bay of Fundy to the Bering Sea, in the whaler Athol *with her husband, bearing two children aboard along the way.*

1987 as *Following the Sea: A young sailor's account of the seafaring life in the mid-1800s.*

It was to be a long, arduous, sometimes dangerous expedition and young Doane had a romantic interest at home, so he was in a blue mood as the departure approached. He boarded in Saint John with his cousin Olive Kenny and her sea captain husband. Olive Kenny had been on many voyages as a captain's wife and as Doane prepared to depart, she handed him a glass of wine, saying, "Cousin Ben, before we say goodbye, I am sailor enough to take a parting glass with you. May you have good health and fortune and may we meet again." They all knew that the casualty rate for whalers was high, and it was perhaps especially so for Ben, who had signed on as a boat steerer: he would go out on the sea harpooning whales from a small boat at the risk of being towed about the ocean on a "Nantucket sleigh ride" by an angry, harpooned whale.

Athol sailed out of Saint John on July 12, 1845 with the crew shaking down and Mary Coffin making a snug home in the cabin aft. They follow the usual route across the Atlantic to the Azores, the Canaries, and Cape Verdes off Africa, then back across on the northeast trade winds to the Abrolhos Bank whaling grounds off the bulge of Brazil. They do not tarry on these no longer rich hunting grounds, but sail on around Cape Horn and up the coast of Chile.

In April 1846 they come into pleasant weather. On the morning of the ninth, Doane records their position: sixty miles off the remote island of Juan Fernandez,

Saint John whalers Canmore *and* Margaret Rait *in the South Seas. Dirty and odorous, and making extended voyages, the whaling ships were looked down upon by seamen in regular cargo vessels.*

Robinson Crusoe's island. The crew is loitering about the deck, waiting for the cry, "There she blows!" from the lookout. The captain has not been on deck all morning nor has Dr. MacDonald. The mate, Mr. Thomas, has been walking around with little Esther in his arms, doing his best to interest her in the porpoises under the bow or with amusing activities on deck. Suddenly there is a strange and far more startling cry than "There blows." All work stops and the seamen stand about expectantly. The captain comes on deck to relate the news quietly to Mr. Thomas, but all ears hear him: "It's a fine healthy boy." Esther is taken below to be introduced to her new brother, James Fernandez Coffin. The ship is dressed with flags and the crew sings songs in honour of the new hand.

The first stop for the Saint John whaler, nine months at sea, is an anchorage at Guafo, on the island of Chiloe, Patagonia. This location was a rendezvous where whalers could replenish fresh water and pick up mail brought by new arrivals from home. *Athol* meets four Yankees and *James Stewart* out from Saint John with mail and some charts that Captain Coffin had left behind. Here, there have the usual whalers'"gams," ritualized social events, like a mating dance between ships, designed to ensure a safe and convenient meeting at sea. In a gam, one ship, usually to windward, flies flags to indicate availability for an invitation. The downwind vessel's master signals agreement and backs his main yards to stop his progress. The upwind vessel runs down and cuts close across the other's stern, a potentially

Saint John Harbour was a forest of masts in the heyday of the sailing ship, a world port where many ships were built, owned and engaged in trade, and the centre of the prolific Bay of Fundy seafaring community.

dangerous maneuver. As they pass, the two masters exchange formal compliments, starting with, "What ship is that, pray?" An invitation to visit follows and one ship's master crosses in a boat to change places with the mate from the other vessel. An exchange of visits among the rest of the crew ensues. The sailors are very hospitable, exchanging gifts and serving meals, and the seamen in the fo'c'sle even open their sea chests and invite their visitors to take what they need.

Gamming was a great opportunity for a captain's wife to act as hostess, and was especially enjoyable to her when there was a woman aboard the other vessel. Even for masters without their wives, the chance to enjoy the company of women and to experience a home-like atmosphere were treasured. Ships carrying women were called "lady ships," and after identifying a newly met vessel through the telescope, the first thing the seamen looked for was a figure in skirts to indicate whether this was or was not a "lady ship." Gamming was particularly strong among the whaling vessels because they tended to congregate in known hunting grounds to exchange information on whale sightings and the number of barrels of oil recovered. The larger the number of full barrels, the more successful the voyage and the sooner the vessel would turn for home. All too aware of the importance of these numbers, the women kept count themselves.

After the gams at Guafo, *Athol* moves north to the Galapagos, where there is more gamming, fishing, and collecting turtle for food. Along the way, they meet the United States troop transport *Thomas Perkins*. They ask the transport to stop so an army surgeon can examine a seaman who has a knee injury too serious for Dr. MacDonald to treat. The result is a formal visit to the *Athol* by Captain Arthur and a number of army officers to pay their respects to Mrs. Coffin. They come across to the grimy little whaler in glittering formal dress uniform. But, according to Doane's account, even their elegant bearing does not outshine the dignified Captain Coffin in his rarely worn dress uniform, and the self-possessed Mrs. Doane as they dispense the hospitality of their little ship. There is an exchange of gifts, food, scrimshaw, newspapers, and novels.

March 1847 finds the Canadian whaler heading into Honolulu, a rough settlement in the Sandwich Islands frequented by whaling vessels. Here fresh water, fruit, and vegetables can be restocked while crews rest and ships are refitted. The captain and Mrs. Coffin move ashore, boarding with a missionary because there are no hotels in Honolulu. It is early in the whaling era for Hawaii; in another decade, Honolulu Harbour will be a forest of masts, and the busy harbour will afford an active social life for women, many long-time friends through whaling. Some American captains' wives stay in Honolulu while their husbands go to Japan and the Bering Sea; they are picked up again on the ship's return, if there is one.

Mary Coffin is a good sailor; she stays with the ship in its onward search for whales over the seas. Whaling takes her to the primitive islands of the South Pacific and the seas of Japan and Okhotsk where the *Athol* visits with Siberian

Russians, Kanakas, and Japanese before turning south toward Australia. Regrettably, Mary leaves no account of the places she visited, the people she met, or her impressions of them both; to learn about Mary and her travels we have only Ben Doane's notes and Captain Coffin's logs to turn to.

On this part of the voyage, the friction that arises among people confined together over a long period of time results in a confrontation between the mate and the captain. After Captain Coffin accuses the mate of cowardice and inefficiency, the moody mate seizes a whale lance and lunges at the captain, who fends off the attack with his telescope while a boat steerer tries to grasp the lance. Hearing the shouts, Mary rushes on deck, and with a scream confronts the mate, begging him not to kill her husband. Her distress brings the mate to his senses; he drops the lance and walks away. He is demoted and discharged at Sydney.

Arriving at Sydney in December of 1847, Captain Coffin puts his crew to work refitting his vessel, and moves his family ashore to a boarding house. In February, the Coffins' daughter Esther, now four years old, falls ill and dies. The child's death is a great blow to the parents, to Ben Doane, and to the rest of the crew, who had enjoyed the company of the little girl who lent a touch of family life to an otherwise cold existence. Having had enough of whaling and not happy with the new mate, Doane signs off from the *Athol*.

The Coffins sail back north seeking more barrels of whale oil. Having an unsatisfactory return and discouraged by the loss of family and officers, including one killed by a whale, they return to Honolulu to sell their oil. They sell *Athol* to the Governor of Goa, who also offers to adopt the Coffin's son "Nandy"; however, in Doane's words, "the parents selfishly clung to their offspring." The boy, just three years old, has spent most of his life on board *Athol*.

The whalers and other plodding, blunt-bowed ships of the time were not glamorous, and as they began to disappear from the scene, the first of the celebrated, high-flying clippers were launched in the United States. Some of these ships, their masters, and, uniquely, a few of the women aboard them would have their moments of fame in the years to come.

II
THE GLAMOROUS CLIPPERS

Famous not only for its speed, but also for its beauty, the clipper is the antithesis of the grubby whaler. The clipper ship's golden era is the decade from 1845 to 1855, when urgent demand for fast transportation to the Californian and Australian gold rushes and access to the profitable Chinese tea trade prompted American shipbuilders to design these new and beautiful greyhounds of the sea. British builders, hampered by restrictive legislation, did not achieve their own clipper era until later in the century.

The new ships were highly wrought thoroughbreds. Their fine lines, tall masts, and wide sails gave them speed, but they required highly skilled handling and were easily damaged when driven hard, which was usually the case. Individual ships and masters were well known to the public: like modern America's Cup challengers or Indy racecar drivers, they were the heroes of the day. It was in the clipper ships that women came nearest to popular fame. Often overlooked by histories of the period, records show that women sometimes navigated and sailed the ships for their husbands in both normal and emergency situations.

The first impetus for developing a faster ship was the California gold rush and the rapid opening up of the west before the railroad. Not only was the voyage around South America from the populous eastern states long, but the stormy stretch below Cape Horn was also a supreme sailing test. There was also the "tea race," the yearly rush to transport the first cargoes of the new tea crop from China to London, where they fetched premium prices. New record passages received much publicity and the fastest masters, many of whom were hard-driving taskmasters, were prized by shipping management and owners. Histories of these ships, their captains, their record passages, and their disasters have had little to say about the women who travelled aboard the clippers, when in fact a few of them did a lot more than make the after cabin comfortable.

For signs of women's involvement with these ships, one could start by looking behind the most famous designer and builder of the American clippers, a man whose name is synonymous with clipper design: Donald McKay. Celebrated for his renowned, pace-setting vessels, McKay was a Nova Scotia boy who went to New York to learn the trade before launching his own company in East Boston. Seldom is it mentioned that for all his genius, he was poorly educated and did not possess the mathematical skills needed for designing the hull of a high perform-ance vessel. But he was smart enough to marry a woman who did. His first wife, Albenia Boole, was from a family of shipbuilders. She was well educated and had a special knack for laying off the complex curves of a ship's hull plan, a skill vital to the competitive speed of the clipper. With her mathematical sense, Albania also kept the company accounts. After his wife's death, Donald McKay acquired a repu-tation as a poor businessman.

Life on the clippers was much different from that on whaling vessels. First, the clippers were larger, cleaner, and sweeter smelling than the whalers. Also, clipper voyages were usually less than a year in length and were taken as one long haul at sea, without the intermediate stops or dawdling that afflicted the premium cargo carriers. In the whaler there were leisurely visits with crew and passengers from other ships to break the monotony of the long voyages, and crews stayed together for several years. The clipper crew, on the other hand, typically signed off after arriving in port, and a new lot of seamen was signed on when the ship was ready to sail again.

One of the first women to go to sea with her husband in a clipper was Char-lotte Babcock. Captain Charles Babcock was master of the well-known extreme clipper *Swordfish*, which set sail in 1851 with Charlotte, her nine-month-old daugh-ter, and a nursemaid aboard. Charlotte's husband was eager to beat the recent record established by *Flying Cloud* from New York to San Francisco. He pushed his vessel hard, which meant a rough voyage, but came into San Francisco's Golden Gate in ninety days and eighteen hours, less than a day longer than *Flying Cloud's* best time. *Swordfish* then continued across the Pacific to China.

Charlotte Babcock kept a diary and wrote fine descriptive passages that show her appreciation of the sea life. *Swordfish* carried a few passengers on the fast 1851 voyage, but Charlotte remained aloof, finding them uninteresting. After an initial bout of seasickness, she writes:

> *I shall never forget the wonderful sight, nothing but the sky above and the water be-neath, as far as the eye could see, and the immense waves following each other in un-broken succession. As they came toward us it seemed impossible for us to escape being overwhelmed by them. I grew very fond of this sea life and my chief delight was to sit on deck with my husband on pleasant evenings watching the waves and the ever chang-ing sky, talking of home and friends, and singing old familiar songs, My days were al-ways occupied with my baby, my sewing or a book, so that the time never seemed tedious or monotonous to me.*

Charlotte Babcock lived the seafaring life for seven years.

At nineteen, Sarah Low married a prominent skipper from a wealthy shipping family and went off to sea with him in the famous *N.B.Palmer*. The custom among seamen has long been to refer to the captain as "the old man," regardless of his age or their feelings for him. Sarah Low was amused at being called "the old woman" though she was not yet twenty. She was a great beauty and a great hostess who entertained lavishly in the Chinese tea ports. The Lows' beautifully maintained ship became known as "the yacht."

Sarah went to sea because she loved the life. She was not spared the seamy side, either, seeing her genial husband quell and disarm mutineers and flog them on the long Cape Horn passage. She bore two children at sea, the first arriving in January 1853, while the *N. B. Palmer* was racing into Batavia. The ship had run onto a reef in the South China Sea and water from a shattered bow was gaining on the pumps. Captain Low was simultaneously nursing a damaged ship and a wife in labour. The second boy arrived a year and a half later off Sandy Hook, New York, just as *N.B. Palmer* met the pilot at the end of a long voyage.

Throughout sailing history, experienced shipmasters have kept private logs and notes on their sailing experiences. The data accumulated in the course of their plotting was in fact useful and commercially valuable, as Lieutenant Matthew Maury of the United States Navy recognized. Maury collected the data he could find, organized it scientifically, and published it in two-volumes under the titles: "Wind and Current Charts" and "Sailing Directions." This collection of data on where the winds and currents of the world were likely to push a ship was received skeptically by many, but some enterprising navigators used it to their advantage in the highly competitive period of the Yankee clippers.

CORDELIA (STERLING) WATERMAN

As the younger sister of a sea captian, Cordelia Sterling of Bridgeport was not unfamiliar with the world of ships and sailing. She would gain firsthand knowledge of this world and go to sea herself through her marriage to Robert "Bully" Waterman, one of the first captains to gain renown as a hard-driving, record-making clipper master. Actually, Cordelia's brother picked up Waterman as just a young lad after finding him hanging about the ship, and took him under his wing to train him in seamanship. The boy spent twelve years at sea, rapidly climbing the ladder to master. After serving in the tough trans-Atlantic packet trade, Waterman hit the California boom, sailing clippers around the Horn to San Francisco and across the Pacific to China. Using Maury's guides, Waterman established record times to California in *Natchez*. Once famous, he became a dandy, strutting about the "in" places in New York. But he forgot the city girls when he met Cordelia Sterling, the sister of his old mentor. Nevertheless, another of Waterman's long voyages on *Natchez* was permitted to interrupt the couple's courtship.

In 1846 a state-of-the-art clipper was launched from the yards of Smith and Dimon in New York with Bully Waterman as master. The ship was launched on the day before Cordelia and Robert were married, December 7, 1846. Cordelia was thirty-four, Waterman thirty-eight. Cordelia launched the ship, which she named *Seawitch*, and burst into tears. She probably had a clear idea that she had launched a formidable rival for her husband's time. There was a very short honeymoon and Waterman rushed off to sea in a blustery northwester to test *Seawitch's* speed. He looked forward to even faster voyages in this beautiful vessel, with its black hull, gold stripe above the waterline, and black dragon figurehead. Showing no real interest in going to sea, Cordelia stayed behind. But as was often the case, her resolve changed after long months waiting on shore, and she decided to accompany her husband on *Seawitch's* next voyage to San Francisco and Canton. Ever the record-maker, Waterman returned triumphantly from Canton in an astonishing seventy-seven days. *Seawitch* represents the commencement of the golden decade of the fast American clippers.

Cordelia comes to resent her husband's long absences at sea, but she does not go on another voyage. It is possible that she finds an astonishing difference between the urbane gentleman Robert Waterman is on land and the tyrant he becomes as Captain Waterman. He is prosperous but is forced to retire after being tried for abuse of his crew en route to San Francisco. The couple settles in California, where the captain invests in ranching and lays out the towns of Fairfield and Cordelia.

Following her husband's trial in 1852, Cordelia takes a steamer from New York, and to save the long trip around South America, elects to cross the Isthmus of Panama with a small group and some local guides. It is a long, arduous, and frightening hike through the jungle. One night, just short of their destination at the port of Panama City on the Pacific side, Cordelia suspects that the guides are planning to rob her of her jewelry, so she flees the camp. She becomes lost, finally stumbling out onto the coast, sick with yellow fever. After recovering in hospital she seeks a vessel to take her up the coast to San Francisco. Meanwhile, hoping to meet his wife's original ship from New York, Captain Waterman fortuitously arrives at the Del Rey pier where she is waiting. She collapses in his arms.

Other women who went to sea only to be with their husbands found themselves fascinated and seriously interested in the navigation and operation of the ship. One young woman became sea-sick on the ferry between Boston and Cape Cod; her name was Hannah and she married Captain William Burgess in 1852. When the captain's new ship was ready, Hannah was happy to let him go off alone on the first voyage. But a year's absence was enough for her and she went along on the next trip, finding that she was not seasick at all in the big clipper. She loved the life, and learned to keep the log and determine the vessel's position. Eventually, she took over the navigation entirely. For some masters, navigation was an onerous part of the job, and they were happy to hand it over to anyone capable.

The Burgesses next voyage was around the Horn in the larger clipper *Challenger*. Hannah's husband and his officers agree that Hannah is among the best navigators. Eighteen months later, on the Horn route, Captain Burgess takes ill and is never able to resume command. The mate, perhaps unable to handle the intricacies of navigation himself, agrees that Hannah should assume command. The ship heads north along the Chilean coast toward Valparaiso, with Hannah both nursing her husband and running the ship. In sight of Juan Fernandez Island, Hannah's husband dies. Hannah completes the remaining two-hundred-mile journey to port, having held command for three weeks. The emergency passes, and Hannah Burgess disappears ashore.

ELEANOR CREESY

A keen interest in navigation distinguishes Eleanor Creesy from the women who went to sea but were happier ashore, women like Cordelia Waterman. Their husbands differed too in their views on navigation. Robert Waterman was a gentleman sailor and a fashion-plate, and was inclined to refer to the wisdom of Matthew Maury in plotting the course of his spectacular voyages. Quite different from Waterman is his rival for fame and profit in the clipper racing stakes, Josiah Creesy, a master who was concerned neither with how he looked nor with the information that reference guides had to offer; he preferred to sail guided by instinct. Creesy's wife Eleanor, however, was enthusiastic about Maury's ideas and saw to it that his two publications were on board their own new clipper, *Flying Cloud*, for Eleanor Creesy was Josiah's navigator. Her position as navigator was likely another case of a captain who was only too glad to have someone else with proven competence do the calculations. Eleanor was a confident navigator, plotting time-saving but risky courses for *Flying Cloud*. She also had a reputation for watching the interests of the crew, keeping an eye on the cook and nursing the sick and injured.

A great race between captains Waterman and Creesy took place in 1851, the former commanding the new *Challenge*, the latter *Flying Cloud*. The races, which were time-elapsed, starting perhaps weeks apart, resulted in fame and profit not only for the speediest of captains, but also for the owners, who secured offers of premium cargo. Creesy sets sail from New York a month ahead of Waterman, booming down the Atlantic and picking up the favorable trade winds and ocean currents. The navigator plies her tools, sextant, chronometers, Bowditch's logarithm tables, and Maury's texts. She chooses the fastest routes, and, guided by Maury's notes, directs her husband to sail close to dangerous headlands such as those on the Brazilian Capes, courses that more conservative sailors usually gave a wide berth. The westbound trip is the greater trial due to the prevailing high winds coming from the west, and fog, rain, and snow. Prudent shipmasters commonly passed around the outside of Staten Island near the Horn. Only in the occasional clear weather with favourable winds could the shorter inside run through the treacherous tides and contrary winds of the narrow Strait of Le Maire be ventured. Captain Creesy approaches the strait and spots Cape San Diego, but a storm blots it out and he tacks off to the northeast where he waits until morning for improved visibility.

In the meantime, Eleanor rechecks her dead reckoning position and consults Maury and the charts, bringing *Flying Cloud* back to the entrance of the strait by daybreak. And there it is, with visibility improving. Josiah pilots his vessel through the narrows, making use of the crosswinds and counter-currents when he can. Sailors passing through the narrows in clear weather have noted the jagged rocks holding the bleached bones of numerous ships unsuccessful in their attempts to make the passage. *Flying Cloud's* passage takes only twelve hours, but it is a hair-raising sail until the clipper comes out into the open ocean south of Cape Horn.

Even Maury's advice followed the established wisdom of sailing far south of the Cape to gain westing beyond the tip of South America. But Eleanor Creesy takes the short run, bringing them only five miles south of the dreaded island promon-tory and its jagged rocky islets. Visibility is fair, Eleanor is sure of her location, and icebergs are to be expected only further south. By late July more sail is set and easier weather comes as the ship moves northward. A rising wind from the south-east raises their speed to a log reading of eighteen knots. Eleanor calculates the day's run at 374 miles, more than 15 knots average, the record to that time.

Their luck holds (luck is always part of a record in sailing), and *Flying Cloud* follows the navigator's directions through the Golden Gate into San Francisco Bay, having completed the run from New York in eighty-nine days, twenty-one hours. This record is never beaten, except by *Flying Cloud* itself. The trip is sensa-tional news for the New York and San Francisco newspapers. The Creesy's retire in 1856, come back for one more trip in *Flying Cloud*, then retire again until Josiah joins the Union Navy in the Civil War. Eleanor's role as the de facto navigator of her husband's ships is recorded in some accounts, but ignored in the official docu-ments of the day.

MARY ANN PATTEN

There is no evidence to suggest any of these women went to sea with the initial expectation that they would navigate or perform regular ship duties like standing a watch. It was unthinkable to these nineteenth-century women, their husbands, and the crew that "ladies" would participate alongside men in the running of a ship. Some women remained determinedly domestic at sea, apparently content with playing the role of companion and homemaker. Others probably surprised themselves by discovering a bent for actually sailing a great, square-rigged ship. The most famous of the women clipper-era sailors was Mary Ann Patten. She married Captain Joshua Patten in Boston in 1853, at the age of sixteen. He was ten years her elder. Two years later, she joined him in the large clipper *Neptune's Car*. At some point on the long voyage to San Francisco, undoubtedly full of tedious and dull days for a bright young woman, Mary Ann Patten commenced teaching herself navigation. *Neptune's Car* went on across the Pacific to Hong Kong to load a cargo of tea for London and then return to New York. Mary Ann made herself useful on the voyage—when some crew members were injured by a lightning strike on a mast, she nursed them—and by the end of the voyage she had become a proficient navigator. Captain Patten is said to have then commented that his wife could have passed the examination for a master's certificate if she had wanted to. He reportedly also said the following of his wife: "Mrs. Patten is uncommon handy about the ship, even in weather, and would doubtless be of service if a man." On their next voyage to San Francisco Mary Ann Patten proves equal to his confidence in spades.

Neptune's Car sets sail again for San Francisco on July 1, 1856. As is usual when two or more well-known fast clippers set out about the same time on an important run like this, it is billed as a race and bets are taken among the shipping fraternity. *Neptune's Car* has *Intrepid* and *Romance of the Seas*, both very fast ships, as racing mates. The three leave within a three-day period. Mr. Keeler, Patten's first mate, begins making trouble early in the voyage, abusing the crew, sleeping on watch, and shortening sail without orders. Suspicions arise about Keeler's hand in a possible scheme to tilt the odds in the race in favour of some of the bettors. Nearing the Horn, Patten finally has Keeler relieved of duty and confined to his cabin. The second mate is a good seaman but illiterate and unable to perform the maths required to navigate, so the job is given to the next capable person: Mary Ann Patten. The voyage has been relatively easy, but as Mary Ann takes over navigation, things begin to get difficult—her husband becomes increasingly unable to command as his illness, which turns out to be advanced tuberculosis, debilitates him.

Approaching Cape Horn, the captain is on deck day and night, battling the strong westerly gales, but he soon exhausts himself; he becomes delirious, and lapses into intermittent comas. Mary Ann assumes charge of *Neptune's Car*, with the second mate agreeing to serve as her first mate. Former first mate Keeler offers to take the ship through the difficult passage around Cape Horn and on to California. In a moment of lucidity, Captain Patten rejects the idea, and Keeler threatens to set the crew against the pregnant, nineteen-year-old Mary Ann. Not to be daunted, she summons the crew to the break of the poop deck, the traditional place for masters to harangue their men, and explains the situation: she needs their help to get around the Cape and north to California, or, she offers alternatively, they can look to a passing vessel for help. The crew voice their confidence in her navigational abilities and answer with three cheers for the acting captain.

It is one of the toughest winters off the Horn, where the Chilean winds meet the south Atlantic gales in a foggy, rainy, snowy maelstrom. Ahead of *Neptune's Car*, *Rapid* is fighting the battle to get west past old "Cape Stiff," and losing. After losing ten men and having another ten injured, *Rapid's* captain gives up and flees back east for repairs, passing *Neptune's Car* heading into the same heavy weather with a new master in command.

With help from a willing crew, something not too common in those times, Mary Ann Patten fights for fifty days to gain westing, actively commanding operations from the poop and navigating mainly by dead reckoning under leaden skies. She struggles to get some sail to stay up, but it keeps blowing out. She keeps her ship head to the seas, not stopping to change her clothes and sleeping only a few hours at a time. In one storm, she remains on deck for forty-eight hours straight driving her charge into the mountainous head seas. Along with the ship, she has her husband to take care of. She tries to alleviate his suffering with what is available in the medicine chest and with advice from the *Sailors' Guide to Health*. Joshua Patten, for the most part comatose or delirious, is tied into his bunk as the ship pitches about.

The wind eventually abates and Mary Ann gets some sail up to make progress west. In the ship's log, she records, "A hard beat to windward under reefed topsails and foremast topsail." Then the skies brighten and a position check shows *Neptune's Car* far enough west to turn north to the Pacific Ocean. Captain Patten begins to recover a little and is able to help, but his wife continues to command on deck. The mate is released from confinement to help with the watches, as Mary Ann is exhausted. She discovers a few days later, however, that he is heading the ship towards Valparaiso. He is returned to confinement and Mary Ann lays a course toward San Francisco. By this time her husband has lost his sight, and Mary Ann is left with the whole responsibility of command once again. After a frustrating final ten days idling about with little wind, Mrs. Patten sails her vessel through the Golden Gate, a respectable 134 days out of New York. She beats *Intrepid* by 12 days, but is beaten in turn by *Romance of the Seas* by 22 days.

Mary Ann takes her husband ashore and then by steamer back to New York via the Isthmus of Panama and on to Boston. The insurers of the ship send Mary Ann a letter of commendation and a cheque for $1000. There are many remarks about how penurious they are when she has saved a vessel worth one hundred times that amount, but she writes a modest reply to the underwriters in which she says:

I feel very sensibly, gentlemen, that kindness which has prompted you to commend the manner in which I have endeavoured to perform that which seemed to me, under the circumstances, only the plain duty of a wife towards a good husband, stricken down with what we now fear to be a hopeless disease, and to perform for him, as well as I could, those duties which he could not perform for himself, especially when it was to carry out his own expressed wish. But I am, at the same time, seriously embarrassed by the fear that you may have overestimated the value of those services, because I feel that without the services of Mr. Hare, the second officer, a good seaman, and of the hearty cooperation of the crew to aid our endeavours, the ship would not have arrived safely at her destined port.

On March 10, 1857, Mary Ann's son was born. Two months later, on July 25, Captain Joshua Patten died, never knowing he was a father. Boston's feminist movement used Mary Ann Patten as an example of women's real capabilities and asked her to join their cause, but Mary Ann declined. Soon suffering from consumption, or tuberculosis, herself, she died four years later at the age of twenty-four. Mary Ann Patten, uniquely, is rated an outstanding woman in American maritime history, and a hospital at the Maritime Academy in King's Point, New York, carries her name.

III
ON THE WORLD TRADE ROUTES

ACCOUNTS OF A FEW WOMEN IN THE WORLD-CIRCLING SQUARE-RIGGED SHIPS
THAT ESTABLISHED GLOBAL SEABORNE COMMERCE IN THE 1800S.
WOMEN'S LOVE AND DISLIKE FOR THE LIFE. A TRANS-ATLANTIC SEAFARING
COMMUNITY IS ESTABLISHED.

European colonization and the industrial revolution led to the expansion of trade across the world throughout the nineteenth century. Although primitive steamships were developed early in the century, most of the goods transported continued to be carried in sailing ships. The increasing length of voyages and the development of more commodious trading vessels prompted more women to go to sea with their captain husbands and to take their young children along with them.

SARAH ANN (OSBORNE) SMITH
One day in 1874, twenty-six-year-old Sarah Ann Osborne packed her trunk, said her good-byes, and left the little shipbuilding port of St Martins, New Brunswick, for Saint John. There she met family friends Captain Jim Wishart and his wife Jennie, boarded their ship, and sailed across the Atlantic to Liverpool on her first long trip away from home. At twenty-seven, she would sign on for the vigorous life of a captain's wife at sea.

Sarah Ann and Captain David Smith were married in Birkenhead, across the Mersey from Liverpool. Sarah Ann immediately set up house in the saloon of *Prince Eugene*, a St Martins built vessel operated by the Morans of Liverpool and St Martins. The honeymoon voyage took the Smiths back across the ocean to Quebec and back again to Liverpool with a load of lumber. After delivering their cargo, they set out on the long voyage down the two Atlantic oceans, around the Horn, and up the west coast of South America to Callao, Peru, for a permit to the desolate guano ports. *Prince Eugene* was ordered to Pabellon de Pica, where there was the usual wait for the chance to load, and the ship lay at anchor among other vessels off the port for many weeks.

During this period there were two events of note: the Smith's firstborn—a daughter Jessie—arrived on board, and the earthquake and tidal wave of May 9, 1877, hit and virtually destroyed the town. The ships at anchor were driven ashore; seven were sunk and many lives were lost. *Prince Eugene* was among the many vessels suffering damage. Captain Smith managed to make his way to Callao, where repairs took five months because of the limited facilities and supplies available there.

Sarah Smith sailed on across the world with her husband. There was an aborted mutiny that ended with half the crew locked below, and the ship sailing on shorthanded for another ninety-four days. In September of 1878, a second daughter, Maggie Mabel, was born at sea. The registration of her birth at home in St Martins shows the place of birth as simply "21 degrees south, 23 degrees west." Delivering his own children was one of a captain's requisite skills. In November of the following year, the Smiths were able to go home on leave.

David Smith continued his career at sea, changing to ships of the Troop & Son fleet, one of the last operators of Canadian square-rigged sailing ships as steamships gained in popularity. Smith retired in 1909, after forty-two years at sea. His personal and official correspondence records the events of his career, but no mention is made of Mrs. Smith after the first few years. It is likely that she went ashore to raise her family, focusing her attention on them and learning to live with her husband's long absences.

As the world was opened up by trade and colonization in the nineteenth century, ocean shipping became key. At first the sailing ship carried all the cargoes, but through the century the steamship gradually developed a reliable shipping service, particularly suited to liner or scheduled runs between specific ports. The sailing ships were left to operate through the latter half of the century largely in tramp cargo service, which meant delivering cargoes to any specified destination, then sailing onward wherever the next cargo took them. Crews had little assurance as to when they would get home again. This tramping life was hard on both the homesick women on board and the women who opted to stay on shore while their husbands worked at sea. However, motivated by the love of sailing life and their devotion to their husbands, some women were content wherever they were.

Virginia (Walker) Slocum

Virginia Walker of Sydney, Australia, a good horsewoman and crack shot, was from a gold rush family out from New York via the California Gold Rush. Described as a handsome woman of regal bearing with some Indian blood, she loved the outdoor life and the freedom of Australia. The tall, lean American sea captain who came to Sydney and spied her would provide the chance for further adventure and travel.

The well-known name of Captain Josh Slocum immediately brings to mind a lone sailor battling storms on a great empty sea in a small boat. He became famous for daring, adventurous voyages in which he crossed the oceans of the world all by himself. Not so well known is his earlier career as master of full-sized ocean sailing ships. After his marriage, Slocum was accompanied not only by a crew, but also by his wife and growing family, and later, by his second wife.

Virginia Walker and Joshua Slocum met, courted, and married while Slocum's ship was in port at Sydney. Though it was normal for sailing ships to spend at least a month in port unloading and loading cargo with the primitive means available to powerless vessels, Slocum was a fast worker and managed to balance work and matrimonial duties with time to spare. Virginia went to sea with her husband in vessels large and small, even living in a thatched hut in the Philippines while he built ships. When he was paid off with a small schooner, she and the children sailed with him on trading and fishing expeditions to Hong Kong, Yokohama, the Siberian Kamchatka Peninsula, and, with a huge catch of cod, 8000 miles across the Pacific to Portland, Oregon.

The twenty-one-year-old bride joined her husband aboard *Washington* and sailed with him for the rest of her life. They were said to be very close and well-matched, often oblivious to those around them. Virginia was certainly devoted and long-suffering.

After *Washington* ran on a reef in Alaska in a gale and stuck fast, Captain Slocum was given command of the barkentine *Constitution* aboard which Victor, their first child, was born in San Francisco Harbour in 1872. In another vessel the next year, a second child was born, followed by a third in 1875 in Philippine waters. Captain Slocum, in his own free-wheeling way, started to trade in small vessels about the eastern seas. Virginia gave birth to twins off the Siberian Kamchatka Peninsula. After acquiring his own 350-ton vessel *Amethyst*, Slocum sailed to Manila. He hired his brother as cook and a sister to assist Virginia, who was now busy schooling her children. Virginia also busied herself with sewing and playing the piano, though she still practiced her marksmanship. Reports say that she would have seamen attract sharks to the ship for her to kill with one shot from a .32 revolver.

The twins died and, in 1881, another baby—the seventh—arrived while the ship was in Hong Kong Harbour. Not yet forty, Slocum traded up to a much larger vessel, purchasing the eighteen-hundred-ton *Northern Light*, and sailed proudly home to New York. During a mutiny on a move from New York up to New London, the mate was fatally stabbed. Virginia's proven ability with firearms stood her in good stead as she held the mutineers at bay with a pair of pistols, protecting Joshua until the Coast Guard arrived on the scene. On sailing to the Orient in 1884, another mutiny was forestalled, but there was a lawsuit and a need for major repairs to the ship. Disgusted, Slocum sold his shares in the vessel and took his family home to Boston.

But the whole family was soon off again in a smaller vessel, *Acquidneck*, sailing to Buenos Aires in 1884. Virginia fell ill off the coast of Brazil, and died aboard while her husband was on shore in the Argentine capital trying to secure cargo to Australia so that he could take his wife home. At thirty-five she was buried in an English cemetery in Buenos Aires, having ended a devoted, but surely strenuous life.

Slocum, who could properly be described as eccentric, picked up his career again, sailing to South America with his second wife, Hettie (Henrietta), a pretty twenty-four-year-old cousin from Nova Scotia. Victor Slocum, now fourteen and a veteran of the sea, was mate, and his younger brother Garfield was with them. The ship stranded at Paranagua, Brazil. In true Slocum style, Joshua used materials salvaged from the ship and hand tools to build what he called a sea canoe. The canoe looked like a large, covered dory, with three short masts and square sails like a Chinese junk. He and Hettie, with the two boys as crew, sailed north all the way to Washington, D.C., a trip that convinced Hettie to stay ashore thereafter. Joshua Slocum's finances had been in decline and he headed "on the downhill course toward fame" as a solo round-the-world sailor in small boats. His books recounting his voyages make little mention of his wives. Hettie was left for protracted periods at home in Massachusetts, without word from him. She was ultimately obliged to have him declared missing and presumed dead.

Emily (Morris) Spicer

Emily Spicer was a woman who went to sea in the usual fashion—to accompany her husband instead of living life ashore alone. She moved ashore when her five children needed the benefits of a regular school, but Emily Spicer was determined not to see her children return to sea as adults. Like Cordelia Waterman before her, Emily Spicer had not approved of the hard-driving style on ships like her husband's. Determined though she was to have her children choose lives on land, she did not quite succeed.

Emily Jane Morris grew up in the village of Advocate, Nova Scotia, near the small but prolific shipbuilding port of Spencer's Island on the eastern shore of Minas Basin. In 1868, she married twenty-three-year-old Captain George Spicer, a ship's master of two years standing. Like so many young men who achieved this exalted status, George Spicer was big, self-reliant, and brimming with self-confidence. At the same time, he had learned humility and religious reverence from the sea. Hard-working and largely self-taught, he came from lowly rural origins, making his way up the ladder of jobs available aboard ship from the age of twelve as cabin boy on a schooner.

Emily ultimately moved ashore so the children could have regular schooling. Then came the years of George's long absences and worrying for his safety. He was one of the masters known as "drivers" because they sailed their vessels hard and pushed the crew to perform hard as well. But getting good seamen in the 1880s was difficult.

s on board the Spicer ships and on one occasion a young mate,
e captain's relation, was stabbed to death. It seems quite likely that
rd ship was not as pleasant as some others, though she did hold
s on Sundays, with invitations to the crew to attend.

as for the coarseness of life that she discouraged her two daughters
from entertaining ideas of returning to the sea. They largely obliged:
married landsmen, one son went into business, and another became
third son, Whitney, wanted to follow his father at sea, but George
d Emily that he wouldn't take him. Emily died in 1890, and when
ned eighteen a few years later, he persuaded his father to take him on
his full-rigged ship *Glooscap*, the last of the great sailing ships built in
n. According to the Canadian custom, Whitney signed on as a lowly
ge Spicer lived to regret going against Emily's wishes as a stark entry in
November 14, 1898, off Luzon in the Philippines indicates:

*Hard squalls and rain coming down in torrents all day. A high sea going. At 4 p.m.
Whitney and three others went out on the jib-boom to secure the jib. The ship took a
sea over the boom and they all went. My son drowned before my eyes and I was not
able to do a thing.*

Abigail Ryerson

The striking feature of this era in commerce is that thousands of vessels were
powered about the world entirely by the sailor's ability to manipulate whatever
winds happened to blow. One need only ponder a vessel one or two hundred feet
long, loaded with a thousand tons of cargo, being coaxed across oceans, through
tricky, rock-strewn passages with swirling currents. And all managed by putting
up canvas sails to catch whatever breeze or gale there might be, from whatever
direction it chooses to come. Navigation aids were minimal in much of the world
and there was no radio. Considering the perils, it is not be surprising that many
ships simply disappeared. Yet in their writings, many women present sailing as a
pleasure tour of the world's exotic ports and their frail ship as their snug home.
Excerpts from the journal of Abigail Ryerson demonstrate the near helpless de-
pendence of the shipmaster on the vagaries of wind and current and the blindness
imposed by fog. Abigail's journal recounts events on a voyage from Saint John to
Greenock aboard *Nova Scotian*, captained by John Ryerson. Captain Ryerson,
Abigail, and the crew set out from Saint John on August 27, 1847. Wary of being
blown further up the Bay of Fundy and trapped there by the prevailing southerly
winds, Ryerson anchors off Partridge Island at the harbour entrance. He wanders
about trying to get down the bay, hindered by the lack of useful winds and blind-
ing fogs, and threatened by rocky coastline and islands all around. Ten days later
Nova Scotian finally emerges from the Bay of Fundy off the tip of Nova Scotia at

Seal Island; luckily, Ryerson knows with certainty where they are. Abigail's journal records their perambulations with a good understanding of their movements and difficulties. Some of her entries differ little from that written by a captain in his official log. She has certainly mastered the discourse:

Friday, August 27, 1847
Took leave of our friends at the City Hotel and embarked aboard the Nova Scotian, weighed anchor and was towed down to Partridge Island by the steamer Maid of Erin, Capt. Livitt, master. The wind being south, obliged to anchor. Not being accustomed to the sea was a little sick this afternoon, there being a heavy sea for a ship at anchor, but soon revived and assisted in arranging the necessaries for the voyage.

Partridge Island is a beautiful little island situated at the mouth of St. John Harbour. There is a light-house, a fog bell and a telegraph station upon it beside three hospitals and a few small houses with some fine shade trees. At present there are a great many tents pitched upon it for shelter for the Irish immigrants which have recently landed from the old country, and many, many have died there with the immigrant fever, while numbers are still suffering under the disease.

Saturday, August 28
This day commences with a thick fog, moderate breeze from the southeast   attended by a little rain. Crew employed in cleaning decks and preparing for sea. Am perfectly well and much pleased with my new home. This afternoon will busy myself by making new curtains for the stateroom. Captain goes on shore or up to look on business leaving me in the master's care. Captain returning safe finds us at our unusual amusement, cooking cake and pies for Sunday on board of a ship, it being the first thing of the kind I then had the pleasure of doing. So ends this day.

August 29
This day commences with moderate breezes from the northwest. Roused all hands half-past five. Weighed anchor and set sail for sea in company with three other ships outward bound and all sail set to a fair wind. Middle part winds died away, took in studding sails and hauled the ship by the wind. So ends this day.

August 30
This day commences with thick fog, wind to the south, at noon fog clears and nearly calm. Crew employed in ship service, at two made land which proved to be Grand Manan about 12 miles off. This afternoon (to add to the comfort of the captain and myself) employed by stuffing the rocking chair. After tea went on deck and exercised by jumping the rope, rehearsed the compass. Wind still to the south, fog returning. So ends this day.

Tuesday, August 31
This day begins with a thick fog and wind to south. Moderate breeze. Still beating down the bay, the wind and tide alternating ahead, have not gained many miles. At ten fog cleared up and found we were just on shore at the Petit Passage, probably not quarter of a mile distance. Tacked ship immediately, bore round and soon found ourselves out of danger. The latter part of the day have been knitting. Crew employed in ripping up sails for a purpose I have now forgotten. The term, being a green hand, expect it will take me some time to learn all the ropes as the sailors call it. Feel very much grieved to see the captain with so much anxiety and care upon his mind. But hope Providence will send a north wind to clear the fog that we may get out of this dangerous place. So ends the day.

September 1, 1847
Still find ourselves in the same state, it being very foggy and wind still from southward, judging ourselves up with Brier Island, looking out for land. Rehearsed the compass but have not yet committed it to memory. Latter part commenced raining, hope this will wash the fog away. Employed in mending socks and knitting with other domestic chores. Seamen doing ship's duty and trying to catch a cod. So ends the day.

September 2
Again we perceive with fog. We are surrounded. A short calm this morning. At seven p.m. a moderate breeze from the southeast. Soon after spoke a schooner laden with wood bound for Boston and had been deeper in the fog than ourselves, having not seen land since Tuesday night, heading southeast by east. Crew employed in scrubbing decks latter part of the day. At 4 p.m. discovered a school of mackerel under our lee and prepared a line and by the time t'was over, our ship had run away from them. Amused ourselves hauling it in several times. Usual work knitting for our shipmate the captain and assisted the steward in making a bread pudding for dinner, and toast for tea. It being quite wet, have not had chance for exercise. The captain having read to me for a good part of the day from the ladies' magazine. Have passed the day very pleasantly. So ends this day.

September 3
This day commences with a light breeze from the southward with fog. At six p.m. discerned a sail through the fog, in a short time came up with her. She was bound for Boston, load of cord wood from Digby. Left Brier Island last night at 4 p.m. Judged Brier Island to bear east about 18 miles. Gave us quite a dish of conversation as he was highly blest with the gift of the gab, which raised some laughter among the crew. Crew employed in ship service. Employment for ourselves much as yesterday. So ends this day foggy as usual.

September 4
This day begins with a moderate breeze from the southward still attended with fog. Not having been very well from a slight cold I had taken while attempting to fish, I know but little as regards today's affairs except that by sitting at our stateroom windows, overheard the captain give orders for the helm to be put hard down and some of the crew to catch some fish. My curiousity led me to remain in the same position to see if their attempts proved the same as mine, fruitless or no, having my appetite satisfied by seeing them haul three or four in with ease. So ends this day.

September 5
This day begins as bad as the last ends, with thick fog and wind still from the south, the wind having been at the same corner for seven days. Were in hopes that by the eighth there would certainly be a change as it had not varied over three points during that period of time. At four, the mate went into the top to see if he could discern land as the fog seemed to lighten a little. He did so, it being so thick he could not tell what it was, apparently four miles distant. As we were still beating, tacked ship and stood off. So ends this day.

September 6
This day begins with a little better prospect than usual. At half past five the sun appears to be finding his way through the fog. A strong breeze from the south which makes more sea than we have yet had. At noon got the sun and found we were about three miles south of Seal Island. The captain feels a little better in his mind than he did last night at this time. At four out all sail to a fair wind. Latter part commenced raining. So ends this day.

Although they have been wandering back and forth blind between the hazardous shores of both sides of the Bay of Fundy with its swirling, powerful tides before finally clearing the south end of Nova Scotia, Abigail Ryerson is still able to concentrate on routine events.

September 7
This day begins with a strong breeze from the north. At 2 p.m. took in the studding sails and braced the yards. The day has been very pleasant, scarcely a cloud to be seen in the horizon, and upwards of twelve vessels have been seen, eight of which have been ships and the remainder barques and schooners. At four set the studding sails. Crew variously employed. Have been variously employed myself. So ends this day.

September 8
We have had very fine weather today with the wind to the east. At 9 a.m. took in the studding sails and shaped our course to the southeast at 5-1/2 a.m. past, tacked ship

and stood to the north. The captain having wished me to learn to take the sun, complied with his kind request by practicing at 12 p.m. I am highly delighted with the idea of any practical branch of education. This afternoon have been employed in the cooking line, having baked tarts and gingerbread. We have a very attentive steward as regards the baking line. We have passed the day very pleasantly. it has been so very fine, with scarcely a ruffle on the ocean or a cloud to be seen in the sky.

September 9
This day begins with beautiful weather and the wind is in the east, light and baffling. This being directly opposite to what we would wish, have tacked ship several times during the last 24 hours. We are now in Latitude 41°-42' and Longitude 61°-30' by chronometer which in all probability makes us in the Gulf. It has been delightful beyond any descriptive powers to describe this day's scene upon the ocean. Our ship gliding so smoothly over the proud waves which roll so calmly, one after another, that it has awakened within our breasts some sweet thoughts as regards being wafted to our future home, that being one of the most delightful topics for meditation.

We amuse ourselves after dinner by tabling some birds which have been following us for the last day or two. I believe they are called petrels or mother Carey's chickens. By throwing over grease it was amusing to see what numbers we would have about us so soon as they tasted of this great luxury, and what was still more as to see with what greediness they would catch at the small particles which would be so soon dispersed after throwing it to them. We pass the time very pleasantly, but think we should much more so had we our darling boy with us, whom we regret to have left behind. The weather having been so fine thus far, and being blest with our health in such a comfortable degree. Been employed much the same as yesterday. Crew differently employed. So ends this day.

It took *Nova Scotian* thirteen days to get clear of the perils of the coast and beyond the ships' graveyard of Sable Island, half of the time required for the whole voyage to Liverpool.

W.D.Lawrence, A Man Left Ashore
William D. Lawrence, a shipbuilder from Maitland, Nova Scotia, had produced six ships by 1868, launching them into the swirling, muddy tides on the Shubenacadie River. He learned his trade under the celebrated clipper-builder Donald Mackay in East Boston. One of his later ships was the 1120-ton *Pegasus*, which sailed off on the usual world-wide itinerary to earn a profit for Lawrence on its construction. The captain, Jim Ellis, had married Lawrence's daughter Mary and taken her with him to sea. William Lawrence had been recently widowed and was not happy to be without the company of Mary and her three children in his big house on the hill above the river. This time it was not a wife who was left

alone on shore, but a father. *Pegasus* took the typical long tramping route to go where cargo was or might be offered, ending with Philippine sugar bound for Boston. After four years and three months afloat, Captain Ellis turned over his command and the Ellis family took a steamer home via Halifax.

Upon the return of his daughter and her family, Lawrence hatched a plan to hold his family to him. First he would construct a very large ship. It was to be the ultimate wooden sailing ship and his ultimate investment in shipping. In 1874, after two years of building, he completed what turned out to be the largest wooden square-rigged vessel ever built in Canada and the largest in the world at that time. The ship was 2459 tons, had a 200-foot keel, carried 8000 square yards of sail canvas, and was given his name, *W.D.Lawrence.*

Lawrence kept his daughter and son-in-law captain at home for two years to help supervise the construction of his great ship. Then Captain Ellis took the new vessel to sea; with him were his family, including his owner and father-in-law. Because Lawrence could not have his family at home, he joined them at sea and arranged that they live in style: there was a huge, paneled main cabin and spacious sleeping cabins in the big vessel, including one for the children's tutor. Lawrence stayed aboard with his family for two years, enjoying sightseeing in ports around the world.

The Liverpool Connection

After a great part of the port city of Saint John, New Brunswick was destroyed in a conflagration in 1877, one of the most prominent sources of monetary assistance was Liverpool, England. The connection between these two ports was very close through most of the nineteenth century. Numerous Maritime women from small towns visited and knew Liverpool well. New Brunswick and Nova Scotia captains moved their families to Liverpool and other British ports because these would be their principal ports of call. Names like Moran, Haws, and Wright were prominent in ship-owning and brokering on both sides. With its ability to capitalize on the industrial revolution and the resulting spread of commerce across the seas, Liverpool became one of the world's most important seaports. Saint John was the heart of the wooden shipbuilding industry that satisfied the growing demand for ships and the timber to build them. A pattern between these two important port cities developed: Liverpool entrepreneurs emigrated to Quebec, Nova Scotia, and New Brunswick to engage in shipbuilding, then returned to operate in the shipping trade at its hub in Liverpool. Many of the vessels built by the British in the Maritimes went to associates and relatives back in England and Scotland. The wives and children of ship owners, brokers, and masters were caught up in these peregrinations, giving birth to the trans-Atlantic seafaring family, at home on both sides of the "Western Ocean."

Many of the men involved in these enterprises were master mariners who moved ashore to build and broker vessels after serving time at sea, often in the company of their wives and children. Women were not unfamiliar with life aboard ships, and most relationships and marriages were made from amongst the captains and mariners and their daughters. An example of one of these building, sailing and owning clans is that of the Hawses.

Calista Calvert, daughter of a prominent Loyalist family in Saint John, married an enterprising young shipbuilder who found success among the prolific builders there. John Haws became established in shipbuilding in Saint John around 1820. His shipyard and home were in Portland, adjoining Saint John. After his death, Calista visited and finally retired in Liverpool, which had become the headquarters of the family business. Haws' sons and grandsons built and sailed family ships from bases in Saint John, Quebec, and Liverpool.

In a slump after the Crimean War, the first son of John and Calista, John C. Haws, sold the shipyard and moved to Liverpool to become a shipbroker and operator with his brother Richard. A successful businessman, Richard built a fine home, known as Portland House, on the outskirts of Liverpool. Here, his wife Eliza staged marvelous Dickensian Christmas celebrations for their six children and, eventually, their grandchildren. The area in Liverpool where the Hawses lived was known as the "New Brunswick Settlement" because other former shipbuilding and sailing families such as the Vaughans, Morans, Nevins, and Wrights from the Saint John area were also established there.

John Haws' third son, George William, was the second master mariner in the family. George went to Quebec City to serve the Haws shipping interests and there met and, in 1860, married Elizabeth Taylor Davie. The marriage established a connection between the Haws family and the major shipyard entrepreneurs of Levis, the Davie family. The one condition of the marriage, however, was that George had to agree to give up the sea and the command of his splendid vessel *Calista Haws*.

When Haws shipmasters were accompanied by their wives, Richard's daughter Eliza "Bessie" Haws went along as a guest. It was said she travelled for her health, but she seems to have enjoyed the sea and the view of the world it gave her. The son of George and Elizabeth was Allison Davie Haws, who went to sea as well. One rule of the Haws shipping firm was that one must become a master mariner before being admitted to senior management. Allison Haws was duly apprenticed in the Haws ship *Traveller*, in 1881. There he found he had the company not only of the captain and his wife, but also of his own cousin "Bessie."

When appointed later as mate in another ship, cousin Bessie was again enjoying a voyage with the captain and his wife. As soon as Allison gained his master's papers in 1887, he married Bessie and took command of his old ship *Traveller*. A honeymoon voyage around South America to San Francisco ensued, with Bessie spending a good deal of the time rounding Cape Horn lashed to the leg of the cabin table to keep from being thrown about. The passage around "Cape Stiff" was living up to its reputation for wild storms. But Bessie was not unprepared, for she had travelled as a young woman with her brother Captain John R. Haws, and probably as a child with her family.

Bessie and Allison Haws returned to England, then sailed out to Rangoon, but Bessie returned by way of the Suez Canal by steamer "for reasons of midwifery." Allison returned to Liverpool, the new father of a baby girl. On a voyage to Calcutta in June of 1893, Bessie and Allison's second child, three-year-old George William, missed his grip on a hand rail in a North Sea gale. He fell down the poop ladder and suffered a severe concussion. Captain Haws put his wife and children ashore by way of a passing trawler and continued his voyage. George never went to sea again except for short trips around the English coast. George would have liked to have stayed at sea in the family tradition and was envious of other children who sailed. His sensitivity to his own lack of experience aboard ship comes through in his story of Nelly, a friend, climbing a mast:

> Other families were more fortunate and Nelly, only daughter of our old family friend Captain Burchell of the Oweenee went to sea up to the age of fourteen years with her parents, at which age she was sent to school. We were close friends and she was greatly envied by me, especially on those occasions when the Oweenee visited Liverpool and I went on board and was shown her curios and treasures. The last time was in Wapping Dock, Liverpool. On climbing high aloft, I had to take the cowardly route, passing through the lubber's hole, while she, being thoroughly used to it, went up the outside over the ratlines like a sailor.
>
> I can remember how shame-faced I was at being beaten by a girl and by the surprise expressed by Captain Burchell at my evident ignorance in ignoring the correct path going straight up from the top of the shrouds.

The Haws family's company made the inevitable shift to steamships, which were built in Britain. Their role in shipping ended with World War One, but the surname spread across Canada and was highly respected in Liverpool.

IV
THE PARKER WOMEN

A DAUGHTER WRITES HOMESICK LETTERS TO HER MOTHER IN NEW BRUNS-
WICK FROM STEAMY CALCUTTA. HER SISTER-IN-LAW HAS MARRIED A FAMOUS
CAPTAIN, BUT FINDS THE NORTH ATLANTIC OCEAN TOO ROUGH. THE FATES
BRING TRAGEDY TO ANOTHER BROTHER AND HIS WIFE.

The Parker family of Tynemouth Creek, New Brunswick
consisted of a number of seafarers, men and women alike.
Bessie Parker's collection of correspondence, received from
a number of her seafaring children, provides a rare record of one family's travels
all over the world.

BESSIE PARKER

Although Bessie Parker can be counted among the Parker women who never went
to sea, she was intimately concerned with the lives of those who did. The tri-
umphs and perils of this precarious trade were part of her everyday life; her husband, John Parker of Tynemouth Creek, New Brunswick, built ships and her sons
sailed them. Bessie's first born son died of fever sailing in the Caribbean while still
in his teens. At least six of her sons went to sea at one time or another, and she
carried on correspondence not only with them, but also with her daughter Annie
and her sea-faring daughters-in-law Lilly and Ida. She was a source of strength to
them all, and their devotion to her is evident. Regrettably, few of her own letters
to them have survived. In 1845, Bessie Parker gave birth to the fourth of their
eight children—Annie, their first daughter. Almost nothing is known of Annie's
early life, but it was most likely domestically oriented and it certainly took place in
a village shipbuilding and sailing atmosphere. Annie went to sea like her three
younger captain brothers, and became a significant contributor to the body of
family correspondence.

ANNIE (PARKER) COCHRANE

Young women often went to sea with family members, but staying at sea for any real length of time as adults usually meant marrying a sea captain. The selection of potential bridegrooms in Tynemouth Creek would have been small, though reasonably enough both Annie Parker and her sister Alice married men from the nearby village of Quaco (later St Martins). Quaco village was a busy shipbuilding centre for its size. Settled early by land grantees with some shipbuilding know-how, the Vaughan and Moran families vigorously pursued the most promising line of commerce in the primitive young colony of New Brunswick. They built ships from the ample forests at hand. The number of ocean-going ships produced in St Martins was prodigious for a mere village—about sixty. The most prolific builder was James Moran, who built twenty-four square-riggers between 1855 and 1874, mostly for the firm Moran-Galloway of Saint John and Liverpool.

Annie married Captain Daniel Cochrane, from a less established family of builders and seafarers in Quaco. He was ten years her senior and sailed for most of his career with Moran Galloway. Despite being a home-loving daughter in a close-knit family, Annie joined her husband aboard, although she never overcame her home-sickness. In 1876, Bessie Parker mentions a report that "Moran's are going to have a new ship built for Dan." The ship turned out to be the splendid *Prince Lucien*, one of the larger vessels of the time at 1549 tons. Dan Cochrane sailed the *Prince Lucien* about the world for many years, accompanied by Annie and, when very young, their children.

Annie (Parker) Cochrane joined her three brothers in a life at sea by marrying a captain. She liked her home afloat, but was homesick.

This portrait of Annie (Parker) Cochrane, with son Parker and Captain Dan Cochrane, was taken in Liverpool, their home port.

At first, Dan sailed in the trans-Atlantic, American, and Caribbean trade, permitting several visits home each year. But then the trading patterns for Canadian sailing ships changed to accommodate the steamers that started carrying the premium cargoes across the Atlantic. The slower sailing ships took the world-wide bulk cargoes around Capes Horn and Good Hope to the Pacific and Indian Oceans, the Pacific Northwest, Australia, and the Orient. Possibly the first very long voyage for Annie was from London to Callao, Peru. Her mother Bessie writes to son Leonard in November of 1876, saying "Poor dear Annie is going to Callao, write her there she says (with love to you), about middle of January. Poor thing, I feel sorry for her going on such a long voyage."

There was reason for concern as it was a long, difficult voyage around South America to Peru, even in the southern summer. The wreckage of sailing ships strewn along the jagged coasts was fair warning of the peril. A call at Callao meant loading guano from bleak, treeless islands lying off the coast while at anchor, with no piers and no city to visit, not even a sheltered port. Long waits for a turn to load and primitive, hand-loading methods meant a stay of up to several months.

By the time Annie and Dan Cochrane sail to Callao, they have a son and a daughter, Parker and "Little Annie," who may or may not have been born at sea. (On a trans-Atlantic schedule, Annie likely stayed home a voyage or two to give birth.) The children sail with their parents, taking to the sea life as the natural way of things.

The new ship *Prince Lucien* arrived in Liverpool, the home port of Moran-Galloway and many other major shipping lines. It was common with Canadian-built vessels that some final fitting such as coppering the wood bottoms against tropical wood borers be done on first arrival in Liverpool. Annie uses the time in Liverpool to make final improvements to the after cabins, her new home.

The Cochranes sail to Antwerp in April of 1878, likely with a cargo of grain, a profitable run for sailing vessels in the trans-Atlantic trade. With the usual slow pace of unloading, they are still in Antwerp at the beginning of May. From Antwerp, *Prince Lucien* embarks for Bombay with coal, an extended voyage that exacerbates Annie's homesickness. It is plain from her correspondence that she longs for her old home and the company of her mother. In Bombay, Moran's places the new ship in the competitive eastern rice trade out of the Bay of Bengal until a good cargo back to Europe or America can be found. Signs of the coming decline in the availability of cargoes and, consequently, a decline in the viability of sailing ships, are everywhere evident. Sailing ships lie idle or sail home in ballast for want of a cargo contract. Eventually, a contract is set for home *and Prince Lucien* departs. Annie writes her mother from her temporary accommodations at 50 Nelson Street in Liverpool. She has made the important decision that it is time for their son Parker to stay ashore to attend a proper school. Daughter Annie will continue to live aboard the big square-rigger:

May 24, 1878

My Dear Mama,

I know you think I am not writing so regularly as I might do, but I have been very busy. I have not had a moment. We arrived here from Antwerp on Saturday, had a rather rough passage across the North Sea arrived at Grimsby at 6 p.m. Sunday and started for L'pool at 6 a.m. Monday, arrived here at noon and found Nelson Street just in the same place.

Parker is quite pleased at the idea of going to boarding school. He will begin school on Monday so that he might be nicely settled before we leave. We have made arrangements for him at such a nice school. They only take six boys as boarders and make their own of them. They have no family and are the nicest people I have met for a long time. They will take Parker with them to Wales for a month in midsummer during the holidays. I have been so fortunate to find out this school. It was very highly recommended to me the last time I was here, but we thought it too much to pay for Parker then.

You will not neglect writing him sometimes, dear mama, while we are away from the dear. He has no one but you to write to him. I am sure he will be pleased to get a letter from my grandma. I have almost everything he will want as regards clothing. Mrs. Robertson will buy him anything he requires while we are away. She is so kind and motherly, I'm sure he will grow fond of her. The five boys who are there now are

This barque, Prince Lucien, was home for Annie Cochrane and her young children as they sailed from England to India and back. The splendid full-rigged Moran ship was built in St Martins, New Brunswick in 1877. Annie supervised the interior decoration of the family quarters of the newly built vessel.

all so happy and so nicely behaved I think Parker will be all right, and perhaps learn better than he would if he was with me.

The weather is very cold and wet. We will be here about three weeks longer. Our new ship is very nice. Good night my own dearest Ma, God bless and keep you. With kindest love to all, I remain your ever loving and devoted daughter - Annie.

Annie writes a short note just before departing for India. She is somewhat conscience-stricken at leaving her young son behind:

My Dearest Ma,
We are all ready for sea, and will go out of dock tomorrow morning at 9 a.m. I am going over to Birkenhead with my things this afternoon and am very busy packing up this morning. I don't like leaving everything for the morning. Parker will come home tonight and spend tomorrow, Saturday, with Mrs. Carlow. Poor dear, he will feel it very much and how I feel to leave him dear ma, you can well understand. I must try and not let him see how hard it is for me. He will be well cared for and it must be done.

Mrs. Robertson will see that he writes to you once in two months or oftener perhaps and, please ma, write to him as often as you can. It will be four months before he can possibly get a letter from me. He is going to Wales to spend the holidays with Mr. and Mrs. Robertson. They go every summer and will take him with them. I have a few friends here who will see him occasionally and if any of my brothers come here I know they will call to see him.

How I long to see you each time I leave here. I feel how long it is since I saw you. That photo has never come yet. Annie is out with Pattie. She is quite well. Dan is well and very busy today. Address our letters c/o Jehanisphee Jehangee, Apollo Street, Bombay.

Give our kindest love to papa, grandma and all the family and believe me as ever, your most devoted daughter - Annie. Excuse haste. We sail tomorrow, 15th.

On October 9 *Prince Lucien* sails into the harbour at Bombay to anchor before the teeming city and awaits a turn for unloading.

Prince Lucien Bombay, Oct. 10, [18]78
My Dearest Ma,
We arrived yesterday all well after a pleasant passage of one-hundred-and-fifteen days which is considered very fair for this season. We were eight days becalmed just a few hours sail from the port, which appeared longer than the whole passage to that point.

I received two letters from dear Parker. He writes me that he is very happy and does the best he can to learn which is a very great satisfaction to us. I rec'd a letter from Mrs. Robertson who writes very highly assuring me that he is just the good boy he always was, and that I need not feel at all worried about him. He is such a sensible boy, he knows it is for his own good and I think the last voyage was quite enough for him.

Well, Ma, with what pleasure I received your kind letters you can never imagine. I got it into my head that something had happened to you and that I was never to hear from you again. Your last letter rec'd the morning we sailed made me feel so badly that the whole passage I thought of scarcely anything else and dreamed constantly all sorts of bad dreams about you. I seemed possessed with an evil spirit that gave me no peace, and though I wanted my letters so much I was afraid to look at them. I could scarcely believe my own eyes when I saw one in your dear handwriting. I know it was foolish of me, but dearest Ma, when we are at sea so long and everything just the same day after day. We have so much time to worry and think over what people on shore forget in a few days.

Dan is quite well but not a little troubled about what is to be done with the ship. There is nothing for steamers to do here and several ships have gone from here to New Orleans for orders (without cargo). Just fancy that. I expect we will lay here a long time unless something turns up. Our ship is so nice it is not like being on board ship at all. We have everything that heart can wish to make us comfortable. We had everything fitted up so nicely in L'pool and I am quite proud of my nice cabins.

Women who chose to accompany their captain husbands at sea in the deep-water sailing ships needed courage and strength. They could make a cosy home, but rarely was another woman aboard, and she might not meet another woman for several months. Life aboard ship was often confining even when in port.

Lying at anchor week after week in steaming Bombay Harbour, waiting to fix a cargo contract is frustrating for Annie. It is the hottest season and the ship, although well-appointed, is naturally without electricity, refrigeration, or plumbing. Annie Cochrane, lonesome for the close society of Tynemouth Creek, depends upon correspondence from her mother and family for news. She writes home regularly, and, while she acknowledges that her mother is very busy, regularly pleads for letters in return. Annie has time to write, whereas her mother is the "queen-pin" of her community and has half a dozen children besides Annie scattered about the world to correspond with.

Altho' I haven't any news I must write something as I can't expect you to write unless I answer some of your letters which are so welcome. We are slowly discharging. Have not done much yet, the weather is so fearfully hot the men can't work well. Under the awning the thermometer is about noon up to 106 degrees. When it is so warm in the shade, I don't know what it would be in the sun. I never felt anything like it, and at night it is almost as warm. Some nights we are on deck all hours in the night trying to find a cool place. I believe this the hottest month of the year in India.

We had a terrible thunderstorm night before last. The thunder and lightning was frightful and, talk about it raining in buckets-full, I think it rained casks-full at a time the most of the night.

We were invited to Jehanisfee's day before yesterday, which was their New Year's Day, to see the grand ceremony of opening the new books. Six sheets of paper wouldent half hold it all, so I can't begin to tell you about it. I will only say Jehanisfee was flying around in a new pair of yellow satin trousers and scarlet slippers and all his children were there with 30 others, all relatives. He gave everyone a rupee for luck and a daub of red stuff like red paint on their forehead. Annie wouldn't keep it on. I don't think the old fellow noticed it though. We had champagne icecreams and enjoyed it all vastly. I haven't seen such a grand performance before and never expect to again.

I have no idea of how long we may have to lie here. There is nothing for ships on this coast (as opposed to steamers). There are some lying here seven and eight months—can't get anything to do, and Calcutta is the same. Unless there is a good crop of rice there will be nothing else for us. The rice season doesn't come in till February. It is not known yet whether there will be a good crop this year or not. There never was such dull times known before and no prospect for any improvement. I can't understand what inducement there is to build more ships when there is nothing for them to do and not likely to be. However, some wonderful change may take place next year. We will hope so.

In November, the oppressive heat eases, Annie makes expeditions ashore, and her health and outlook improve.

Prince Lucien, Bombay, Nov 12, '78
My Dearest Ma,
I am afraid you have only written two letters thinking we would not be longer than a month here. Now, by the time you receive our first and answer it, we will be without letters about three months. Our letters will be forwarded to the next port, but I hoped to have had more than two. None have come by the last four mails. We have an English mail every week.

We are all enjoying good health and hope you are likewise. The weather is quite cool and pleasant now: I am a different person. Didn't know till now that I haven't been well since we arrived. The weather was so fearfully hot I was good for nothing, had no appetite and felt miserable. Now I am so well and feel like a new creature. Mornings and evenings are quite cool and so pleasant. Even the middle of the day is not so warm in the shade. We went to church last Sunday, which I enjoyed very much. It was held on board one of the ships in the fleet. A number of ladies were there, several from shore.

We are discharging very slowly, have only one-thousand tons out yet. We expect to lie here till the rice crop is ready, which will be in Feb., but it will take a month, or six weeks, perhaps, to go round to the rice ports—if we go.

The harbour is crowded with ships. Some have lain here nearly a year, can't get anything to pay expenses, expecting something to turn up, which so far has not. I be-

*lieve ships will have to lay up before long unless something makes a stir. I am sorry to
hear Pa is building another. I am afraid he will rue it.*

*Dear Ma, I have no news worth writing. How much I would like to see you today.
Take good care of yourself, give my love to Pa and Grandma. Hope they are both well.
Annie sends you a dozen kisses. She calls you grandma now. She remembers Grandma
Ellis darning stockings and putting an apple in the heel. She is as black as a little coolie
and generally a very good child. I don't remember the last time I had to whip her. I
will answer Sarah's letter soon, give my love. Dan unites in kindest love to all. Ever
your affectionate daughter, Annie.*

The new ship that John Parker is building is *J. V. Troop*, for Troop & Son, with
the builder retaining some shares as was customary. Bessie Parker complies with
Annie's request to write Parker Cochrane at his boarding school and he replies,
mentioning a visit with his Uncle Raymond who has arrived in England in his
swift new barque *Cyprus*, in which he makes some astonishing trans-Atlantic runs:

174 Chatham Street, Liverpool, 13th November, 1878
My Dear Grandma,
*I thank you very much for your kind loving letters which make me so happy each time
I read them. Uncle Raymond gave me the pretty story book that you sent me and I like
it very much. I have read it through. I spent two evenings on board the Cyprus and enjoyed the visits very much. Uncle Raymond thinks that I have grown very much. I had
two letters and a story book from Uncle Willie and Alfred. Their ship (Abram Young)
was in Bristol when they wrote to me. I had two long letters from dear Mama which
delighted me very much to hear they were quite well. Mr. Moran invited me to spend
last Saturday and Sunday with his family. I had quite a treat, his house has so much
ground around it and I ran about a great deal with the big dog. His name is Nep. Mr.
Moran told Mrs. Robertson that trade is very dull in Bombay.*

*I had a grand sight this morning. Mr. Robertson took us to see the procession
formed to escort the princess and the Marquis of Lorne to the landing stage to embark
for Canada. Pat Poodlay for me!*

With very fond love to dear grandpa and yourself, your affectionate grandson,
Parker Cochrane.

Anne Robertson, who runs the school with her husband, writes reassuringly to
Bessie Parker as she no doubt does to Annie Cochrane. She says the boy is behind
in his education after being aboard ship, but does not seem so concerned with
theoretical learning from books; she sounds very progressive, wanting the children
"seeing as much as possible all that is going on in a public way. It enlarges their
ideas and gives them subjects for thought, making lessons afterwards a pleasure
instead of a toil, which is often the case if children are kept too much to it."

Annie tells of the arrival in port of another Moran-Galloway vessel, a ship she had sailed in previously, *Prince Eugene*. David Smith is now master and his wife, Sarah Ann Smith, who has sailed with her husband since they were married, is also aboard with her two young children. Social visits with people from home are a tonic for a lonesome expatriate like Annie. However, in contrast with other seafaring couples, the Cochranes are noticeably less outgoing.

On January 19, 1879, Annie writes to her mother that they are at last leaving Bombay:

We are fixed at last. On Tuesday 21st or Wednesday we will sail for Diamond Island for orders—which will be one of the rice ports. We are very glad as the weather will be warm again before we are loaded and we are anxious to be on our homeward passage. We will be away before the next mail arrives. Jehanisfee will forward our letters. Parker has written me two letters every month. He writes much better than he did. I think he is doing very well at school, poor dear. How I long to see him. It is seven months since we sailed from L'pool.

Annie and I were on shore yesterday and saw a Mohammedan wedding procession which consisted of two carriages. The first contained four children, gaily dressed, scattering flowers before the carriage containing the bride and groom, the former so closely veiled nothing but her pretty white hand was visible. The latter an old fellow about sixty, bride about fourteen. That is the age they marry here. Two children were in the same carriage, one throwing flowers at the bride, the other at the groom, and the bride and groom then throwing flowers at each other. Sensible, wasn't it? Next came the native band and then four men carrying a bedstead all ready for use, trimmed with green and yellow gauze. Nothing white about it, all colored silk. Fancy how pretty it was. No other article of furniture came so I suppose that was all that was necessary.

The rice loading port turns out to be Rangoon, Burma. The vast delta of the Irrawady River was a major source of export rice. Ships lay at anchor in the river to be loaded from barges. Annie writes from Rangoon on March 19th

We are almost loaded. We will be ready for sea in a few days. I thought it hardly worthwhile writing on arrival here, as we would be only a short time here and I wrote so often from Bombay that I have very little to write about. We had a very fine passage round, much too fine to make a good passage, we were becalmed for several days.

I am quite well dearest Ma, don't imagine that going to sea is injuring my health. I am always well. My nervous system received such a shock in the earthquake (likely that at Pabellon de Pica, Peru) that my eyes are weakened by it. I am very nervous. I suffer very much from it sometimes. the least noise or excitement puts me in such a state. I may possibly get over it, but if my eyes were not so bad I wouldn't mind. I never read fine print or do any kind of fancy work. I do as little as possible to strain them. I know my nerves are all unstrung and my poor eyes are most affected by it. If we go to London I'll see if something can't be done to strengthen them.

Annie has two little girls about her age spending a week with her. They are making so much noise I can hardly write. I had a letter from dear Parker by last mail. He is getting along nicely at school, he says he is working hard for a prize, poor dear. We call at Queenstown (Cobh) for orders for London, Liverpool or Bremen. May be looked for about the middle of July. With fond love, your affectionate daughter, Annie M. C.

Annie and I spent yesterday on shore and it was so warm I feel quite 'done up'. To-day my head aches and I feel miserable. Dearest Ma, how much I want to see you. It is the only bitter drop in my cup, being separated so long from you. I have everything to make life happy and should be more thankful than I am. God has been good to me and I am not deserving of it.

The Indian voyage is too much for Annie and she swallows the anchor, staying ashore with her children in Liverpool and taking a house in suburban Wavertree. Dan is off on another voyage, carrying Cardiff coal to India. Annie writes on April 16, 1881 to Leonard, who is courting in Tynemouth Creek:

My Dear Brother,
Dear Len you haven't written me for a long time, does Miss get all the letters? Now you might spare time to write me just once in a while and tell me how you are getting along, and when the wedding is going to take place, etc. I like to hear all the news and you write me nice newsy letters.

I am awfully busy these days getting things straight before I go to Queenstown to meet Dan. I have to lock the house up and I must be already to start at an hour's no-tice. I expect him about the middle of next month. That is just a month longer now. I wish he would come here to discharge.

Unlike Annie's brothers, who continually move around among the Troop ves-sels, Dan Cochrane is master of *Prince Lucien* without change or relief. Nor does Dan Cochrane's ship's voyages take him to the North American seaboard, where Annie might have the chance to visit her old home. Annie settles down in Liver-pool, but at least has visits from her seafaring brothers on occasion. When Dan arrives in England from his long voyages it is usually at Queenstown (now Cobh) in Ireland for orders. With no wireless aboard ship and no accurate way of esti-mating arrival time (due to the vagaries of the wind), Dan can only send word once he arrives. Annie hurries to Queenstown as soon as she hears he has arrived. They have short visits at least, and, if the orders are for a convenient port like Liverpool or Antwerp, she sails with him.

In May of 1881, Annie Cochrane apparently sails aboard *Prince Lucien* from Queenstown to London. While in London, brother Will Parker arrives in his ship *J. V. Troop* and Annie spends a day aboard with him for the first time in some years.

He writes home that she hasn't changed any but in age. On May 22, Will and J.V.Troop are whistling for a wind to get off down the English channel when they are overtaken by *Prince Lucien.* Dan Cochrane has the advantage of a tug, which will tow him around to Cardiff to load coal for India again. Will reports, "Prince Lucien passed me yesterday towing to Cardiff. She is a fine looking craft. Dan is a fine fellow, I like him better all the time."

By mid-1881, Annie is settling in as a homemaker after the early years at sea. On board ship she worked to create a domestic atmosphere to the afterguard's quarters in an otherwise almost always male environment, but she did not have to cook or clean—that was the job of the ship's cook and the steward. Thus she establishes herself as a cook only upon settling in her home in Liverpool. Dan is now alone, taking *Prince Lucien* on a new routing around Cape Horn into the Pacific. On August 21, Annie writes to Leonard:

> *I have now got the nicest little home, Len, you could wish to see. I only wish you could come in and take tea with me tonight. I am getting to be quite a good cook too. I haven't spoiled anything so far and the children think anything I make delicious. Everything so far has gone on nicely. The children are doing well at school. I am making home as bright and pretty for them as I can. I want them to think it the dearest spot on earth.*
>
> *I wonder how poor Dan is getting on. I hope he is making good day's work. How I long to see him. It seems six months already and he is only gone two. I expect he will be between four and five months going out. Winter time and westerly gales off the Horn, he might be a month beating round. The currents run so strong with the wind there and in winter the wind is westerly most of the time. He is chartered for the round and should do well this voyage. Nearly all the Princes are going or have gone that round this year, some open and some chartered, not one doing badly.*

Like owners and others with family members at sea, Annie keeps track as far as possible of her husband's progress in the newspaper shipping reports, which include arrivals and departures at the world's ports as well as sightings by other ships. She writes, for example, to Len in March of 1884:

> *I am writing Dan this week. I hope in another month or so to hear of his arrival at Calcutta. He made a quick run to the line (equator). He was spoken on the 21st of January in 5_South and 19_ West. That was a month and five days, or thirty-five days out. He will have the northeast monsoon against him in the Bay of Bengal. I don't expect him to make good passages this season of the year.*

It is evident that Dan Cochrane has been at sea steadily for years without respite and that his earnings from shares in his ship or on personal enterprises on his voyages are not large. In September 1882, Annie says to Len, "I only wish Dan could stay at home for just one voyage, if not more. You never saw any one so thoroughly appreciate a home of their own as he does, I can tell you. What those few days were to him! He was only here ten days. We have always been either in lodgings or some other person's home ever since we were married and a real home of our own is fully enjoyed more so by him than myself. As home I shall always call my mother's ever a true home to me."

Annie Cochrane's correspondence drops off and little is known of her later life. She has another son, Georgie, in 1883, and Dan is laid off in 1885. He becomes despondent over the end to his unspectacular but exemplary career. His brother-in-law Raymond Parker would say, "Dan has been shabbily treated by Moran's." The Moran-Galloway company went bankrupt in 1905, one of the many casualties of a slump in cargo markets and other problems for the wooden ships at the end of the century.

Dan takes out other ships as late as 1896 in the prosperous case oil trade from the American east coast to the Orient, and his morale improves. Annie is still struggling to get in visiting time with her husband, travelling to British ports on his arrival to be with him for his short stays. Dan retires again and lives until 1906. Annie does not appear ever to have returned to Tynemouth Creek, but lives out her days in England, pleading an inability to afford the trip. She writes her mother on May 24, 1885, "How much I would like to go out and see you all. It is not to be thought of at present, the money is so scarce. If the ships would make anything there would be a chance. We must hope they will soon."

They never do improve. The days of the wooden sailing ship are numbered and Dan has probably lost considerably on his ship shares in the collapse of his long-time employers. Times are hard for the Parkers too; apart from occasional visits from her three sailor brothers when they bring their ships into English ports, no one comes across to visit Annie. Most of her contemporaries have long gone from Tynemouth Creek, many to New York. There, a nephew, Ned Parker, gets rich and gains renown for his countrywide chain of dental offices under the name "Painless Parker."

LILLY PARKER

Appearing suddenly in the Parker family scene in Tynemouth Creek, New Brunswick was Lilly, who married Raymond Parker, the glamorous captain sailing for Troop & Son. There is no information on Lilly's background other than that which comes out incidentally through family correspondence. Her family name eludes us, but she is believed to have been a member of a prosperous family of the Liverpool shipping fraternity. It is easy to picture her social introduction to the famous captain from a village in the colonies and her attraction to an exciting, travelling life at sea. For a few years she experiences life on the glamorous, pace-setting barque that is at her husband's command and basks in the admiration of the shipping fraternity.

Ray Parker was a natural seaman, capable of getting the maximum out of a vessel

Lil Parker, a refined lady of Liverpool, married a famous, fast sailing New Brunswick sea captain, Ray Parker. After a few hard-driving voyages across the infamous North Atlantic, she retired to raise their large family in Liverpool.

Raymond Parker, a shipmaster for Troop & Son, got home frequently when on the North Atlantic run, but missed his family on later long voyages to Asian ports.

In the barque Cyprus, the hard-driving trans-Atlantic sailings became too much for Lilly Parker. Her husband Ray Parker was celebrated for record passages between New York and Europe.

without losing sails or spars to the gusts. He becomes famous for his achievement of five round trips between North America and England in one year. But this kind of all-out sailing is not conducive to the comfort of a lady and her young children, so after a few years Lilly moves ashore, taking a house in Egremont near Liverpool. Although she sails with him to Canada for visits to Tynemouth Creek, her life is lived predominantly on land. She raises her six children in comfort, apparently on a secured income of her own. Raymond is financially successful until the decline of sailing ships when he loses much of his income through shares in Troop & Son ships. He is eventually engaged in supervising construction of British-built steel ships for the company. Lilly christens the first of these the barque *Troop*.

Raymond suffers substantial losses on his shares in ships and falls out with his old mentor, Howard Troop. He enjoys family life while his six children grow up, but in later years, as master of steamships sailing on long voyages, he and Lilly grow apart. One daughter, Vera, accompanies her father on several voyages in sail and steam. He eventually retires in a farm in Vermont.

IDA PARKER

Like Lilly, Ida appears in Tynemouth Creek through her marriage to a Parker. Ida grew up in Bathurst, on the north shore of New Brunswick. Beautiful but apparently not of robust constitution, she captured the attention of Will, the handsomest of Bessie Parker's many sons.

So many of the young British North American ships' officers married soon after they achieved master status, which usually occurred when the bright young officer was in his mid-twenties. William "Will" Parker of the shipbuilding and seafaring Parkers was in no rush to marry. He was the despair of his sister Annie and brothers, who clucked over his reckless romantic behaviour in their correspondence from scattered ports. In 1878, when he was master of the veteran ship *Abram Young* berthed in New York, there were comments about his spending a lot of time visiting at the home of a Captain Cox, known to have an attractive daughter. A year later it was reported in the family that he was at Cox's every night in December while his ship was in dry dock. On another occasion he was criticized for toying with the affections of a girl in Scotland. He was in the grain trade between New York and Britain and could easily have relationships with girls in ports on both sides.

His sister Annie writes their mother from Bombay:

> I received a letter from Willie who has dropped another girl. When I see the wives some ships' masters have, can't help thinking that of all men in the world they are the easiest deceived and one out of a dozen makes a good choice. I was pleased to think Willie was getting such a respectable good girl, I feel quite vexed with him, but I suppose he will suit himself. We will try and think he may find another as good.

In 1880 Will was important enough in the eyes of Troop & Son to be given command of the beautiful new ship *Nellie G. Troop*, but he proceeded to run ashore off Holland on the ship's maiden voyage. This was a traumatic and sobering experience for the young captain, and whether the event had any bearing or not we do not know, but he had a fairly abrupt change of heart soon after and married Ida on February 1, 1881. They proceeded on the usual seafaring honeymoon in his next ship, *Jacob V. Troop*, making the round trip to London and New York. In July, Will set off on a long voyage to Bombay, sending Ida to stay with his family in Tynemouth Creek, commenting that she "might be sick" on the long voyage. She was pregnant, we know.

Will Parker expresses the feelings of a seaman on an extended absence from his wife in a letter to his brother Leonard from Bombay. He has arrived there with case oil from Philadelphia.

> *I would like this trade if I had my wife. I won't come out here again without her—too long to be alone. Might as well be in jail. Imagine, nobody to speak to for five months. It was a hard thing to send her home and start on a long voyage like this, but I am glad now I did send her home as she is likely to be sick and if anything had happened to her I would of never forgave myself.*

Ida may have been a poor sailor, or Will an undue worrier, but he is frustrated during a long delay in Bombay, and is concerned about her health when writing on March 29, 1882. In fact, a daughter Nellie is born to Ida in March, with complications. While stuck in Indian ports, Will confesses to being a changed man since marrying, admitting that he had been foolish as a bachelor and bragging about his celibacy in foreign ports. He writes to his mother on January 3, 1882, from Bombay:

> *We arrived here on the first after a tedious passage of 145 days. Ships that left before us has not arrived yet, so don't think I got off the track. You have no idea how I missed Ida. I would not come on a long voyage again without her if they gave me the ship. I have more feeling than I ever gave myself credit for. She has made a man of me. I was only a foolish boy, like what Lennie is until he gets in "court-house." If he can get the young lady my advice is for him to hook on and I hope father will give him a chance to make a living for he deserves it. He is no longer a boy and would be much better married.*
>
> *I am sorry to hear of your being so ill mother, you must take better care of yourself. I am pleased Ida was of use to you. She is a woman I have a great regard for, as Billy Riggs said when his mother died. Kind love to all. I rem. your loving son - W. Parker*

Will was home in the spring of 1883 then made a voyage to Britain while Ida showed off her daughter on a visit to family in Bathurst and Chatham. In due course he arrived home to take over another new ship of Troop & Son at Saint

John. *Herald* was a fast vessel, built by Will's father and launched in July. He was proud of this beautiful vessel but was frustrated trying to make record times.

He picked up his wife and daughter and set sail from Saint John. In October *Herald* was chartered for coal to Acapulco, setting Ida and Nellie on a long voyage around Cape Horn into the Pacific. In July of the following year they were in Valparaiso and all was well. But the correspondence that records their lives together is limited and irregular, ending with a letter edged in black from Will at Hamburg to his brother Len in Tynemouth Creek. It is a follow-up to previous, lost correspondence with his mother and thus frustratingly incomplete. Will writes on January 8, 1885:

> I wrote mother a few days ago, since then I have chartered for Philadelphia—empty barrels. We are making slow progress discharging. The custom is fifty tons per day. I was very fortunate getting upriver without ice. The river is full now and wooden ships are getting badly cut. This is a murit spot in winter.
>
> Nellie, I am thankful to say, is well, poor little girl. On board ship is a hard place for a child. I have engaged a man and his wife. I hope they will turn out better than the last.
>
> My friends here are persuading me to send Remains of my poor wife and child in steamer that leaves here for Halifax. They seem to think I would have trouble travel-

Frail Ida Parker married a sea captain, Will Parker, and went with him to sea, only to be ill. She eventually died at sea, probably following childbirth.

Captain Will Parker of the shipbuilding Parkers at Tynemouth Creek, New Brunswick vanished with his ship Herald and crew in a typhoon shortly after the death of his wife and baby.

ling through the States. I don't know what to do. The boat leaves on the 20th of January. I will make up my mind before she starts. I dont feel as if I wanted to come home you can well understand. I will do my utmost to get out, but it will be well on to the last of February before I can get away from here. Kind love to all and hoping you are enjoying good health. I am your loving brother - Wm. Parker

Captain Parker stays at sea, immersing himself in the preoccupation of handling a sailing ship at sea. He has little Nellie with him. In September, he sails from San Francisco for China or Japan, leaving Nellie behind. In December he makes his way up into the East China Sea. A typhoon is reported in the area about the time he is expected to be there, causing his two brothers increasing concern as time passes by without any report of his arrival in port. Several months later, the shipping columns carries acknowledgement of the presumed loss of *Herald* and all the crew. A search locates some flotsam, but it was unidentifiable. It is an easy speculation that Will Parker, having lost his interest in life and frustrated in setting some fast sailing marks in what should have been a fast ship, held on to too much sail a little too long in the teeth of a rising storm.

V

GLORANA (PRICE) FOWNES

A YOUNG BRIDE FROM AN INLAND VILLAGE FINDS HERSELF EMBARKED ON A
LONG PLEASANT LIFE AT SEA SEEING THE WORLD WITH HER CAPTAIN HUS-
BAND. THEIR CAREER IS HAPPILY FORTUNATE IN CONTRAST TO HER BROTHER-
IN-LAW'S, WHOSE LIFE AT SEA ENDS AS HIS SHIP FOUNDERS IN A TYPHOON. A
SEAFARING CAREER RECOUNTED BY A WOMAN WHO ACCEPTED AND ENJOYED
THIS CONSTRICTED BUT ADVENTUROUS LIFE.

If things had been different, Glorana Price would have married a
local boy and spent her life near home, but her relationship to a sea
captain brought her around the world and a life far removed from
her home village. Born in 1859, Glorana Harding Price grew up in the little farming village of Havelock in eastern New Brunswick. She was the lively, outgoing
daughter of the local squire, John Cliff Price. In due course she went off to the
Normal School and returned to teach in the village school, about as well as an
intelligent village girl could have hoped to do.

In later life Glorana tells her story in a narrative account, but time possibly
dulls her memory, for she recalls only how easy and enjoyable the life was. Nevertheless, she paints an interesting picture of everyday life at sea in her time. Glorana
comes across as a lively, social person whose life is touched on all sides by the
influence of the sea. Even at the age of seventy-eight, for example, she always refers to her late husband as "the captain," or if there are two captains involved, "my
captain." Although she learned to shoot the sun and was venturesome enough to
find her way across New York alone, she never had occasion to do anything bold
in the running of the ships. But her writing leaves the feeling that, if given the
chance, she could have. Her life at sea was simpler compared to most other women
in that she was childless; there was no on board school to run, no pressure to stay
ashore to secure quality education and medical care for her children.

Glorana Price's story starts when she is about nine years old and the beautiful, young Thomasina Fownes comes to Havelock from St Martins to teach in the village school. The children all fall in love with her and there are many squabbles as to who will hold her hand and walk beside her to and from school. The children are not the only ones to admire her; most of the young men around fall for her too. Eventually she chooses one, Ben Keith, whom she marries and settles with in Havelock. Thomasina's sister Hannah comes to take her teaching position at the school. Hannah in turn marries her sister's brother-in-law, Elias Keith.

The St Martins people were primarily occupied with building and sailing ships. Benjamin and William Fownes, brothers to Thomasina and Hannah, were sailors and like all sailors, liked to head inland when taking a leave, so they too each make a visit. Ben, the younger, arrives first, and it does not take him long to fall in love with Alpharetta Keith, the sister-in-law of his two sisters. In due course they are married and sail away to a life on the briny. A few days after Will Fownes' arrival in Havelock, the young sailor is sent across the road by his sister to fetch a pail of water at the well of Squire Price. On the way he meets teenager Glorana Price and asks directions to the well. She points it out and he replies, "I see said the blind man and he didn't see at all." Thinking this hilarious, she repeats it to her friends, and soon the visiting sailor is a great favourite with young and old, full of fun and always with an amusing story to tell. He joins in the work and frolics when the squire holds a barn raising. At the dinner table, the men begin naming local girls they think will make him a good wife. Will smiles and listens awhile, then says, "You need not bother choosing a wife for me, for I am going to wait for one of the squire's girls." They have a good laugh and think it a great joke. Glorana is sixteen, ten years younger than Will.

Will Fownes returns to sea, but periodically comes back to Havelock, eventually as a saucy second mate. Pulling Glorana onto his knee, he asks, "When I get to be a captain will you be my wife and go to sea with me?" She replies, laughing, "Yes, if you leave that smelly pipe at home." The sailor goes off to join his ship again and Glorana forgets him and his pipe. She finds a boyfriend and he a girlfriend. She goes to Normal School and comes home to teach, but breaks eventually with her boyfriend. As a first mate, Will is understudying the famous setter of trans-Atlantic speed records, Captain Raymond Parker in his fast ship *Cyprus*.

Four years pass and mate Fownes is now a captain. He blows into town, welcomed by all. But he has eyes only for Glorana; he walks her to work and takes her driving, and, to the disgust of the older girls who have their caps set for him, he proposes to Glorana. They are married August 3, 1881, when she is twenty-one. They spend the winter in Havelock, waiting for a call for the captain to take a ship.

The call comes from his old company, Troop & Son, in Saint John, offering him command of the barque *Electa*. He meets the ship in Philadelphia, sails to Havana, and brings sugar back to New York, where Glorana meets him on their first anniversary. She is thrilled with the big city, and with her husband's seafaring friends and the shipping fraternity. No hotel is necessary as Glorana, setting foot for the first time aboard a ship, moves aboard her new floating home at once. Because sailing vessels spend weeks loading and unloading, there is plenty of time for the couple to see the metropolis and have a round of gay parties.

Electa loads case oil for Plymouth, England, and sets sail. Glorana makes nothing of it, but adapting to the pitching and rolling life must have been a testing experience. At least she does not suffer from sea-sickness—not yet. She writes:

> *It was a great experience for me to be aboard a ship for I had never even seen one before I was married. The captain and mate told me all sorts of incorrect things about sails and the sea, but I kept my eyes and ears open and I soon learned the ropes, as the sailors say. I also learned to work sights with the captain in order to find out the position of the vessel. We had a very pleasant passage of twenty-three days.*

From the start, Glorana Fownes makes the most of her visits to foreign ports, finding friends among the captains, the shore agents, and their wives, and sightseeing. *Electa* is loaded with premium Cardiff coal for Havana. Glorana describes the weather typical on the route down past Portugal and across the Atlantic on the northeast trade winds as *Electa* makes its way to Havana with a load of premium Cardiff coal:

> *The first part of our voyage was rather stormy, especially crossing the Bay of Biscay. We then ran into fine weather for the rest of the passage. When we arrived in Havana, we were towed to a little bay called The Cattagat and anchored. The coal was unloaded into lighters and taken ashore. As there were several other captains and their wives in port, we enjoyed ourselves very much. I especially enjoyed the fruits and flowers and plants of the tropics. We went from ship to ship in row boats and some of the more devout captains had prayer meetings aboard with good singing.*

Coming out of Havana in ballast and rounding Morro Castle after a sojourn in calm harbour waters, *Electa* strikes heavy swells and Glorana gets her first dose of seasickness. Good weather returns as they sail towards Galveston to get cotton for Liverpool, but a cold and strong norther strikes in the Gulf of Mexico. All sails are furled in a hurry. After forty-eight hours anchored in shallow waters, Captain Fownes takes his vessel into Galveston Roads. Soon after docking, *Electa's* crew run off, a common occurrence in ports that promise good jobs. However, having to ship and train a new crew was routine for a sailing ship captain.

The Fowneses sail to Liverpool, seeing icebergs on the way, and return to Cocagne, New Brunswick to load lumber for England. Glorana goes home for a summer visit and rejoins the ship on its return to Saint John. *Electa* continues on its way to New York, then is off to Spain. As a tramp vessel, *Electa* goes wherever cargo is offered, giving Glorana a wide-ranging tour of the world's ports. She is fortunate that the ships of Troop & Son return home periodically so she can visit family and occasionally sit out a voyage to spend time at her old home. But sailing involved much more than visits abroad and return visits home. Heading in through the usual rough swells of the Bay of Biscay toward a small port called Passages, near San Sebastien and the French border, Captain Fownes falls ill and is confined to his bunk. The winds die and the heavy swells push the barque towards a lee shore, one of the seafarer's worst fears. There is no wind to use to claw off and the situation, as Glorana recalls, is critical:

> We were helpless for twenty-four hours, then a breeze sprang up, which carried us to within five miles of our port, but it left us with flapping sails. There were no tugboats and the coast was a solid wall of rocks with deep water to their edge and we did not know what to do. The mate had not much confidence in himself, so the captain simply had to get out of bed and come on deck. Talk about praying, if ever I prayed it was then, and would you believe it, my prayers were answered, for what should we see but the smoke of a little steamer coming out between the reefs at the entrance to Passages. It was a little fishing steamer starting out on a trip. But when her captain saw our predicament he came to us and my captain made a bargain with him to tow us into port. It cost some hundred dollars and took the cream off our freight, but it was better than losing the ship and our lives. We all had thankful hearts when we heard the anchor go down in that quiet, peaceful little harbor, surrounded by very high hills then covered with yellow cowslips.

An English doctor is summoned from San Sebastien and Captain Fownes is put to bed for a week. However, he is soon able to go ashore to walk on the hills and pick cowslips. The case-oil—kerosene for the lamps of Spain—is unloaded and the *Electa* receives orders from Troop & Son's to go across to St. Thomas in the Virgin Islands. Getting out of the little port is another trial. There are no steam tugs, so the locals use a pair of large rowing boats and twenty to twenty-four oarsmen to tow *Electa* out through the narrows. When they reach the headlands, a head wind hits the vessel. In spite of the rowers' efforts, the ship is turned around and blown back into the narrows. A second attempt fails a couple of days later. The wind eventually relents enough to allow the *Electa* to start a pleasant run across the mid-Atlantic pushed by the northeast trade winds.

The *Electa* anchors off in a small port in Puerto Rico to load sugar for Boston. Here the hospitality is overwhelming; in gratitude, the Fowneses give their fine black retriever, Black Jack, to an admiring hostess. The dog has not been consulted, however, and runs off into the hills. A few days later in early morning, the dog is seen sitting on shore, looking towards the anchored ship. Glorana recounts the dog's triumphant return to the *Electa*: "The captain laughed at the idea, but I got up just the same, looked on shore and there was our Black Jack. It did not take the captain long to get men in the boat and row ashore for him. The dog was so delighted to see them all that he nearly upset the boat, and when he got aboard the ship his joy could not be described." Evidently Black Jack could recognize the ship from a distance, but knew he could not swim that far. Needless to say, the dog remained aboard, retiring ashore only when the Fowneses leave *Electa* years later.

Departing Boston, Captain Fownes sails his vessel up the narrow Penobscot River to the anchorage for Bangor, Maine. It is July, 1884 and, so close to home, he decides to quit Troop's barque with the idea of looking for a larger command. He and Glorana take leave until January when he assumes command of *Sunshine*, a ship operated by Herbert Olive of an old Saint John shipbuilding and operating family. Fownes makes a voyage to Liverpool and back. Glorana prudently does not go on this mid-winter North Atlantic trip, but joins her husband on his return to Saint John in the spring. In the meantime there is for Glorana renewed acquaintance with family and friends.

Sunshine visits Dundalk, Ireland; Sydney, Cape Breton; and Shediac and Ayr, Scotland. In Scotland, they exchange a load of lumber for coal, but on the day the loading is finished, Fownes discovers that the shore crew has loaded *Sunshine* too deeply. To avoid the expense of unloading the excess coal he decides he can carry it, despite the fact that the ship is riding below the Plimsoll safe load mark. All goes well in fine weather, but trouble comes when the bad weather hits: "We ran into a gale and we felt sure the vessel would never weather it. When the heavy seas came aboard we could feel her settle under us and then she would plunge and throw it off. When the gale was over, all aboard wondered how she lived through it."

When *Sunshine* is towed into the old port of La Boca at Buenos Aires, the people on the dock decide the captain is a fool to load a vessel that deep. In Buenos Aires, Glorana meets numerous captains, captains' wives, and their children. Inter-ship visits are usual and on one occasion a group takes a steamer to the island of Tigre for a picnic. With a more cautious captain, the *Sunshine* sails on to Pernambuco, Brazil. With their ship at anchor, the Fowneses stay with friends aboard a docked ship for convenience. For company on expeditions ashore, Glorana spends her time with the other captain's two daughters. In the smaller and less interesting port of Maccio, Glorana has no one to visit, so she stays on board the ship most of the time. To help relieve the tedium, a local ship chandler presents her with a beautiful parrot, which she treasures and brings home with her to New Brunswick. In the spring of 1887, after another round from Cardiff to South America and back to Halifax, the Fowneses turn their vessel over to another captain and take leave. The leave is short as Captain Fownes is pressed to take command of the brigantine *Arbutus*. *Arbutus* is a small, three-year-old vessel again belonging to Herbert Olive and Associates. There follow routine sailings across the Atlantic, one trip taking them as far as Bahia, Brazil. The

Fowneses' travels in *Arbutus* are mostly uneventful except one particular night in Cardiff when Glorana is being helped across a dredge from the ship to the shore by a Captain Sanders. As he reaches for her hand, he says, "I will give you a little pull, Mrs. Fownes, so you will not fall between the vessels." As he steps back, he slips and falls into the dredge hopper full of soft mud, pulling her in after him. Glorana describes the scene:

> *The captain was in his shirt sleeves, so it was not hard for the others to see him and haul him out, but I had on a black coat and they couldn't see me. I did not lose my head and heard them say, 'Can you see her?' Then I heard one say, 'I will get down and feel and see if I can find her.' So I put my hand up through the mud and they grabbed it. I was so heavy with the mud that it took three of them to pull me out and they nearly pulled my arm out of the socket. But they got me out and were talking of putting a rope around me to get me back on the ship. I said, "If you can take off my coat, I can go up the ladder myself." So I climbed up and back to the cabin, giving Mrs. Sanders a terrible scare, for she could not imagine what had happened.*

Meanwhile, Captain Fownes, who has tired of waiting for Glorana on the wharf, comes back to see what the delay is. In the dim light, he sees Glorana covered in sticky red mud, which he mistakes for blood so he clasps her in his arms, mud and all. He becomes so incensed at the dredge company that the investigating policemen nearly arrest him. Everyone gets cleaned up and stays the night in the Sanders ship.

More serious is an episode with their friend, Captain Ray of the Troop barque *George E. Corbett*, which arrived in Santos (Brazil) ahead of *Arbutus*. Smallpox has broken out in Santos and captains are asked to keep their crews aboard. Taking his second mate to task for going ashore without permission, Captain Ray is stabbed in the abdomen by the mate, and is not expected to live. Glorana recalls the incident:

> *When the Guarda Mor, chief of the customs house, came aboard to look at our papers and saw that our vessel hailed from St. John, he asked us if we knew Captain Ray of the Corbett. We said yes and he seemed very much relieved. He told us that Captain Ray had been stabbed in the abdomen by his second mate and could not live. When the captain chastised him for disobeying orders the mate pulled out his knife and stabbed him. The officer said that when we had dressed and had our breakfasts, he would come with his motorboat and take us to see Captain Ray, which he did, and if anyone was ever pleased to see old friends, it was Capt. and Mrs. Ray. The captain lived until 9 p.m.*
>
> *The Guarda Mor and his men were more than kind to us all, stayed aboard all night and helped make arrangements for Capt. Ray's burial next day. The flowers*

came by the bushel basketful. As soon as the funeral was over, we brought Mrs. Ray aboard our vessel and our mate was made captain of the George Corbett. The various ships' captains rallied round, helping arrange his funeral. Flowers came by the basketful and the captains and the Masons of Santos bought a small monument for him.

Mrs. Ray boards the Fowneses' vessel and remains for six months while they make the rounds of several ports before arriving at Philadelphia. Turning the ship over to a substitute master for the next voyage, the Fowneses and Mrs. Ray return home to Saint John by train.

On the next voyage, which is to Ireland, the Fowneses take along twelve-year-old Leonard and fourteen-year-old Walter Olive, sons of the ship's owner. Glorana takes them sightseeing in Belfast and Dublin. Following that voyage, Glorana's sister Minner joins her in hopes that the sea will cure her lagging health. They tow out of Saint John Harbour, but when the tug drops the towline off Partridge Island, *Arbutus* begins to bob around in the Bay of Fundy's swell. The weather turns fine in the tropics and the voyage goes well until they arrive at the channel that leads into the port of Buenos Aires. The River Plate is heavy with silt and the port must be entered by way of a dredged channel extending many miles to sea. A lightship marks the entrance. Glorana describes the difficulties they encounter as the ship tries to enter the channel, referring to her husband and the mate as "they":

It was the day before Christmas and all were eager to get in port for Christmas Day, but the fates were against us. As we sailed up the Plata they were watching for the lightship to show us the channel through which we were to pass, but as the river is muddy looking and there was a haze, they could not see distinctly, but thought they could see the masts of the lightship and steered for it, when all of a sudden, we bumped on a sandbar, the waves came over the deck and there was a great commotion. Supper was on the table, a real good one too, for we had been cooking for Xmas. Everything went helter skelter, even ourselves, so we had to hold on to keep from being hurt. The captain closed the doors to the deck and called to us not to be afraid, but how could we help it!

After they took off some of the sails, the vessel seemed to back off the bar into deep water. They sounding all around and finding deep water, they anchored. Then they got busy over the chart and found out just where we were, in a deep spot surrounded by shallows, and also found out that the masts they saw were those of another vessel that had met the same fate. Later we discovered that she was one of our owner's other vessels, the Jumbo, and that the lightship had been removed for repairs.

We lay at anchor all night, keeping strict watch and when the haze lifted, found many vessels anchored out in the river. At daylight the mate and our two most able seamen took our big boat and rowed across to the other vessels to see if they could get a pilot to come and get us out of our trouble. They were gone all day, coming back with the news that the pilot said, 'The captain might as well abandon the ship, for he could never get her out of that hole.' The captain and the mate studied the chart some more and decided to make a try at it themselves.

The anchor chain is unshackled and tied to a hawser running to the vessel's stern. All sail is set and, when the wind brings *Arbutus* up to the anchor, the hawser is cut. *Arbutus* bumps on the bar once and sails clear on momentum. The vessel was likely kedged around against the anchor with the windlass, so the hawser had to be cut to avoid losing way. Such is the kind of ingenuity needed where the only power available is that of wind and the muscle of sailors. Glorana remembers their relief at making it through:

> A happier crew never sailed that river before or since, I am sure. We reached the other shore and anchored with our remaining anchor among the other ships that night. During the night a terrific Norther sprang up and of course, the captains and pilots of the other vessels thought we had gone to Davy Jones' locker and were quite surprised to see us riding at anchor among the other vessels in the morning.

When the storm abates, *Arbutus* sails into Buenos Aires Roads and is towed to the dock. The Christmas of 1889 is delayed, but very happy for the various captains and their wives in beautiful Buenos Aires. The ship seems undamaged, but once dry docked upon return to Saint John, they discover rudder damage and the loss of twelve feet of false keel. Although Glorana's sister continues to be seasick after each departure from port, she arrives home in good health. *Arbutus* is in need of repairs and the Olivers offer Captain Fownes a deal: if he buys shares in the new barkentine under construction at Edward McGuiggan's shipyard in Carleton, the command of it is his. Glorana writes of the outcome:

> So he bought some shares and left the *Arbutus*. He stayed in Saint John and watched the building of the new, smallish, three-hundred-and-sixty-four-ton vessel, which was christened *Woodbine*. There was a grand celebration at the launching. She was then towed to the wharf where they started in to rig her, finish her cabins and get her all ready for sea. We slept aboard of her for the first time on September 22, 1890, a very sad date to us later on. They loaded *Woodbine* with laths and sent us to Washington, D.C., U.S.A. There was great rejoicing as the new vessel towed out of the harbour with flags flying. Many of our friends were on the wharf to bid us 'Bon Voyage.'

They have a pleasant voyage down the coast, towing up the Potomac to berth near the presidential yacht in Washington, then a seaport. Glorana sees the sights of the capital, but is "too bashful to go aboard the president's yacht, even though we [are] invited." *Woodbine* is towed around to Richmond, Virginia, where the usual throng of chandlers and other merchants swarm aboard looking for business. One merchant approaches Captain Fownes to ask him if he knows Captain Fownes of the ship *Lizzie Troop.* "I should, he is my only brother," responds the captain. "Well the ship is lost with all hands, September 22," replies the merchant. Captain Fownes drops everything and goes to the cabin to tell Glorana about his brother's fate. "I want never again to see a man in such agony," writes Glorana, "I thought he would surely die. Soon more considerate men came into the cabin offering their sympathy."

The Fowneses sail on to Rio Grande du Sul in South America. Outside the entrance bar, the *Woodbine* is caught in a gale waiting for the tide to turn and for a tow into the port. The captain eventually sleeps, but not his nervous wife: "All of a sudden I realized that the ship was going astern and dragging her anchor so I called the captain at once. When he went on deck, he found the second mate asleep on watch. He flew forward as fast as he could and gave the vessel more chain, which stopped her dragging. They were watching our lights from shore and reported that we would soon be lost, but our anchors held and kept us off the rocks or sand bars until the wind abated and the tug arrived in the morning."

Returning north, most of the crew signs off at Baltimore and *Woodbine*, as is frequent practice, tows up to New York with a skeleton crew. Glorana mentions that while the few seamen aboard are busy handling the towline, she must take the wheel as the tug and barkentine are thrown about by a coastal storm. They arrive home from the sea for the winter and Glorana begins to pine for a permanent home on shore. Will's mother offers him a farm and he gives in. The Fowneses spend their spare funds on a team of ox, cows, sheep, pigs, hens. and farming implements and optimistically set about farming. Glorana is "so happy to be on land instead of sea that [she] did not mind how hard [she] had to work."

Masters at sea often fall into the dream of farming, but the dream ends as soon as the master starts to miss the sea. When *Woodbine* returns from a voyage to Africa under another master, Captain Fownes hires a couple to help on the farm and he runs off to sea. On the coast of Brazil, however, the *Woodbine* is lost on a reef off Cap St. Roque, because, unknown to the captain, a navigation light has been under repair. This misadventure forces his return to the farm for another winter, but the sea bug is still in his blood. When he is offered the big barque *Kate F. Troop* in the spring, he loses no time in accepting, going back to where he is the sole master of all he surveys except for the weather.

The Fowneses have some difficulty finding good help for the farm and they come to admit that sailors do not necessarily make good farmers. They sell the farm and furniture and Glorana bids goodbye to her fond dreams of a home on land.

In February 1897, Glorana starts life at sea again. At 1,096 tons, the sixteen-year-old *Kate F. Troop* is a somewhat bigger vessel than the *Electa* and the *Woodbine*. John Parker built the ship in 1881 at Tynemouth Creek, a few miles from the Fowneses' home-town of St Martins. These bigger Troop-fleet vessels—well-built and with comfortable quarters—operate all over the world. Glorana Fownes embarks on new seas toward Australia and the East Indies.

Travelling new seas is an exciting prospect, one dulled only for Glorana by the length of the absences from her family: "It nearly broke my heart to think of going so far from home and my dear mother, so I wept very freely at times." She also feels distant from her husband, as his attention is on the long voyage ahead. The day they finish loading general cargo in New York, Captain Fownes' cousin says to him, "Will, the American clipper *Conqueror* is coming here to load for Sydney as soon as you pull out, and I'll bet you two Pounds that she will be there before you."

Glorana (Price) Fownes and husband Captain William Fownes sailed the world together from their marriage in 1881, when she was twenty-one, almost continuously until 1903 or 1904, when he died. She returned to New Brunswick and lived until 1954.

Glorana and William Fownes voyaged to the Orient in the barque Kate F. Troop. *The Parker brothers also commanded this fine example of the Maritime wooden ship builder's art.*

"I'll take no one-sided bet like that," Fownes replies, "but I'll bet you the two Pounds I can make as good time to Sydney as the *Conqueror*." The *Kate* is no fast clipper, but Fownes knows that with a little luck, a competent captain can make up for speed on a long voyage.

Glorana recalls the voyage with typical understatement: "When I looked at the long, long charts and saw how short a mark we made on them each day, I felt we would never get there, but we did it in 89 days." A New York newspaper account gives a little more color and detail:

> *The barque left New York February 16 and had light to fresh southeast trade winds from the line, reaching the Cape of Good Hope meridian on April 1. She ran her easting down between 42 and 43 degrees south latitude, experiencing strong gales from the northeast to northwest with strong seas. She ran across the southern ocean, shipping heavy bodies of water in stormy weather, but suffered no damage. She had very good running from the Cape of Good Hope to Cape Otway, Australia, averaging two-hundred miles a day, and up to two-hundred-and-forty miles in a single day. Then there were light to variable winds up from Cape Otway to Athol Bight. The wooden ship and her master beat all the iron ships to Australia that season.*

Some trips take much longer. The *Conqueror's* was one of the slowest, with a final time of 110 days. Impressed by the magnificence of Sydney Harbour, the Fowneses enjoy the city and, as always, find old and new friends. They tow up to Newcastle in New South Wales for coal, then head off to Manila. They journey through the

Rock Terrace—*one of the big wooden sailing ships nearing completion on the stocks at Saint John*—*was one of several Troop and Son ships, including* Lizzie Troop *and* James Elwell, *lost at sea in dramatic circumstances.*

exotic island archipelagos and the Cannibal Islands, threading their way through the famous straits, Basilan and Mindora, and the small seas, Celebes, Sulu, and China.

At Manila, they unload coal from Newcastle, and load up hemp for New York. One day at noon, the skies abruptly become black and the wind begins to howl. A cyclone has struck, leaving the captain and his wife in a familiar, but most trying position. While Glorana worries about her husband getting back, he, unable to put out in a small boat, is worrying about his wife and ship. He is not able to return until the next morning, but fortunately the anchors held without dragging and the mate kept careful watch all night.

Heading west from Manila, Captain Fownes takes his barque through Sunda Strait and into the Indian Ocean. They pass Krakatoa, where a recent volcanic eruption has left pumice stone floating in the water. The crew scoop up bucketsful of pumice for use in scrubbing the decks. They travel across the Indian Ocean, around the Cape of Good Hope, and up to the very remote island of St. Helena. *Kate F. Troop* anchors off Jamestown to purchase fruit and vegetables from the local bumboats, a common practice. The Fowneses make a quick visit home while the hemp is unloading in New York before setting out to Adelaide with general cargo.

Glorana is not one to vividly describe the sailing of her ship at sea, but the thrilling run across the bottom of the world on the continuous westerly winds to Australia moves her to comment:

> We proceeded on our way, through storms and calms, fair winds and fowl (sic). Then came the long stretch the sailors call 'running your easting down', across the Indian or Southern Ocean, where you have a fair wind and never meet a ship coming the other way. Sometimes a faster ship passes you and only rarely you pass a slower one so it is not a very cheery part of the voyage.
>
> When we were a few hundred miles from Adelaide, we ran into a heavy gale and seas. The men were sent aloft to furl the sails and, sad to say, a young German boy lost his hold and fell, striking the rail and then going overboard and sinking near the vessel. They threw a lifebuoy and stopped the ship as well as they could, but he was gone. Never will I forget that cry, 'Man overboard!'. Only the night before he had been telling the steward that his parents did not want him to go to sea and as soon as we got back he was going home to them.

This same southern route—the "roaring forties"—is the track for today's ultimate danger sport of round-the-world sail racing. In 2001 a Canadian woman placed second in this race.

In the after cabin of her ship, Glorana Fownes has a very small social group; she has her husband and one or two mates for company and at dinner, one of the men is always on watch and therefore absent. She does not venture forward on deck—the crew's preserve—and the conversation she has with the crew is always

circumscribed. Glorana does not have the children that busy most women at sea—
a circumstance that frees and impells her to actively pursue social connections on
shore. At Christmas, she makes parcels for each of the crew and is solicitous of
their welfare as far as is circumspect.

On one occasion, Glorana is sitting on deck in Acapulco when a young stranger
appears on the steps of the poop. Removing his hat, he speaks to her: "I don't
suppose you remember me, but I will never forget you. Do you remember," he
went on, "one very hot day on the *Arbutus*, a boy who had a sore foot and could do
no other work but stand at the wheel and steer, became almost blind with the sun
shining in his eyes and you went below and brought up your big sun hat and put
it on his head? Well I am that boy and I will never forget your kind act." Glorana
recalls: "I had forgotten all about it, so it shows that kindness is not always wasted.
His name was Brown when he was a boy, but he had married a Mexican and
living in Mexico as a man he was Mr. Moreno which is Brown in Mexican."

After the ship arrives in Puget Sound, Washington for lumber, Glorana takes a
ferry to Victoria to visit relatives over Easter. As she talks with a captain at the rail
of the steamer on her return home down the Sound, he notices a sailing vessel
towing up, and says, "Why, that looks like your vessel!" "It can't be," she laughs,
"Will would never go and leave me." Arriving at the pier, she is met by the ship's
broker instead of her husband. When she asks the whereabouts of her husband,
she is shushed and told to follow. Glorana knows the man's wife, has been to their
home, and it was there she supposes he is taking her. It is midnight when he lands
her aboard a tug and tells her that the captain has had trouble getting a crew. Men
are so scarce and the captain so worried that the men they do have will skip if he
stays at the wharf, they decide it is best to tow the vessel out the Sound slowly.
Glorana is to follow in the tug and overtake them at daylight. The ship Glorana
passed on her ferry ride had in fact been her husband's. Ushered aboard the tug,
Glorana spends the rest of the night in a dark little cabin. At daylight they approach *Kate F. Troop* in a heavy sea and blowing wind. "I began to wonder how
they would get me aboard the ship. The tug steamed as close alongside as she
dared and they put planks from the tug to the ship and I walked across them. It
was a dangerous business, but it had to be done. The captain of the tug held one
hand and as soon as possible my captain reached out and took the other, and I
think there were thankful hearts on both vessels when I was safe on deck."

In ports like the Pacific Northwest with good employment opportunities, Captain Fownes' subterfuge was not unusual. Most of the crew sign off, or desert the
ship, for better jobs ashore. However, once a ship is out of a port the crew cannot
leave, physically or legally. Towing up Puget Sound, Fownes and his mate size up
the crew that the shipping master has. According to Glorana, it is the usual rabble
supplied by the agents:

They found they had jailbirds of all kinds. They were all drunk but one young fellow from Pennsylvania. He was a railroad man and had never been aboard a ship before. The shipping master had persuaded him to go to help the Captain out, telling him the trip would take only six days. After the tug left us, they put that young man at the wheel and taught him how to steer. It was well he was apt to learn. In a short time the others got sobered up and, as they were sailors, we got along all right and had a fair passage to the equator. There we were becalmed for days and days and had no rain. Ships always expect to fill their fresh water tanks at the equator where it almost always rains.One day the young railroad man said to the steward, 'The shipping master said we would only be six days on the trip. We have been out over a week and I can't see land yet.' He had to wait many more for it took us ninety-six days to Guayaquil, Ecuador, our destination.

By then they are very short of water and Glorana often goes thirsty so her husband can have a drink.

The squire's daughter from Havelock has seen much of the seafarer's world, but there is another experience yet, a storm off Cape Horn. The eastbound voyage is easier than westbound because the prevailing winds are more favourable. *Kate F. Troop* leaves Vancouver with a full deckload of timber destined for Cramp's dry docks at Philadelphia. The passage south begins calmly, until they encounter rain, snow, ice, and wind, as expected, at the cape. The seas hove the heavily laden vessel almost on its beam ends and it will not answer its helm. In the midst of this storm in the huge expanse of the southern ocean, they find themselves on a collision course with another sailing vessel with the right of way. It is the first vessel they have seen since leaving the Strait of Juan de Fuca. Captain Fownes, struggling to keep clear, finally orders down the topsail they have been sailing under. This brings some response to the helm and the two ships pass clear. The other master is so taken aback to meet a heavily laden timber carrier heading eastbound down there that he signals Fownes to ask if they are lost.

One hundred and twenty-nine days out of Vancouver, their anchor touches down in the anchorage below Philadelphia. Going up to the city in a tug, their first concern is to get letters from home, but the news is not good. Will's youngest sister is seriously ill and he is asked to return home. After Fownes wires Troop's for a relief captain, Glorana and he leave the sea again.

When Will's sister dies, Will and Glorana move into their little farm cottage for the summer with Will's mother. However, they soon elect to join the rest of Will's family in San Francisco. Besides visiting with family, Will sees the move to San Francisco as a chance to get command of an American ship, something he had wanted. They arrive in the autumn of 1900 and Will quickly obtains command. The barque *Challenger*, of the well-known California ship operators Hind, Rolph & Company, sails immediately for Sydney, leaving Glorana to tend to Will's mourning sister and mother. However, he is too lonesome on such a long and tedious passage without her and asks her to take a steamer to Sydney to join him. Her trunk misses the steamer and she does not go.

Will and Glorana remain apart for quite a long time. The *Challenger* is slow returning across the Pacific and is put on the missing list. Although Glorana is unaware of the status of her husbands' ship, she becomes anxious when she receives a phone call from Mr. Rolph about an unusual event. Her husband's ship has just sailed across the turbulent entrance bar, and through the Golden Gate without the aid of a tug! Will receives a warm welcome at home and among the shipping fraternity who believed him lost. Glorana puts to sea again, this time to Vancouver with a personal friend and Bessie Rolph—the owner's daughter—as company. From Vancouver, the voyage continues around the Horn to Delagoa Bay, Africa, Newcastle, New South Wales, for coal to Mazatlan, and finally back to Victoria.

More bad news plagues the Fowneses as news of death in both their families causes them to leave the ship and take the train back across the continent to San Francisco. While in San Francisco, Captain Fownes' deteriorating health convinces him to say good-bye to the sea forever. They settle on a chicken farm in Petaluma, California, and enjoy making a home with eight hundred hens. Soon Will's unspecified illness grows worse and a team of San Francisco's best surgeons are brought out for surgery. Glorana describes her husband's end:

> *Our Petaluma doctor prepared our front room and fumigated for the operation. It was too late, they could not finish the operation for fear he would die on the table, so they put him to bed and he only lived a few hours.*

Will died October 11, 1904. He was fifty-five-years old. Glorana returned to New Brunswick to live with her mother. She lived until 1954 to the age of ninety-five. Life at sea had evidently been good for her health.

VI
SURVIVORS

A TYPHOON, MUTINY, AND FIRE IN THE SOUTH ATLANTIC AND TAKING TO
THE BOATS OFF CAPE HORN. THE COURAGE AND ENDURANCE OF THREE SEA-
FARING WOMEN.

As a result of the awesome and capricious power of a great storm
at sea, many ships disappeared without a trace or left a mute
mass of splintered timbers on a rocky shore. Others foundered,
were wrecked, or burned following human error to vanish into the deeps. Whether
they drowned or died of exposure in open boats, women and children perished
alongside the men, leaving family at home mourning for all those lost. But by
chance, some survived to tell the story of their harrowing experiences. Among
them are the dramatic cases of two Saint John vessels belonging to the prominent
shipping line Troop & Son.

ORDEALS IN OPEN BOATS

Since Captain William Bligh's epic voyage, there have been numerous long and
tedious runs to land in lifeboats. Oftentimes, one lifeboat from an abandoned ship
is successful in reaching land while another is lost at sea. Only a few of these
lifeboat voyages involved women, but their participation and resilience in these
situations frequently surprised their male companions.

One example of such a situation involves the Troop vessel, *James W. Elwell*, a small-
ish, 550-ton barque built in 1870. On September 15, 1872, *Elwell*, commanded by
John Wren, sailed from Cardiff with a load of Welsh coal towards Valparaiso. Among
the crew is the first mate, Pope, the cook, Edward Farrington, and the stewardess,
Mrs. Sarah Farrington. The run down to the River Plate goes well until they meet
the usual heavy gale. Pope is severely injured in the storm and soon dies. Wren sails
on, sighting Staten Island and rounding the Horn to sight Diego Ramirez Island

without incident. Ten days after passing Cape Horn, Farrington also meets with an accident from which he contracts an infection and dies.

Pope and Farrington are both buried at sea. Captain Wren describes the events that follow:

> While burying the cook, I had occasion to wear ship, and when thus brought before the wind, I noticed, to my surprise, that smoke was issuing from the after ventilators. Examination revealed the coal cargo to be on fire and I decided, after consultation with the crew, to run for the Straits of Magellan, where was located the nearest port and the likeliest place to meet passing vessels. The wind was averse for three or four days, then a heavy westerly gale set in and we had to heave to under lower topsails at midnight. The cargo appeared by this time to be all on fire. Smoke was issuing through every opening and the water from the pumps was hot.

Far in the desolate Southern Ocean, Wren and his crew face the seaman's worst dread—fire. It was common to have coal cargoes ignite spontaneously from internal heating during a voyage. The usual tactic was to keep it enclosed and away from a fresh air supply, and to make for port. Wren tries to head up the west coast for the Straits of Magellan, on which is the Chilean port of Punta Arenas, but he is stymied by lack of wind. The fire gets worse, threatening to burst through the decks. After trying for six days to sail on and hoping the fire will stay bottled up, another ship passes near them, but keeps on despite the *Elwell* crew's frantic signals. Then, about midnight, a rushing sound then a bursting open of the hatches over the coal forces a decision; Wren gives the order to abandon ship. Two boats well-stocked with food, water, a compass, and sail are launched. The crew members drop from the taffrail into the boats when the crests of the swells are high up. Wren describes the scene:

> A heavy sea was running, and added to the darkness of the night was the smoke, which enveloped the ship. We dropped into the boats from the barque's stern, watching our chance to jump as they rose on the waves. The cook's wife, while standing on the taffrail waiting her chance to jump, did not leap when ordered to, but jumped as the boat was receding. She fell twelve feet, spraining one of her ankles and otherwise injuring herself, she being rather a heavy woman.

The boats stay near the now blazing *Elwell*, hoping the glare of the flames will attract a rescuer, but the only other vessel to appear ignores the burning barque and slowly disappears into the distance. At daylight, their ship, having burned to the water's edge, sinks, leaving the crew, the cook's wife, and the captain alone on the sea, 160 miles off the Patagonian coast of Chile. This coast, rough, barren, and cold, is among the most forbidding in the world.

There have been many long and difficult, but ultimately successful, voyages in open boats. The *James W. Elwell* boat's voyage was by no means the longest, but because of the extreme southerly location, it was very cold and there was no food to be scavenged from sea or shore. There was plenty of land around, but it was so inhospitable as to be of little succor. Wren consolidates his supplies and crew into the bigger of the two boats and makes a good four-day sail to a small bay on the north coast of the Strait of Magellan. Totally inhospitable, the coast features high mountains topped with snow and sloped with ice rising right out of the sea. The weather is tempestuous and wretched. Two weeks of continuous storm with rain, sleet, and hail keep the group cowering there without shelter for two weeks, all the time suffering from exposure.

The boat moves on along the coast when the weather moderates. The crew is suffering from want of food, which is starting to run short. Two young seamen die of exhaustion and are buried on shore under stones and brush. The group continues making its way along the strait under sail, interrupted by storms and exhaustion. They venture ashore to rest and pick mussels, now almost their only sustenance. Some of the crew die along the way, others give up and lie in the bottom of the boat, letting the spray come over the side. Wren mentions Sarah Farrington as his only help; she bails out the sea-water while he steers. Men become delirious and have to be lashed down to keep them from leaping overboard. Limbs begin to turn gangrenous. Captain Wren recounts Sarah Farrington's role in the adventure:

> *Our provisions were almost exhausted and we were slowly starving to death. The only one of the crew I could depend upon for assistance was the stewardess, the cook's wife. Her powers of endurance and pluck were the admiration of all, particularly myself, as I had to look to her as my chief assistant. She had no favors shown her in the distribution of food—we all shared alike—moreover, she was still suffering from the injuries she received when jumping from the ship, yet she never murmured, but on the contrary, worked, cheered and encouraged the others.*

This is apparently a major statement for a taciturn seaman not given to hyperbole. The land beyond a few bits of beach is generally inaccessible, but the fear of meeting the natives of the region, who are reputed to be fierce, is really what keeps the ship's crew from venturing inland. For this reason, Wren lights a fire on shore only once. The number of survivors shrinks day by day. They work their way slowly along the strait among islands, hoping to encounter a steamer on the main channel. At last, with their number reduced to four—the captain, the stewardess, the carpenter and one seaman—they stop on an island for four weeks. After the carpenter dies, Wren reflects on the stewardess' determination:

I now became despondent myself. It was ten weeks since leaving the ship. We were in an uninhabited country, always exposed to the weather, with no warming fire and nothing to eat now but shellfish. Could nature endure much longer? Though blessed with a tolerably good constitution, I had witnessed stronger men yield. Possibly the responsibility of my position somewhat stimulated me. But the cook's wife was a puzzle. She, a woman, and therefore not expected to have the endurance of hardy seafaring men, had worked, shared the same fare and was exposed to the same hardships as all of us, yet she was physically stronger than any. Really, she was becoming a heroine in my estimation. Moreover, she was always ready with a word of cheer and, with the object of keeping up our spirits, though in a most tantalizing way, would enumerate the many good things in store for us when picked up. She would often describe a dish that a certain American captain was very fond of and one that I was very partial to, and I had to beg her to stop to spare my feelings.

The mussels are becoming scarce so Wren moves his small crew on, the three of them with scarcely the strength to get in the boat. Again he sails, heading for what he thinks is a main channel; Sarah Farrington bails, and the young seaman sleeps in the bottom of the boat.

When about half way over, an extra swell of the sea tumbled me over into the bottom of the boat through sheer weakness. In getting up, I happened to look round in the direction from whence we had come. Though dazed and bewildered, I thought I saw smoke. Yes! It was a steamer! I broke the news by singing out, 'Ship in sight!' The prostrate sailor, whom we thought was taking his last sleep, raised his head and cheered feebly. The woman clapped her hands for joy with the characteristic exclamation, 'I told you so! I told you not to despair!'

The White Star liner *Tropic,* bound from the west coast to Liverpool, lifts the pitiful little group aboard. Under the care of the ship's surgeon, the three survivors of *James W. Elwell* slowly recover from their seventy-two days of hardship, peril, and near starvation in a climate Wren describes as similar to New Brunswick in October. Strange to say, he says, Sarah Farrington stood it better than any. She would have been the last to succumb. She was an Englishwoman, strong, robust, "good-sized," and about thirty-six years of age. Despite this terrible experience, she went to sea again, shipping as a stewardess on a voyage around Cape Horn. She married the ship's carpenter and eventually settled in Digby, Nova Scotia.

CRICCIETH CASTLE'S PEOPLE

Another lifeboat ordeal is that of *Criccieth Castle,* a British full-rigged ship that receives damage in the usual mid-winter Horn weather in the Southern Ocean.

Late in the era of the commercial square-rigged sailing ship, July of 1912, Captain

Robert Thomas is just rounding the infamous headland carrying a cargo of guano from Ballestos, Peru, toward Queenstown (Cobh). At 2 a.m. on the July 15, in a violent pitch, the rudder breaks loose, holing the stern. In an attempt to gain time, Thomas puts his crew to work vigorously pumping out the inflowing sea. After twelve hours, water floods the cargo hold, turning the guano into a viscous slurry that in a few hours gums up the manual pumps and seals the fate of *Criccieth Castle*.

There are twenty-two people aboard, including the wife of Captain Thomas and their four-year-old son. In appalling weather, the captain succeeds in launching two boats. The larger longboat, carrying sixteen, tows the smaller so they don't lose each other. Thomas sets course for the Falkland Islands to the northeast, a safe refuge for so many vessels defeated in the battle with the storms of Cape Stiff. On the morning of July 16, the longboat is alone on the sea—the other boat is not within sight. During the morning a large barque is sighted, but a snow squall comes between them and blocks the view. Captain Thomas sits high in the stern at the steering oar and at one point is washed overboard. The seamen struggle to haul him back in, their hands numb with cold. Only the frantic encouragement of Mrs. Thomas pushes them to succeed, and some of them even hang on to his clothes with their teeth.

At seven in the evening, a seaman, the cook, and the cabin boy die of exposure, while the rest pass another freezing-cold night. Even rum does not help. The next day, two more die, and their oilskins are passed on to the survivors. Mrs. Thomas lies between the thwarts on the bottom of the boat in the water that keeps sloshing aboard, cosseting her young son, a sight that gives the men more will to survive. An icy wind drives them north, and the captain and mate begin to hallucinate. On July 19, they make barren Beauchesne Island, about thirty miles south of the Falklands, and warm themselves before a fire overnight. They stop briefly on another small island where snow must serve as food and water.

On July 20, the group's seventh day of suffering, Thomas gains the coast of East Falkland, but is held off by contrary winds for two days. Finally, a shift of wind into the south blows them right into Port Stanley two days later. Two of the crew die in the hospital from gangrene, and some of the nine others lose toes. The Thomas boy comes close to losing his feet, but circulation returns and he soon recovers. His father hobbles about on crutches for a while, though his mother is well and, two months after their return to England, she delivers one more survivor of the epic voyage: a baby girl.

The Milton

Another unborn child survives an epic lifeboat voyage in the case of the ship *Milton*. En route from Shields, England, towards San Francisco, Captain Henry MacArthur of Maitland, Nova Scotia, loses his ship in the Pacific Ocean from a fire caused by spontaneous ignition of the coal cargo. MacArthur abandons his vessel, dividing

Captain and Mrs MacArthur and boys pose with crew of Milton. *Mrs MacArthur suffered a long ordeal in an open boat while pregnant.*

the crew among three boats. The steward's boat is picked up by a passing vessel twenty-six days later. The mate's boat, however, is not so lucky: it joins the disappeared. The captain's boat, aboard which is MacArthur's wife and two young sons, sails and drifts an astonishing 2619 miles over a period of forty-six days before meeting a ship. Food and water have long since run out, though the captain manages to contrive a condenser that produces a few drops of fresh water. The younger boy dies of exposure as do two seamen. As their rescue vessel enters harbour at Guaymas, Mexico, Mrs. MacArthur gives birth to a three-pound baby boy, who grows up in good health.

The Loss of Lizzie Troop

The second ill-fated vessel of the Troop line, the full-rigged ship *Lizzie C. Troop*, is smashed by a typhoon in the Kurile Island chain south of Japan late in 1890. The master is Benjamin Fownes from St Martins, New Brunswick, who is accompanied by his wife, Alpharetta and their two-year-old son, in addition to a crew of about twenty. The 1391-ton ship, built in 1873 has just left Nagasaki en route to Puget Sound, carrying ballast in lieu of cargo. The first mate, John Troop, describes the coming of the storm for the newspapers:

> *We left Nagasaki for Puget Sound on September 15 with 600 tons of stone and dirt ballast on board. We soon found wind, and at ten o'clock on the night of the 16th it increased to typhoon force; we were in fact, in the typhoon that wrecked the* Ertougroul

and other vessels. For thirty-six hours the winds shrieked and roared such as I have never heard before, and our lower topsails soon went. We kept our spars intact, however, but the copper sheathing began to wash off the ship outside.

From that time on until Sunday, noon, it blew a gale continuously, when it again increased and by the afternoon we were in another typhoon. We had set all our strong, heavy sails, and for seven hours we had managed to keep her off the shore, but with the increased fury of the storm they were blown to pieces. The morning of the 22nd, at about 6.20 we sighted the tops of hills; we could just see them sufficiently, that is to say, to distinguish there was something there besides sky. We struck almost at once, and after three bumps we were in pieces. The main and foremasts were iron, and the former broke in the middle.

Alpharetta Fownes writes to her sister-in-law, Mrs. E. A. Keith, in Havelock, New Brunswick, from Okinoerabujima Island where *Lizzie Troop* has driven ashore, telling of her harrowing adventure and of the deaths of her husband and baby:

We met a typhoon which lasted three days, during which time we could carry no sail and were steadily drifting towards the islands until Sunday morning when it cleared a little, but at noon, shut in again and blew and rained as hard as ever. However, they got a little sail on and hoped she might drift below or between the islands; that seemed our only safety. The captain and mate remained on deck all night Sunday, dreading every moment that she would strike. The wind roared and the rain poured so that it was terrifying. I watched the barometer all night for them and at daylight saw that it was beginning to rise. I ran to tell the captain when he shouted, 'There is the land! My God, we are lost!'

I ran and got my baby out of bed and put some warm clothes around him, put on my boots and shawl and called the cabin boy who was seasick. I took my baby and started to go on deck, but met the captain in the door and he said, 'It is no use. In two or three minutes it will all be over, not a soul can be saved in this fearful sea.' He took the baby in his arms, bade me goodbye and with a prayer to God to have mercy on us, the sea came in on us, the deck gave way under our feet and we went down in the wreck. I was under the water long enough to go thirty or forty feet towards the bow of the ship. Next I knew, I came up in the light, but was fast in the wreckage. I tore my clothes off me and freed myself and looked for my husband and baby. I heard a groan, but could see nothing. Just then I saw my husband on top of the deck house alone. I called to him asking where baby was, but he could not tell and I saw he was hurt. He motioned me to get on the rock. I said, 'No, not till you come.' He said he would do so.

The mate and some of the men had got on shore and were calling me to come. I tried to get my shawl as I was nearly naked, but could not, and ran for the rock on floating pieces of wreckage. It was with much difficulty I got on shore and we found shelter from the wind and rain in a hovel. When they laid my husband down I saw he was badly hurt. He said it was his back, but I did not think he would die. He never seemed really conscious, but would ask if our little one was saved, and the men. He suffered terribly for an hour or so. Some of the natives brought him water off rice, which he drank and asked for water. He then lay down and shortly breathed his last. He was terribly injured; his ribs were broken, his head hurt and the doctor said he was hurt inwardly. He died on the 22nd and was buried on the 23rd.

After he died we all went about a mile through the storm and in water to our ankles, over rocks and coral to a house for shelter. I had nothing on me but an old blanket for a skirt, an old coat of one of the sailors and a straw hat that was picked up. When we got to the house they gave me a native dress. The mate and most of the men that were saved were injured more or less. On the fifth day the carpenter died. The natives were very kind. Our cabin boy was a Japanese and could talk English so he interpreted for us.

We are the first Europeans on the island and thousands have come to see us, and the women will come around me and cry and try to sympathize with me in my trouble. This is a closed port and they are going to send us about sixty or seventy miles to another island in a small boat where there are steamers trading with Japan. We have been here two weeks now and no prospects of getting away as they will only go in fine weather, and it has been blowing a gale for the last three days. We have ridden over thirty miles on horseback over rocks as there are no roads here. I have been to the wreck, hoping to find my baby, but only one of the bodies has been washed ashore. Time seems so long here, sometimes I think we will never get away. We sleep on mats on the floor and have rice, eggs, sweet potatoes to eat and tea. I don't know when you will get this, but it helps me to pass the time away, and if I ever get to Japan will send it to you.

John Troop says that Mrs. Fownes has been "terribly hurt and bruised and received a bad knock on the face," and that all those who were saved were in very bad straits. Their feet are so cut by the coral that it is about three weeks before they can walk. They are weather-bound sixteen days on the island, making three attempts to get away in a small junk to Kumamoto, a small port where a steamer calls. They arrive in the port of Hiogo, Japan, on October 20.

Mutiny and Fire

Mutiny on the high seas was not so common as storm wrecks or fire, but in its way it caused as much distress. A case that involves both mutiny and fire is that of the ship *Frank N. Thayer*, bound from Manila towards New York in 1866 with a cargo of hemp. Mutiny breaks out on January 14, when Captain Robert Clarke brings his vessel up the Atlantic to about seven-hundred miles southeast of the island of St. Helena. The cause of the mutiny is not known, but two seamen involved are described as "Indian coolies" who joined the crew in Manila.

Armed with knives and a harpoon, the mutineers seize control of the deck, and in the fighting kill five men, including the two mates, and wound six others, including the captain. They hold sway for twenty-four hours. When the surprise attack occurred, the master, his wife, and one sailor took refuge in the after cabin, while the rest of the crew was locked in the forecastle forward. An impasse occurs when a sailor in the rigging gets down and releases the loyal crew in the forecastle. They advance on the mutineers while Captain Clarke and his wife, armed with pistols, attack from aft. The mutineers set a fire in the hold of the ship, throw a spare spar overboard, and follow it.

Mrs. Clarke wants the two "coolies" clinging to the spar hung, but her husband can not spare the time so he orders them shot and turns all hands to fighting the fire. But it is too late to save the ship and it has to be abandoned. All the crew, five of them suffering wounds, together with Mrs. Clarke and her small child, set out in one lifeboat for St. Helena, seven hundred miles away. There are seventeen people aboard. Using two blankets for sails, Captain Clarke makes a landfall at St. Helena in four days. Afterward he allows that his wife, "behaved throughout with the greatest pluck and self control."

The Happy Home

Buried in the sparse, journalistic prose of nautical records are hints of men and women's ongoing struggles against the sea. For 1881, the "Yarmouth Record of Shipping" reports one disaster in stark simplicity:

> *The barque Happy Home, Capt. Coalfleet, of Hantsport, N.S., from Hamburg for St. John, New Brunswick, in ballast, struck on Trinity Ledges, 14 miles N. by W. of Yarmouth, at 7.30 on the evening of 3rd January, She remained on the ledge two hours, when she floated off, half full of water, and about ten o'clock, fell over on her beam ends. The captain's wife and daughter—the latter eight years of age—with all hands were lashed to the mizzen chains, the seas breaking over them. The cook perished at twelve o'clock, the little girl at 1 a.m. and the mother at four. The girl was clasped in her mother's arms, in which position they remained until their lifeless bodies were taken off the wreck. The captain's feet and the mate's hands were badly frozen; the second mate and three of the crew were also frost-bitten, but less severely.*
>
> *The next morning the wreck was descried from the shore and boats put off to rescue Captain Coalfleet and crew of twelve men. The dead were also brought to land and an inquest held before N. Hilton, Esq., Coroner, a verdict being rendered in accordance with the facts. The remains of Mrs. Coalfleet and daughter were forwarded by train to Hantsport, in charge of the second mate.*

Happy Home was Hiram Coalfleet's last command as his frozen legs handicapped him for life. The official record does not record Mrs. Coalfleet's given name.

VII
ALICE COALFLEET'S FAMILY

THE DIARY OF A YOUNG WOMAN SHOWS HER DELIGHT IN THE LIFE AT SEA
AND HER INTRODUCTION TO PEOPLE IN FOREIGN PORTS, ONLY TO BE OVER-
TAKEN BY FAMILY TRAGEDY AS SHE RETIRES FROM THE SEA.

The Coalfleets of Hantsport, Nova Scotia, were one seagoing family that had its share of loss at sea, sometimes from disease, sometimes from disaster. There were several women in the Coalfleet clan who went to sea with their shipmaster husbands. The name Coalfleet stands out as unusual today, but it was common for a time in the Minas Basin area around Hantsport and Windsor in the latter nineteenth century. It originated there, the first bearer of the name being Peter Coalfleet, born in the 1770s. The family story, as recalled by Alice, his granddaughter, has it that in the year 1779 a fleet of several ships loaded with coal left England, probably Newcastle, destined for an American or a Nova Scotian port. One of these ships went ashore and broke up in bad weather in the Bay of Fundy. All hands were lost except for one small boy, who was thrown up on the shore tied to a spar or timber. The boy was found by a man named Barker, who could say only a few words, among which was "Pete." Barker brought the boy into Hantsport and named him Peter Coalfleet. Peter eventually married and had thirteen sons and many grandchildren, making the name commonplace around Hantsport for several generations. Today, the name cannot be found in any telephone directory in Canada.

Typically, in these small Nova Scotia ports, families involved in shipbuilding, owning, and sailing were closely associated and their members frequently intermarried. Alice Allen, Captain Hiram Coalfleet's niece and Peter's granddaughter, was born in 1863. She was educated in the German school in Antwerp. Her father was a shipmaster apparently based or employed in Antwerp, in what was then an important port of call for Maritime vessels. Alice lived in a convent there for a time, likely when her parents were at sea. At twenty-two, Alice married George Coalfleet, her first cousin and eighteen years her senior. She sailed with him for most of the length of his command in the barque *Plymouth*, from 1886 to 1892.

Alice Coalfleet recorded life aboard ship during her time at sea in a sprightly diary in which she refers to her husband as "Dodd." She and her husband were full of life, sociable, and musical. Alice and Dodd's ship was the 1312-ton barque *Plymouth*, built in Hantsport in 1879 by John Davison, and owned by John and George Churchill, well-known local ship operators and masters. The diary starts with the first voyage together for this recently married couple (Alice is George's second wife). George's cousin Frank Davison is aboard, probably as an apprentice or junior officer.

Alice's diary excerpts give us glimpses of the social life, travel, and adventure of Alice's six-year career at sea, and the tragedies that ended it. The adventures begin with *Plymouth*'s arrival at Victoria, British Columbia, where Alice meets numerous people in the ports they visit. These are generally the ship's agents, shippers, chandlers, port officials, and a surprising number of old friends from home who have scattered across the country and about the world.

Arriving in Victoria, Alice has the same impression of the city in 1886 as will so many others to follow. She writes in August:

On board bark Plymouth
Anchored in Royal Roads, British Columbia
August 18 1886
We anchor in Royal Roads. Go ashore to Victoria, a very quaint little town nested among lovely trees. We have our lunch at the Oriental Hotel, then go for a drive around Beacon Hill. The scenery is very fine—Dodd and I like this little very English spot and we think it would be a good place to settle when we give up going to sea.

Saturday August 21
We all enjoy our stay here very much—in a quiet way. We are chartered for Port Arthur, China, with lumber. We will probably start loading right away.

Receiving their charter to load for the Orient, the Coalfleets' ship is towed through the islands of the Strait of Georgia to Burrard Inlet on the mainland. Across the inlet from Moody's sawmill, the terminus of the new Canadian Pacific Railway is being built at the new city of Vancouver, a shanty boomtown and construction site in the woods. During the lengthy loading of lumber, there is plenty of time for leisurely sightseeing and social visits, such as they are in this "wild" place. Like other enterprising masters, Dodd has the convenience of a small sailboat carried on board.

August 22
The tug Alexander tows us up to Moodyville—a little sawmill town. Looks a bit for-lorn and dreary. Vancouver, the town opposite, was burnt down a few weeks ago, and is now a city of tents.

August 23
We go across to Vancouver in our sail boat. We meet a Dr. Beckingsale and his wife of London. Quite charming people. They return with us for dinner.

August 26
Dodd goes ashore and comes back with a lovely guitar for me, with a book of instruc-tion, so must learn to play it on our way to China. Mrs. Beckingsale comes on board for tea. The Flora P. Stafford arrives with a load of tea for Port Moody. Lord Durham is on board. We go out in our sailboat nearly every day. We fish, but do not catch very many salmon. The Indians around here told us we used the wrong kind of hooks.

Tuesday August 31
Our new steward and stewardess come on board. She is a strange looking character. We have met the Springers, who have a very fine residence here.

September 9
Dodd hires a horse and buggy and we drive out in the woods. He takes his gun along, but only gets one grouse. The woods are beautiful. Our chief amusement is driving through the woods and sailing.

September 20
We spend the evening with the Springers, their niece Alice Miller, Captain and Mrs. Bridgeman. Senator Nelson and wife are there.

Thursday, September 23
Mrs. Springer and Alice Miller came onboard for tea—Mr. Springer coming later for dinner and the evening.

Sunday, October 3
Dodd and I drive to Westminster, have dinner at the Colonial Hotel, drive back in the moonlight.

October 8
Mabel, Eva and Ruby Springer spend the afternoon on board and we all go up to their house in the evening.

October 12
We start for sea—rainy, dull day. Our new steward and stewardess are not quite as
we should like. They came on last night about half full.

Captain Coalfleet takes *Plymouth* out across the Pacific, passing near Hawaii
and south of Japan into the Yellow Sea off the coast of China. As on their stop at
Moodyville on Burrard Inlet, in the Chinese ports the Coalfleets again enjoy the
hospitality of local agents and officials and their wives. Everyone relishes these
new contacts—the ship's people enjoy getting ashore and the land people seem
happy to be entertained on board a vessel—though it is especially welcome for
the women in their circumscribed social circles.

November 7
We are down in the latitude of the Sandwich Islands. The weather is very fine and
warm, so we just about live on deck.

Saturday, December 4
We see the Loo Choo Islands. See one close enough to see lights in some of the houses.

December 25
A merry Christmas in the Yellow Sea. We have chicken and mince pie for dinner. We
wonder about the folks at home and wish them a happy day. We are having head
winds which does not add to the holiday spirit.

On New Year's Day - "I wish all my friends and enemies (if I have any) a very happy
New Year. We are rejoicing over a fair wind and have made Shantung Promontory
and pass the lighthouse.

January 4, 1887
Anchor in Cheefoo Harbour. Go ashore with Mr. Price and live in their lovely home
until Saturday. We meet Mr. Price's sister Irene. She wants to sell her beautiful piano
so Dodd is buying it for me.
*   We do not have to go to Port Arthur after all as the company our cargo was con-*
signed to have failed. We will probably be here for several weeks.

January 5
My beautiful piano is on board. It is a German piano, made in Stuttgart. Has ten
bronze lamps, two sets on each side, and on the cover are several medals—prizes. Now
Frank and I can have some concerts.

February 20, 1887
Dodd and I go to a bachelors' dinner at Mr. Webster and Clark. We enjoy it very much.

February 21
Mr. Webster sends me a nice banjo. Now I have a piano, guitar, banjo, organ—and Frank his violin and cornet.

February 22
Our last day on shore. Mr. Hansen and Captain Orfeur spend the evening with us at Mrs. Price's We have a nice farewell party. After we have retired, they serenaded us at midnight with 1000 firecrackers.

February 23
Came on board early and got underway for Tientsin.

Plymouth's Canadian lumber is unloaded by one hundred "coolies" at anchor at Taku, which is the actual port just below Tientsin. Alice and Dodd commute up river by steamboat to the city, staying at the Astor House

March 7
We go to the bank. I meet Mrs. Leith, the banker's wife. Later we call to see Mrs. Williams. A lovely home with many Chinese servants. A Chinese "amah" nurses her baby. We leave on steamer Tungchow for Taku. We get stuck in the muddy river— very narrow.

April 6
Go on board S.S. Taku and start for Tientsin. Mr. Smithers (of Wilmington) his son and daughter are on board. Mr. Smithers is to take Mr. Bromley, the American consul's place. The river is full of junks so we go along very slowly. We see Chinese fishing on stilts.

Plymouth arrives in Yokohama in time for Queen Victoria's birthday celebrations. While the ship loads tea for California, Alice passes a pleasant time in Yokohama, staying at the Club Hotel and touring about in her own ricksha, buying curios, and receiving presents from merchants who supply the ship. As often happens early in the season, they have to wait for the tea to be picked before they can begin loading.

June 7
Start for sea again. Our stay in Yokohama was most pleasant. Bought some nice curios and have some lovely presents from the different merchants.

July 7
We are sailing along—nothing of any importance occurring but keep busy and keep well.

July 18
Long. 139°-19'. Lat.36°-59' (about two-thirds of the way enroute from Honolulu to San Francisco.) Dodd and I eat up in the pilot house. He was making bullets for his gun and I looked on. I retire at 7.30 p.m., trying to read, but other matters require my attention. At ten o'clock a little stranger makes his appearance. He is very welcome, a dear pretty little fellow his head covered with black hair. Dodd is doctor, nurse and everything else, washes and dresses the little one, lays him alongside of me then stands and recites funny poetry to make me forget my pain.

July 24
Make the land this morning at eight o'clock. Get to our anchorage at 2.30. The doctor comes on board to see me, says I am fine and have a beautiful baby. The custom house officers are busy sealing up our curios. Dodd brought one of them in to see me and our finest 'curio'. Dodd wants to call the baby William after his uncle William Davison, Frank's father.

Now comes a long period of unloading at Oakland and waiting for a charter to sail to Port Gamble, Puget Sound, for a load of lumber for Melbourne. The Coalfleets have a long round of sightseeing and visits in various towns. Many Maritimers have moved to the Pacific Northwest and there are many friends and relations to visit before *Plymouth* puts to sea for the long run across the Pacific.

November 3
Tow out from Port Townsend in company with Richard D. Buck and Dashing Wave [three ships with one tug].

November 17
Thanksgiving Day. We have many things to be thankful for. Good health, a beautiful baby boy—wonderful good—never cries—no need to—he is so well. Then we have fine weather and fair wind.

December 5
Pass the equator today. Baby weighs over 25 lbs. Is 28 inches long. Is so well—we all are.

December 8
This morning at about three o'clock, a man falls overboard (John Shaw). We lower a
boat and get him. He was an excellent swimmer.

Christmas Day 1887
Merry! and we really enjoy our Christmas dinner—soup, roast chicken, green peas and
corn, mince pie. And just to celebrate, our cat has one little black kitten.

Captain Coalfleet takes *Plymouth* down past Tahiti and the Cook Islands, raising
Deal Island going into Bass Strait to beat against its head winds on January 17,
hauling up to Melbourne wharf on February 4. Life in a tramping sailing ship is
carrying the Dodds and the trusty *Plymouth* around the usual ports of the world,
providing the bulk cargoes suitable for slow, economical sailing vessels. While in
Australia, Dodd and his mate and cousin, Frank Davison, meet Asa Davison, Dodd's
half-brother, also in port at Melbourne. Inter-marriage in a small community has
created a complex of interconnections between the Coalfleets and the Davisons.

Feb. 21
Dodd and Frank leave for Sydney to see Frank's half brother, Gird Davison so I am
aboard alone with the baby Willie. He is such a fine little companion. I took him to a
doctor the other day. He said he was a fine specimen and told me I probably drank a
lot of ale. I told him I only drank water, which surprised him—but cows drink water.

After dry-docking in Sydney to have the ship's bottom cleaned, they re-cross
the Pacific to San Pedro, California. Dodd sails then up the coast to Tacoma to
load grain for Falmouth, while Alice takes a coastal steamer to San Francisco for a
three-week visit with friends in Oakland. She rejoins Dodd in Tacoma.

August 6
Dodd left San Pedro Saturday for Tacoma where we will load grain for Falmouth,
England (for orders). I am rejoicing as I will see my lovely sister Lucy and her baby, a
month older than ours.

Sept 3
Get into Victoria, British Columbia, at two o'clock in the morning. Dodd meets us
there and we get to Seattle in the evening.

Sept 4
Back home onboard Plymouth and glad to be here—everything looks so nice.

From Tacoma there is a long, four-month, voyage around Cape Horn. They leave on October 9: "We tow out at midnight bound for England—I wonder how many days. We are all well."

November 16
We are about two hundred miles to windward of Pitcairn Island. Was in hopes we might pass very close.

November 27
Getting colder, feels like snow. It probably will before we get around Cape Horn. It is daylight now from 3 a.m until 9 p.m. When it is rough I sit on the floor and hold baby. I am reading "Les Miserables." Very interesting.

December 8
A month since we saw the equator. We have hardly any darkness, daylight at 1 a.m.

December 16
A good strong breeze today. We see two ships bound the same way we are. About six o'clock we see Diego Ramirez Island. Round Cape Horn during the night. Snow all night.

December 24
I suppose everybody on shore is making great preparations for Christmas, trimming Christmas trees.

Christmas Day 1888
Our second Christmas at sea. It is nice and fine now so we are on deck nearly every day. Santa Claus does not come this far but we are all well and happy and thankful for it, and safe on our way—Merry Christmas to all.

Sunday, December 30
In the latitude of Buenos Ayres. Baby climbs up the pilot house steps. Needs constant watching, but is so good and well.

February 13, 1889
Yesterday it blew a living gale. We were hove to all night. Today wind and sea have both gone down. I trust it is the last blow this trip.

February 15
See Scilly Light at 3 a.m. Pilot came on board at six. Get in and anchor at Falmouth at 2 p.m. Get our mail.

Alice Coalfleet is one of Captain Richard Allen and Mary Jane Coalfleet's ten children, six of whom die in infancy or childhood. The remaining children are Alice, Lucy, Rena, and Woody.

February 16
Captain Ellis of the Grandee comes on board. Lucy and her baby Margaret arrive on board at 9 p.m. Of course we do a lot of talking, not having seen each other since about five years ago in Antwerp.

March 21
Busy getting ready to start for Nova Scotia. I am enjoying Lucy's visit so much. Only wish Rena and Woody could be with us.

As Alice is expecting her second child, she and William leave *Plymouth*. They will return home in the S.S. *Peruvian* while Dodd and *Plymouth* leave for Montevideo. The weather is rough crossing the Atlantic and the dining saloon empties of passengers except for Alice and Willie, to whom a rolling, pitching world is fairly normal. Alice has the usual round of visits on arrival in Hantsport.

May 5
Aunt Louisa Davison calls. She has been fasting forty-eight hours. She calls it housecleaning. Eats only tomatoes and bran, the bran being the scrubbing brush and to-matoes the soap. They all think she is mentally deranged except me.

June 18
Nell Smith and Allie Campbell call in the evening. Not feeling very well but play Clayton's Grand March for them. Then Nell and I walk up to Sile Mitchener's store for strawberries which I eat on our return but conclude I had better send for the doctor and nurse, Aunt Alice as everyone calls her. The new baby arrives at 1.30 a.m. A fine baby boy weighing nearly ten pounds.

June 19
Send Dodd a telegram (in Montevideo) this morning. Just one word, 'George'. Costs $15.00. A girl it would have been Alice Victoria.

Sept. 26
We leave Hantsport for St. John and Portland—arrive on board Plymouth at 5 a.m."

The next entry reads simply: "NO PLACE LIKE HOME." Even after a long visit among family at Hantsport, Alice Coalfleet considers *Plymouth* her home.

On October 10, the family heads out on another voyage, this time to Montevideo from Portland, Maine. They arrive on December 20. They enjoy a long stay in the Uruguayan capital, the highlight of which is the annual carnival and a visit with Alice's brother Woody, whose ship is also in port. As is usual, there is much visiting with other Bluenose vessels and crews at Montevideo. Alice and Woody part with the hope that the three sisters and brother may all meet together again before long. Alice has the following to say about visiting with her brother:

March 4, 1890
Go on board the Loanda and see my brother Woody. He looks real well and is the same old "Wow" as we used to call him, such a jolly old talk we have about our good times and sad times in old Antwerp. He made me remove my hat to see if I still had my lovely hair. Oh, its heavy and only do it up in port.

March 8
Woody comes onboard and stays all night and we talk some more. Many ships in port so we have lots of company.

Plymouth returns to New York via Barbados and is quickly chartered for Shanghai in the lucrative case oil trade. Willie is three and Baby Dodie is able to stand. Child minding becomes a more serious job.

July 18
Willie is three years old today. Dody is practicing to stand alone. Can come down the pilot house steps. Weather cool and comfortable.

September 8
Various kinds of weather. We are going along tho. We are now in the Indian Ocean with a nice breeze. Long.24°49'. Lat.40°6'.

September 14
Willie throws his little puff-puff [engine] overboard. We are out nearly three months and as Whit Harvey used to say, "it is kind of monotonous." However we are all well and happy. I think if Baby Dodd were on shore he could walk.

September 27 '90
Pass St. Paul's Rocks at about six o'clock this morning in Long.77°35' and Lat.37°. Willie is beginning to learn his ABC's. He calls 'E' the steamboat one. He can sing two verses of "Old Ned".

October 13
Good breeze, quite cool, lots of bonito, but they won't bite. We haven't caught a fish since we left New York. Willie has a mania for throwing things overboard. He has thrown three hammers, one pair of pincers, his bow and arrow, a tin funnel and clothesline. I make him a little oil coat and sou'wester.

October 17 1890
We anchor in Allos Strait (near Bali) at 4.30 p.m. Dodd goes ashore to see about getting some water. Brings back some sweet potatoes, bananas, coconuts and three very meagre chickens. Some of the natives come on board with chickens and geese which they want to trade for knives, scissors or any thing sharp. They all chew betel nut. They talk by making signs, altho I found out that "bagoosh" in their lingo means "good". They all wanted to feel my braids which they thought "bagoosh"—also the children. Weather quite hot.

October 21
This morning we are blest with abundance of rain, so fill up our tanks, much cooler, too—eighty in the shade. We have a young Belgian lad on board, Jan Kenely, lives in Antwerp. I spoke Flemish to him. He seemed real pleased to hear his native tongue. Dody is walking around now.

December 18
Yangtse pilot comes on board at eight o'clock from No.1 boat—Mr. Kofoed, a Dane. Anchor at 3.30 p.m.

December 19
Get underway this morning, fair wind. Just before we get to lightship the towboat Fairy, Captain Roberts['], comes alongside. Wants $300 to tow us to Woosung. Anchor at 6 p.m. Ah Sing comes on board and promises to go get our mail.

December 20
Dead calm. Get underway at 4 p.m., anchor outside Woosung River at eight o'clock. Receive our letters, one containing sad news for me. Poor old Woody died on the passage from Montevideo to New York of fever and was buried at sea. So glad I saw the dear boy in Montevideo. Just we three girls left—Lucy, Rena and me.

In the new year *Plymouth* sails from Shanghai for Manila, a major sugar shipping port, then from Manila in February for New York by way of the Indian Ocean and the Cape of Good Hope.

Feb. 22, 1891
Have tiffin at Mr. Robinson's. Then a lot of us go up the river in a steam launch—
have a very pleasant outing. Mr. Robinson gave me some beautiful jewellery: a bracelet,
broach and earrings. All to match. Gold and pearls. Mrs. Rothbart gave me a beautiful
pearl for a ring. They loved the children, wished they could adopt baby Dodd.

February 26
We make a start for sea bound for New York. Willie throws the little black dog over-
board but we get it back again. We have on board about five-dozen chickens, five mon-
keys and two small dogs.

March 13
North Watcho in sight—quite a pretty green sight in the sea. Willie throws Mr.
Ramesay's [the mate] slippers overboard today so I throw his poukah [bottle] overboard
too.

March 14
Anchor at Anjer at about nine o'clock this morning. Go ashore and spend the afternoon
at Mr. Rairden's. They have two children. Mr. Rairden belongs to Bath, Maine. We
go there for dinner.

March 16
Not much wind all day and very hot. Java Head and Princess Island in sight. The
largest monkey (Sumatran) holds the little pups in his arms most tenderly.

March 18
Awful hot last night. We get up at 2 a.m. and take the children on deck.

March 23
Most every evening we sit on deck under the awning, each holding one of the chil-
dren. Dodd thinks we may go back to Manila some day. Anyway, we make plans
for the future.

April 17
See the Land of Good Hope. Last night we saw Cape Agulhas light.

May 1
St. Helena in sight at 7.30 this morning. A boat comes off so we order coal, sugar, etc.
We leave again at six o'clock. Messrs Solomon Moss Giden and Company come off
with our order.

In June of 1891, on arrival in New York from Manila, Alice and Dodd leave *Plymouth*, their home for six years, and go to Hantsport to prepare for their retirement in British Columbia.

Saturday June 6
We are all feeling good again. Busy ship cleaning—clean out cabin and office.

June 13
The tug Crawford ties us up to our berth at Horbeck Stores in New York.

June 14
We are planning on leaving the Plymouth, go to Hantsport and, in the spring, go out to British Columbia.

June 18
I leave on the S.S. Puritan. Captain Charlie Laurence is on board so helps me with the children. Arrive at Fall River at 4 a.m. Start for Boston where we take the S.S. Yarmouth. Arrive in Hantsport all safe and sound.

June 27
The Plymouth is chartered for London. Poor Lucy will feel badly that we are not going in her.

July 15
Dodd arrives home on the express

August 13
Another picnic, out to Meander farm. A lovely drive. We take some of our good things to the Poor Farm.

September 8
Receive sad news from London—poor Lucy died in childbirth. I cable to father. Well only Rena and I left now.

November 2
The Loodiana arrives in New York. We have wired Rena to come to Hantsport.

November 18
Rena arrives on the six o'clock train. Such a joy for we have not seen each other since we were married. We talked and talked and yearned for Lucy and Woody.

November 19
Rena and I spent the day with Grandmother Coalfleet. At night we just talk and talk. Dodd laughs at us.

November 21
George Churchill wants Dodd to go on to New York and take the Hamburg for one trip to London, so he thinks he better go.

November 25
Dodd leaves for New York this morning. Rena and I both in bed with sore throat. Dodd says it is from talking too much. Dr. Margeson says we are all right.

November 29
Snow on the ground. Rena and I go to church in the evening. She wants me to go to New York with her.

December 1
Hamburg sails for London.

December 2
Rena and I start for New York. First time I have left the children but will only be gone a short time.

December 4
Arrive in New York. Miles is at the wharf to meet us. We go right on board the Loodiana lying at North 10th Street, Brooklyn.

Saturday, December 5
We stay on board all day. Rena shows me all the lovely things she bought in Japan and she tells me about the wedding in London. Such a lovely looking girl and the loveliest disposition. Miles said, 'Enjoy yourselves, girls. No telling when you will meet again.' In the evening Captain Almon comes on board—tells us about poor Woody's death.

December 9
We go over to town for dinner. I feel I ought to get home to the children but Rena begs me to stay. Harry Almon wires to see if they are all right.

December 14
I leave for Hantsport. Rena hates for me to leave, even tried to get me to go with them and join Dodd in London, but I could not leave the babies, and so we say goodbye.

December 16
Arrive in Hantsport at 4.30. Willie is at the train to meet me. Find all well and baby Dodd glad to have his mama back again and now we talk Christmas and Santa Claus. It is quite cold and snow on the ground.

December 25 Christmas 1891
In a way this is not a merry Christmas that is for me. The children enjoy it though.

December 28
The Hamburg arrived in London today—twenty-four day passage. Hope the Loodiana will soon arrive too.

February 3, 1892
Bennet-Smith Co. are beginning to be anxious about the Loodiana, now out forty-three days. Dodd sailed January 29th for New York.

February 17
Go to Windsor to see what I can find out about the Loodiana. A burning ship was sighted off Land's End which seems to be the Loodiana. I am sick over it. Rena's birthday soon. 23. So young to die.

April 6
The Loodiana was burned at sea on January 16th off Land's End, sighted by two British steamers. The S.S. Egyptian Monarch tried to aid them but the ship was aflame. The newspapers [New York papers] gave heart rending accounts of the disaster. She was loaded with naphtha [an organic, flammable liquid].

I am just heart weary and now we are beginning to get anxious about the Hamburg. In less than two years I have lost my only brother and two sisters and now am the only one left. I wonder how father feels about it all.

April 11
A telegram this morning—the Hamburg's arrival in New York and the saddest news of all—for Dodd died at sea on Feb. 28th. I had a premonition that something was wrong but cast it aside as foolish anxiety. But it is all too true. May my little boys be spared me. They do not realize their loss.

April 16
If kind letters and friends could comfort one, I have had many of both. Rena's death seemed more than I could bear and now this. What next? I wonder.

May 4
Dodd's effects arrive today, but none of his papers, letters, photos—not even his memo-randum book. We think Mr. Brown (the mate) destroyed them. I go to see Mr. Churchill about salary, but he claims Dodd drew it all in London. Now I'm getting out administration papers to settle up the estate. We sent all our spare money to a bank in Victoria, British Columbia—about $2000.

May 31
Father is on his way out to see me, left on the 24th on the S.S. Nova Scotian for Halifax.

June 4
Father arrives at seven o'clock tonight. Such a fine looking man—tall and aristocratic looking. He is charmed with my boys. We have a long talk—really never knew him before.

June 5
Father and I walk up to Baptist Church. We are having a nice visit tho sad in a way. We walk up to the old home where I was born.

June 11
Father leaves on a trip to Yarmouth. My grandmother is quite ill and failing fast so go up to see her quite often.

June 15
Grandmother dies this morning (eighty-two years old).

June 17
Go to grandmother's funeral. As grandfather stood at her grave he said, 'I will soon fol-low.'

August 10
Grandfather Coalfleet is buried today—he did follow soon. I am undecided just what to do. Must wait anyway until the estate is settled off. Dodd left no will, nor was he in-sured. I mentioned insurance just before he left for New York. He laughed and said, 'You don't think a fellow is going to die do you?'

Christmas Day 1892
Cold day—plenty of snow. The children are happy as Santa Claus makes his first visit to them and fills their stockings. They love the snow and are out every day. Last year we spent our Christmas in the China Sea.

We go skating quite a bit. Sometimes I take the children to look on when there is a hockey game. They keep so well. I tell them stories I make up. Willie likes to know about going to sea and the funny little things he used to say. He had a swing aboard the Plymouth.

Nell tells me I must plan on marrying again—that I am young and good looking and should marry. Someone with plenty of money. I entertain my thoughts about such things. I know it seems useless to plan ahead for our castles in the air crumble as fast as we make them.

Father writes me very encouraging letters. Tells me I should write. He always said I was a clever girl. I suppose I might try and teach French in some school.

Thus ends the diary of Alice Coalfleet. She had been one of ten children of Captain Richard Allen and Mary Jane Coalfleet. (Six of their children had died in infancy or childhood.) Alice does marry again, in 1897, at the age of thirty-four. She outlives her second husband, Clarence Wiley, dying in Seattle at the age of eighty-eight.

THE TRAGEDY OF THE LOODIANA

Alice Coalfleet's younger sister, Lucy, met an untimely end that proves the all too frequent harshness of fate in nineteenth-century seafaring life. The case of the *Loodiana* might have been recorded as simply another disappearance, but witnesses aboard a nearby steamer tell the tale of their thwarted attempts at rescue and the ship's demise.

The 1874-ton ship *Loodiana* left New York on December 21, 1891, bound towards London loaded with tins of naphtha. Before the development of petroleum tankers, such cargoes were loaded in small crated drums and referred to as case oil. Case oil was an easy-to-handle and profitable cargo—if the drums didn't leak. New York newspapers carried the story related to them by Second Officer Jordan of the steamer *Egyptian Monarch*, first to discover the blazing ship

It was fifteen minutes to one o'clock on the morning of January 16 that I noticed a flare of light about one-half point off the port bow. There was a tremendous gale blowing and we had our sail set double-reefed to keep the vessel steady.

The light disappeared almost as suddenly as I saw it and I concluded it was the flashlight of some sailing vessel which desired to indicate her location to any passing steamship. Immediately after the light disappeared a heavy hail squall struck us. This so enveloped the steamer that nothing could be seen two ship lengths ahead.

After the squall had cleared away, for it went as suddenly as it came, I saw a sudden belch of fire shoot skyward, as though an explosion had taken place some distance off the port side. I could not tell just how far it was. Through the glass I saw a ship on

fire. The explosion was probably the blowing up of her cargo. She was blazing fore and aft, and I at once called Captain Irvin, who came on deck and summoned all hands. He ordered all sail furled and as quickly as possible the Egyptian Monarch was headed for the burning vessel. We reached the ship at half-past one o'clock, after half an hour's hard steaming.

She was enveloped in flames. Her masts had burned away and she looked like a fiery furnace. The only part of her still untouched by the flames was the bowsprit. Out near the end of it was a portly man, whom the agents of the vessel identified from our description as Captain Boyd. Clinging to him was a pale-faced, slightly built woman. Her hair floated in the gale and the picture made by those two miserable beings clinging to the bowsprit of that burning craft I shall never forget. We were near enough to see their faces lighted by the flames, and such agony I never again want to see depicted on a human face.

We were to windward of them and we shouted to them to hold on. Captain Irvin ordered one of the boats launched and called for volunteers to man her. Our crew was a scratch one, picked up in Gravesend at the last moment. They were not good sailors and only three stepped forward. The officers offered to go, but this would have left the ship without officers and an inefficient crew in case the boat was lost, which it in all probability it would have been. There was a terrible sea running. We had to constantly use oil over the bow to lessen the force of the huge waves that rolled in on us.

The boat was not launched, and as it was my watch, I returned to the bridge. The Egyptian Monarch then dropped off to leeward of the burning wreck and we could hear the captain and his wife on the bowsprit calling piteously for help. It was heartrending to hear them and yet know that no succor could be given them.

All that I have related from the time of our arrival at the scene occupied a brief length of time, but the flames had made rapid progress toward the quivering pair on the bowsprit. The heel of the bowsprit was soon on fire, the tough timber was eaten through and then it dropped overboard with the captain and his wife still clinging to it. We caught sight of them once as a big wave caught them up and dashed them against the blazing hull and then they disappeared and we saw them no more. It was a horrible sight and I can see it now as plainly as when I witnessed it.

We remained by the burning vessel until nine o'clock that morning and steamed around her repeatedly. She burned until the waves engulfed the smoking wreck. Then we steamed to leeward for twelve miles, keeping a sharp lookout for any of the vessel's crew, but no sign of any of them was seen. We then resumed our voyage.

VIII
FUNDY FAMILIES

YOUNG WOMEN OF THE MARITIMES MARRY AND GO OFF TO SEA ON THEIR HONEYMOONS FOR SATISFYING LIVES OF SEABORNE ADVENTURE, TRAVEL, AND DOMESTIC BLISS. OTHERS RELUCTANTLY RETREAT TO SHORE FROM THE AGONY OF SEASICKNESS.

Why should women marry sea captains, knowing they will spend most of their lives at sea? The answer could be that captains were of good social standing with good incomes, and to some women, they represented a certain masculine ideal. Many seafaring women married in their late twenties, an age slightly older than was typical at that time. Perhaps working against what captains offered in terms of status was the awareness that life at sea was at best difficult, at worst, deadly. On the other hand, they may have been unwilling to accept relegation to restrictive Victorian domesticity in marriage until this opportunity to travel the world came along.

The Petitcodiac River in Westmorland County, New Brunswick is famous for its tidal bore, which sweeps up over miles of mudflats to fill the riverbed with a powerful surge from the great Bay of Fundy tides. Gone now is all evidence of the busy shipbuilding industry of the nineteenth century. Harvey, on the western shore, was one of the very small communities around the Bay of Fundy that spawned numerous ships and seamen. Henry and James, sons of Joseph Turner, a leading Harvey merchant, went to sea in ships and rose rapidly to become master mariners.

THE MARRIAGE OF JOSEPHINE REID

A bride in 1879, Josephine Reid, like most newlyweds in her position, immediately sets off to sea to be with, and make a home for, her captain husband James Turner. His sister Janie joins them during the year, but when their barque *Kesmark* arrives in New York in January of 1880 it is decided that the ladies will leave the ship to go home. Suffering from seasickness, it does not seem to have been "for reasons of midwifery" that Josephine chooses to sit out a voyage.

It is a sad parting for the devoted couple, but the two sisters, shepherded by Nelson Smith—one of the owners of *Kesmark*—stop in New York for some sightseeing on the way home. In the great metropolis they meet Josephine's brother-in-law, Captain Henry Turner, whose ship *Elgin* is in port. Because sailing ships often spent a month or more in port, handling cargo and waiting for suitable contracts, Henry has plenty of time on his hands. During extended stays it was common to discharge all but key members of the crew to save on overhead, leaving ships virtually deserted. The three tour the town and when Josephine arrives home in Harvey, she writes a long letter to her husband, full of her sadness at their first parting but also full of enthusiasm about her adventures in New York, and of her journey home by train and coastal steamer. Her letters illustrate the vicissitudes of travel at the time, and the entertainment and night life of New York. Famous preachers like Talmadge and Beecher are attractions.

Harvey, January 27th [18]80

How I wish that I could see you this evening. I have so much I want to tell you that I scarcely know how to begin to write. You will doubtless be pleased to hear of our safe arrival to this little village again. I must proceed at once to give you a full account of our journey home. You can easily imagine how sad and lonely I felt the morning I left you. We were a little too late for the nine o'clock train, so we waited until eleven before leaving. Arrived at New York at two o'clock p.m. Met Henry at the station. He had been waiting there for two hours or more.

We all went to the Stevens House to dinner after which Mr. Smith left for the S.B. Weldon, and we only saw him occasionally until after we left New York. Henry stopped with us most of the time, and was very kind to us, did everything he could to make us enjoy ourselves. He went with us that evening for a walk. Sunday morning he came and went with us to Brooklyn to hear Talmadge, who preached a real good sermon as he always does that. His subject was "Hunger in Ireland", his text being Matthew 25:35. I think I must send the sermon for you and Watson [her brother] to read.

In the evening we went to hear Beecher. I did not like him quite as well as Talmadge, but perhaps some would think his sermon the best. Talmadge has the best house and the best music, and the most hearers. Mr. Smith thought the boat left New York Sunday evenings, but it did not. We then talked of leaving Monday morning and come all the way by rail, but Mr. Smith thought it would be better, more comfortable and cheaper to come in the boat even if we waited until Wednesday before we left. He seemed anxious to stop in New York two or three days, although he said he would come any time that we wished. His neck did not get much worse after we left Philadelphia. it kept improving a little all the time after Sunday. He felt rather poorly that day.

Well, we decided to remain in New York until Wednesday, January 21st. Monday, Henry took us to Central Park, we had a ride on the Elevated Railway, spent the afternoon pleasantly in the park, saw all kinds of birds and animals there, lions, bears, elephants, buffaloes, cats, etc. We went back to the Stevens House to tea and then concluded to go on board the Elgin and stop the remainder of the time. Henry said we could go as well as not if we would like to do so. We thought it a good idea, as we would feel much more at home in a vessel, and it cost two dollars a day for our room at the hotel.

We enjoyed ourselves splendidly in the Elgin. Henry has everything about the vessel looking as nice as possible. His cabin looks first rate, I wish ours was painted as nicely. They had no steward aboard, but Mr. Brewster seemed to be well skilled in the art of cooking. I think he has had some practice in that line before. Henry got salmon and all kinds of good things for us. He had a little book on board called "The Young Wife's Own Cook Book" which perhaps they had both been studying after their cook left. Henry made me a present of that book which I have no doubt may prove very useful to me in the future, although I thought it unwise for him to part with it, but he thought he would have no trouble in getting another one if he should need it soon.

Tuesday was a little rainy, but it cleared off in the afternoon and we all went to Greenwood Cemetery. It was quite late when we got back. We were invited to go on board the J.B.Newcomb that evening, but it commenced raining again and we did not go. Captain Newcomb called on us the day we arrived in New York. We had been there an hour or so. His wife was away at her sister's and he was going to see her, called on me before he left.

Wednesday forenoon we went to an artist's and Janie sat to get some pictures taken which Henry will get and send to her. I hope they will be good ones. It was quite late when we got back to the Elgin so we got our dinners as quickly as we could, Henry filled our satchels with cakes, cheese, etc., and we started for the boat Newport. Mr Smith was on hand and about four p.m. the boat left for Fall River. We felt more lonely than ever when Henry left us. And, James, don't you think that after he went around so much with us and did all he could to make us happy, he insisted on paying our expenses in New York. I could not persuade him to take pay for it at all. I felt very sorry to think he would not let me pay at least half our expenses, but it was of no use to talk about it, he would not listen to it. I did not think of his doing so. But I hope we may have a chance to repay him in some way. He paid four dollars for the room and I don't know how much for our meals. I only paid about a dollar for our meals when he was not there, that was for our breakfasts Sunday and Monday.

But I am making a long story about our journey home. We arrived at Fall River about five o'clock a.m., went on the train to Boston expecting to take the boat to St. John, but it did not leave that day, Thursday, but on Monday, the change having been made last week. So we waited at the station until half-past twelve and then took the cars for Portland, arrived there about six p.m. Took the boat for St. John, expected to leave that evening, but it was so dark and stormy the boat, (City of Portland, which is *not at all a new one,) did not leave until ten Friday morning and it was rough enough even then, I can assure you. Nearly all on board were seasick, Janie and Mr. Smith being among that number. You know it must have been pretty rough when Janie was sick. I felt quite sick for a while. We all found that brandy a very useful medicine and I felt glad that I brought it, but dear James, when I was seasick how much I missed your love and care. I miss you all the time, but especially then. The seasickness gradually wore away and I felt quite well the next morning.*

The boat did not get in to St. John until after nine o'clock Saturday morning, too late for the morning train to Salisbury. So we did not leave until afternoon, and as we could not get home that day, we went to Moncton and stopped over Sunday as we thought we would feel more at home there than at Salisbury. We went to Baptist church in the morning and Methodist church in the evening, stopped at Uncle William Robinson's that night and Monday morning (yesterday) he took us to the station.

I don't believe you will have time to read all this scribble before you sail again, but when you get off to sea again you can spend some of your leisure hours puzzling over it. Goodnight—Josie.

Departing the port of Philadelphia, Captain James Brewster Turner and the *Kesmark* move in tow down the Delaware River behind a steam tug until dusk and evening mists cause the captain to anchor for the night. In his log entry for Saturday, January 17, 1880, he notes some ship's business, then turns to what is most on his mind:

Josephine and Janie left for home this morning with Nelson Smith at 8 a.m. I felt very badly to see them leave. I will feel very loanly indeed this voyage. I do hope that Josephine can come with me on the next passage. We left Girard Point at 11 a.m. in tow down the river. We are to pay $40 to tow to Bombay Hook, if to sea $60. The weather has been very fine all day. We came to anchor at dark. It is too thick to go farther.

Sunday - It is Sunday again and I am very lonely. Our little cabin does not appear a bit like home since Josephine and Janie left. How little does it appear like it was last Sunday when we were all together and spent the day so pleasantly. How loanly our little room appears when I come down from the deck and find myself all alone. My dear wife cannot be with me this voyage. I do hope she can come to me when we get back. This is the first Sabbath since we were married that I have been deprived of the pleasure of her company.

The next day (Monday), Captain Turner mentions his loneliness again, hoping that his wife is having a pleasant time on her journey home from Philadelphia to Albert County, New Brunswick. Having vented his feelings onto paper, he gets down to the business of reporting weather and calculations of the ship's position. He is bound on a voyage of possibly many months to the Mediterranean and back.

Josephine ("Josie" to her husband) writes him again on receipt of his letters from Bordeaux, where he has a long wait for a cargo-offering back across the Atlantic. There was a fairly brisk trade in case oil from Philadelphia or grains from other east coast ports, but little going westbound. The "Watson" Josephine refers to is her brother; he works aboard *Kesmark*.

Tuesday, March 23rd

My dear Husband,

I have just received your kind and welcome letter of the 4th and 5th, it is the third I have received since your arrival and hope I receive many more before you sail again. I am sorry you have to stop so long at Bordeaux, but perhaps it is all for the best, I did not expect you would be in port so long or would have sent you another letter or two. I expect you and Watson will both learn to talk French first rate being among the French so long. So you are getting our little cabin and bedroom painted, it will improve the appearance of it very much. I can imagine how nice it looks. I expect you are making so many improvements about the vessel that I will scarcely know her when I see her again.

I don't think I will be very seasick another voyage. I hope to learn to be a good sailor yet and go with you a good many voyages. I trust we shall soon meet again and spend many happy months together. I know, dear James, that you spend many lonesome days in the little cabin where we have spent so many happy hours. Sometimes they would seem to pass altogether too quickly. No wonder Janie and Watson would sometimes say, 'Oh, they would rather stop [stay] than go ashore, they don't mind staying there all day long. We will go ashore without them.'

I can imagine from my own feelings how badly you felt the day we left Phila., I to come home and you to go still farther away. It was a sad parting for us both. I was obliged to keep my thick veil over my face until we got to the station to hide the tears that came so easily. it is so hard to part with loved ones, especially when we know it will be months at least before we can meet again, but my darling husband, do not be too anxious about me. Always think of me as being well and happy. The weeks will soon roll round and we shall soon see each other again. What a happy meeting it will be for us both.

I expect the plants have grown wonderfully since I saw them. That little leaf you sent me looks as natural as possible. I prize it very much because you picked it for me. Has the fuchsia blossomed yet?

Mrs. Gains Turner and Mrs. Charles Dow called to see me today. None of my new relations have called since I came home. It is a great chance if they come at all now it has been so long. But another sheet will soon be filled. When I commence writing to you I never know when to stop. Perhaps you sometimes find my letters tedious, but I know I like to get good long ones from you. I never tire of reading them, wish I could get one every day, will expect another soon.

And now I will again say good night to you my kind and affectionate husband.
May you soon be ready to sail again and have a quick and pleasant voyage.
Yours lovingly, Josie

The last in this series of letters is from Josephine to her husband, who is still languishing in Bordeaux awaiting a paying cargo. Josephine expresses the common frustration of both captains and their wives, whose time is spent mostly at sea or in foreign ports with no permanent home on shore. A wife sitting out a voyage generally had to live with relatives. There are only these four of Josephine's letters, but they are long and make up in description what they lack in number.

Harvey, April 7th '80
My Dear James,
I did not receive a letter from you last week, but got two nice long ones this evening. I am sorry it will be so long before you can get back to New York, but freights are so low in the States. Of course it is better for you not to come back in ballast when you can get a load. It will come out all right at last. I am almost ashamed to send this letter, it was commenced long ago, but I will write again in a few days.

We have had some frightful storms here lately. The train on the Albert Railway got stuck fast in a snow drift last Tuesday, so that we got no mail from that day until Sunday. The snow is piled up in some places nearly as high as Shepody mountain. I am glad you are having such pleasant weather in Bordeaux.

We will not think any more about the house at present. I know you will do all for the best. Do not think, my dear, that I am discontented because you have no house. We will have a home of our own some day and will be so happy there. I hope you will not always have to go to sea, but while you do it is my wish to go with you. I know I am welcome to stop here as long as I wish, but I would rather be with you. It is home anywhere with you. I know I will feel badly to go away again and leave little Josie and all the rest, but I must go with you. It is right that I should do so. I shall be pleased to have you come as far as Portland to meet me if you can conveniently do so. I would prefer going to Portland by rail if I went alone, but if you were with me I would just as soon go in a boat the rest of the way—whichever way you think best.

Josie returns to the sea life to be with her James, joining him at New York. She is determined to adjust to the notorious North Atlantic after the winter storms are past. She writes her sister Mary from Hamburg on October 7, the same year, cheerful and full of the interesting sights she has taken in there. She compares the Hamburg cheese unfavourably with her sister's own and recommends Germany to anyone who likes sausage.

Commenting on problems keeping servants back home in Harvey, Josie observes that the plentiful supply of servant girls in Hamburg should be tapped:

"There's any amount of them here and nice looking as a general thing. Our vessel is chartered or we might take a load across." She admires the "Dutch" as she calls the Germans in the manner of Americans in Pennsylvania. She adores the idea of Watson going to college: "I hope there is something better for him to do than going to sea, although I do not object to a seafaring life myself, although I am still troubled some with seasickness, yet I am well and hearty when in port. You would be surprised to see what rosy cheeks I have now." There is no suggestion that she will not be on the next voyage to Europe.

Seven years later, Josephine writes home from Antwerp to her sister Lottie. She is content and well-adjusted to the sea-going life, even braving the North Atlantic in winter and exploring with enthusiasm the sights of Antwerp. (Perhaps she keeps a brandy bottle handy in the cabin.) But she dies in 1884, and three years later James marries her sister Charlotte (Lottie), who also joins him at sea. In another three years Lottie dies and Captain Turner marries a third time.

DELLA AND JOSIE CORNING

In 1883, Idella ("Della") Corning, twenty, marries a newly-minted captain, Frank Gullison, twenty-five, before he departs on a long voyage as master of the Yarmouth ship *Republic*. Next voyage, she joins the many women who take up the seagoing life rather than "stop" on shore. In May of 1884, Idella travels over to Saint John to join her husband. A number of vessels are in the port loading, some of them Yarmouth ships. Her letter to her cousin Josie Corning reveals a sense of foreboding:

> I'm with my dear Frank, whom I love so dearly that what will come during the voyage—I'll not murmur. Almost every captain has their wives aboard and most of them is going on the voyage.

Two years later, Frank's younger brother, Eugene, marries Josie Corning and they put to sea, having taken over the old *Republic*. Josie is a schoolteacher who goes to sea with enthusiasm. Seven years later, she is still sailing with Eugene. Josie's honeymoon both with Eugene and the sea life seems to be lasting for she writes playfully in her husband's log: "The love of my youth by my side and oh, how he does admire and worship his dear little wife. So nice. So nice."

Della, on the other hand, does not fare so well. She is "not robust" and is ill, try as she might to manage at sea. In 1885 when they call at Cardiff, there is a shipment from the ship's agent in Liverpool of two barrels of beer and a case of claret, medications prescribed for Della by her doctor.

In 1886, Frank and Della Gullison move to a bigger ship, *N.B.Lewis*, and make a voyage that circles the globe. Coming back as far as New Orleans, they face the decision of Della's return to shore. Frank expresses concern for his career and fortunes at sea because he has not yet paid off his shares in the ship. Della writes in their log: "How very lonely I am. May God watch over us and keep us, and if separated, spare us to embrace one another again."

Della Gullison arrives in Yarmouth by coastal steamer in late June, 1888, too ill to leave her berth on the boat. Her mother comes to collect her; she must be carried off the steamer. Whether she suffers from 'mal de mer' or another illness is not recorded, but she is ready in July to proceed to Cardiff to rejoin her husband. Two years later she leaves the ship again, this time at New York, heading home to Yarmouth with a baby son rather than face a voyage to Shanghai. This debarkation seems to have been the end of her career at sea.

Beulah Gullison

Eugene and Josephine Gullison's third child is a daughter, Beulah, born at the little village of Beaver River on the Bay of Fundy in 1895. Beulah's early years are spent at sea and she leaves colourful recollections of life, both at sea and on shore in her journal entries.

The early years of my life were spent mostly at sea. Dad had a number of commands, among them the Euphemia, Otego and later the one I remember best, Bowman T. Law. We had a daily routine aboard. Mornings were devoted to school work for my brother and me, with mother as the teacher. I can also remember doing physical exercises of some kind—a kind of calisthenics. She also taught us music on a small pedal type organ we had in our quarters. We were prompted after meals to brush our teeth and practice our music for a while each day. Mother was talented musically and could play many instruments; she had a lovely, deep contralto voice. There were always books around, particularly the Bible and Bible stories, and both mum and dad read a lot, especially together, as they did almost everything.

Our quarters were away in the stern, just below the after deck. We had a parlour-sized central cabin which served as a sitting/living area, with two bunkrooms off to either side. There was also a "head", consisting of a sink and a small tub, as well as a toilet. Water was very precious and we were careful never to waste it—or anything else for that matter. We also had a small galley where mother cooked on occasion, although we had most of our meals brought to us from the main galley.

I can remember watching dad at work. He had a chartroom close by, where he slept and I can see him still, tapping on the side of his barometer to get an idea whether the needle showing air pressure was going up or down. I could tell by the expression on his face if the indication was for good weather or bad. I can remember, too, looking up at him as he used instruments to shoot the sun or the stars and then watching him write in his log. I was also aware he had responsibilities that went beyond navigation and running the crew. He used to pore over his books as he balanced accounts of cargo sales and ship expenses.

Fred and I weren't usually allowed forward where the crew was, but we often watched them at their work. I can remember them scrambling up the rigging to change sail and then, in calm weather, or in port, mending the sails. They used to sing a lot at their work, especially when they did things in unison. Some of them had good voices, too. In later years, dad and my uncles used to entertain at social gatherings by singing some of those shanties, and the women who had been to sea would join in.

The crew was a rough lot for the most part. In port they would go off and get drunk, and sometimes not get back in time. Dad often had to go hunting for them, or try to hire somebody new if he couldn't find them. Sometimes the ship would have to leave short-handed, which was always a source of worry. Mom and dad saw so much drunkenness, and the fighting it brought on, that they were turned against strong drink.

On one of our voyages, some members of the crew came aft in a very militant manner, demanding the day off from work, as it was Good Friday and their religion called for a day of rest and meditation. My dad, to their surprise, agreed to their demands, saying, "Of course—I respect any man's religion."

Most of them were good to us though, talking to us and teaching us things. I remember, particularly our nice red-bearded German cook, who was so kind to us. He made little goodies for my brother and me and let us tease him with pepper in our hands, when he would sneeze and exclaim, "Oh, my!" in such a comical way. Of course, he spoke with a strong accent, which intrigued us no end. Our carpenter, who was from our home village, made me a nice table and chair and a doll's cradle. I played with my dolls and with my pet monkey. Fred and I each had a little monkey. Jack and Jill, we called them. My Jill fell overboard one day and I felt very badly for some time afterwards.

I remember, too, so clearly, the time a huge whale followed us at sea, diving down under the ship and coming up on the other side with a great blowing of water, so playfully, as if he was delighted to find some life out on the vast ocean. Fred and I loved it, and of course, didn't realize how anxiously our parents watched it all, fearing the huge animal would hit the keel and dislodge the cargo—we were carrying a load of lumber—which would have been very serious. Another memory that remains with me vividly is the sight of the snow-white breast of a great albatross that lay on the deck of our ship after it had flown into the rigging and killed itself.

I do remember some bad storms at sea, but don't recall ever being afraid. I rather liked the pitch and roll of the ship. In those days there was no Panama Canal, so many a vessel was lost at sea, trying to get through the treacherous waters off Cape Horn. It almost happened to us and I have a faint recollection of the high cliffs hovering over the ship, as we were driven by the wind nearer and nearer to shore. It became a family story and, as it was related, dad said, 'I've done all I can,' But mom said, 'there must be something to do, don't give up!' He tried a new tack and we barely escaped certain death. With so many happenings like this in her twenty years of seagoing, it was amazing how well mother did in an emergency—although a nervous woman in everyday living and over little things.

We did visit some interesting places. On more than one occasion I rode in a rickshaw; I can visualize the man running in front of us between the shafts. It must have been either Shanghai or Hong Kong. I also have a recollection of the beggars in the streets and their thin, outstretched arms. When we went ashore, we had to pass through the dockside areas of the cities, which were usually rough and dirty. Even as a child, I was impressed with the squalid appearance of the streets—such a contrast to the tidiness of our ship.

On our last voyage, dad commanded the Bowman B. Law, an iron barque named after and owned by the Law family in our town of Yarmouth, Nova Scotia. We were loaded with case oil and anchored in the harbour at Tegal, Java. Coolies unloading the vessel were warned not to smoke, but someone must have disobeyed, for we were rudely awakened in the night with cries of 'Fire! Fire!' being called by the man on watch. It was a scramble, but quietly done as I remember. We didn't stop to dress or pick up things to take in the lifeboats, but a queer variety of items were thrown into our boat by the crew in their excitement. A rather comical thing, but dear to me, was a 'Tiger Tea' doll that I played with all the time. It was an advertisement for Tiger Tea, which was much used at that time. It was thrown down together with some of the ship's instruments and a silver set which had Bowman B. Law engraved on the pieces. I still have the dented barometer.

Posing with a ricksha in Singapore are Josephine Corning Gullison, her husband Captain Eugene Gullison, and their children, Fred and Beulah. They were awaiting a ship home after narrowly escaping a fire on board their vessel Bowman B. Law *at Tegal, Java in 1901.*

Dad, of course, wouldn't leave the vessel until everyone was off and safely in life-boats. I remember dear mom calling to him as we rowed away from the flaming ship. She must have been terrified, but she came through it as usual, with flying colours. Quite a gal my mom was in any critical happening.

In Tegal we stayed at a hotel for a while, until dad could settle all the business to do with the ship and make arrangements for our long trip home. In September, 1901, we went from Tegal to Batavia, then took the steamship Awa Maru from Singapore to London. So began a new era in my life. Dad and Uncle Frank, who had retired earlier from seagoing, bought out a business my grandfather had followed after his own retirement. This store was located in Salmon River, just a mile or so north of Beaver River.

Ida (Congden) Crowe

Because ships were too large and too deep to tie up where they where built, they were usually launched and towed to a nearby port. The barque *Bedford* took to the water at Clifton, Nova Scotia, in July 1877 in the usual small village manner, into the arms of a waiting tug to be towed to Saint John for rigging and finishing carpentry by specialists.

The difference with *Bedford's* launch in July of 1877 is that, as it drifted out from the shore, Captain John Congden was advised that there was already a stowaway aboard: his daughter. Twelve-year-old Ida, who had come from her home in

Bedford was a full-rigged ship built in Clifton, Nova Scotia in 1877. Young Ida Congden stowed away on board during the launching, later sailed with her captain father, married a captain and pursued a life at sea.

Great Village to see the launch, had sneaked aboard while the ship was still on the ways. Captain Congden succumbed to his daughter's pleading and she was allowed to stay for the voyage across the bay. Her Aunt Jennie arrived in Saint John a few days later, accompanied by Ida's older sister Janey, who was scheduled to keep their widowed father company on his voyage to Europe. Disappointed, Ida was taken home to continue her schooling with a promise that someday she would accompany her father to sea.

Ida does go to sea a few years later, sailing to Bremerhaven where she stays several months and learns some German. Back at sea she studies at a desk set up in the main cabin, then spends two years at Mount Allison Ladies' College. Her father, keen on education, takes with him to sea the Bible and the poetry of Burns, which he enjoys having Ida recite for him. One or another of Captain Congden's daughters sails with their widower father on many of his voyages during eight years in command of *Bedford*. His daughters not only provide him with company, but they reduce the burden of child-raising on Aunt Jennie at home. Fortunately neither girl is with him in 1885, when he desperately (but successfully) controls a fire in his cargo of oil in oak barrels.

Ida is completely happy with life aboard ship, spending nearly twenty years in total on the bounding main, first with her father and then with David P. Crowe (no relation to James), whom she marries in September 1886. Crowe is the son of one of the owners of a brigantine, *Modock*, and at age seventeen, for reasons of health, he sails in it as a passenger on a voyage to Bermuda, Savannah, and England (in 1873). Two years later, he is back at sea as an able seaman and eventually as captain in 1883. Without hesitation, Ida spends her first five years of married life at sea in the barque *Linden*. She experiences a good share of gales, ice, and even mutiny, the only woman in a masculine world. On one occasion, with an infant in her arms, she faces down a drunken seaman intent upon knifing the mate. Her children are born at home, but with her first, John, she sets off for Buenos Aires after only three months on shore. A second boy, Waldo, is born the next year.

The early years of David and Ida Crowe's sailing are spent on the North Atlantic, but as trading patterns change, the couple travels to locations worldwide. Crowe sails a total of 900,000 miles on sail and steam, never losing a ship and losing only one sea-

Ida (Congden) Crowe with daughter Louie, born at sea, and husband Captain David Crowe. Portrait in Shanghai in 1899 shortly before her retirement with her three children after seven years of seafaring.

man. Ida makes many of these trips with him.

In 1892, in the waning days of sail, the Crowes are living on shore—Ida at her husband's family home in Debert, and David in Halifax looking for a command—when a cable comes from Liverpool offering command of *Semantha*, a big, 2200-ton, British-built barque. Four years old and rated 100A1, the best possible classification, at Lloyds, the fast, steel ship is still able to compete in tough times, and is a great break for the Crowes. Rushing to Debert, Captain Crowe asks Ida how soon she and the two boys can be ready to leave on a voyage. "Half an hour," is the quick reply. *Semantha* is their happy home for seven and a half years.

Off they go, to and from England in the trans-Atlantic trade, then, in 1895, on the case oil run from New York to Kobe, Japan, via Hong Kong. Two weeks short of their arrival in Hong Kong, a baby sister, Louie, joins the boys. Anticipating the arrival of a child at sea, Captain Crowe had signed on a stewardess, among whose qualifications was likely midwifery.

Semantha was fast and tender, making excellent time on voyages, but rolling because narrow of beam. On the Atlantic, Crowe took the ship across from Mulgrave to Liverpool in an exceptional thirteen days. Later he made the Portland (Oregon) to Liverpool run in a respectable one-hundred-and-two days. This ultimate sailing vessel had ample room for accommodation, though when it rolled heavily, getting about on board became difficult.

Semantha was a fine late model Scottish four-masted barque commanded for ten years by Nova Scotian Captain David Crowe. Much of this time he was accompanied by his wife and one or more of their children.

A good picture of family life in a square-rigger of the later days is set out by John Crowe in his book *In the Days of the Windjammers* (1959). Drawing from recollections and family logbooks, Crowe describes the much-improved features of the later steel sailing vessels. *Semantha*, for example, had a steam-powered winch for heavy work like raising the anchors, space to accommodate half a dozen apprentice officers, and a pilot house on the poop. The pilot house, in particular, was convenient as a chart house for officers working on navigation. Women like Ida Crowe also found it a pleasant spot for sewing and reading—from it they had a better view of the sails, sea, and sky than they did from the small windows below.

Knowing the precise time of the astronomical observations is crucial to navigation. To ensure accurate times, ships carry a pair of clocks called chronometers, which are cared for with great respect. The accuracy of the vessel's landfall depends on them. Ida Crowe is entrusted with the vital chore of winding the *Semantha's* chronometers daily. Ida takes her role as schoolteacher seriously too. The ship's carpenter builds a double desk into a corner of the main cabin and here the two boys sit for formal classes from nine until four daily. Their mother is musical and encourages singing and reading. When the boys enroll in schools on land, they fare very well.

John Crowe recalls a scene not portrayed in the adventure yarns: when a rolling and plunging ship made walking about difficult, the whole family would surround themselves with cushions and squeeze into the master's bed with its high side board. Captain Crowe would read aloud from literary classics like *David Copperfield* and *Nicholas Nickleby*, while his wife knitted and the children absorbed the English language.

After seven years at sea in *Semantha*, having circled the globe three times and crossed the equator twenty-four times, Ida Crowe and her three children swallow the anchor. They return home to Nova Scotia and regular life. But after finding them a home Captain Crowe promptly leaves for New York and another voyage to the far east, not to return for three years. Upon returning, he retires. The Crowe's speedy globe-girdling home, *Semantha*, sails on until 1915 when, under the Norwegian flag, it is sunk by a German auxiliary cruiser off the Falkland Islands.

IX
AMELIA HOLDER'S DIARY

AN ELEVEN-YEAR-OLD NEW BRUNSWICK GIRL GOES TO SEA IN THE FAMILY
BARKENTINE TO CARE FOR HER INVALID MOTHER. AFTER HER MOTHER'S
DEATH, AMELIA CONTINUES ON VOYAGES AS TUTOR TO HER SISTERS AND
BROTHER AND TO KEEP HER FATHER COMPANY.

Hannah Holder writes from the farm on the Long Reach of the St. John River to her husband Edwin, who is absent on an overseas voyage as captain of a small, family-owned ship, *Mina*. It is February 17, 1867, and while he is on his usual annual runs at sea, things are quiet on the farm. Edwin suggests that Hannah and the two children, Abram, nine, and Susan Amelia, eleven, join him in New York for his next voyage. Hannah, sorry he is not sailing home to Saint John, expresses her reluctance at taking the trip to New York. Since she is in poor health following the birth of their eighth child, she proposes that he visit Saint John while his ship loads in New York. She suggests that Robert, a relative, might take command of the brigantine while Edwin takes some time off. She argues that she has no city clothes, but admits at the same that she wants to see him, saying: "I could go down to town and stay all the time you were there if you did not get tired of me."

Hannah cannot make up her mind and her sister Mary Ann is not there to help look after the family: "People tell me I do not look well and think it might do me good to go to sea, but I do not know how it would be." Hannah is timid, and knows from previous experience that she will be frightened by storms at sea in a small brigantine—she and her eldest daughter Amelia accompanied Edwin on a 1867 voyage to Havana and Stockholm.

Hannah decides finally to go to sea. She is terrified in stormy weather, but is persuaded to go on this voyage in the hope that it will improve her health. Eleven-year-old Amelia Holder accompanies her parents on the voyage as the principal caregiver for her mother, who is suffering from undiagnosed tuberculosis. The family departs from Philadelphia, where the little *Mina*, the size of a large tug at 192 tons and 112 feet in length, loaded case oil for the Mediterranean. Amelia, who reads voraciously and is articulate for an eleven-year-old, keeps a diary for most of her six ocean voyages. Fortunately, her descendants have preserved the teenager's impressions of life at sea in sailing ships and of the exotic foreign ports she visited. Amelia Holder's diary begins with this departure from Philadelphia:

Monday, October 14, 1867
Left Philadelphia today at 3 p.m. in the brigantine Mina, bound for Gibraltar for or-
ders. We had a council just before we left to decide whether Ma would go or not, but at
last she concluded to go. We have just dropped anchor for the night.

October 16
This was a very fine morning and after I cleaned up the room and ate my breakfast I
went on deck. We are in Delaware Bay and I could see no land except a blue outline.
It was calm this afternoon. The mate has a little dog on board and he is very playful. I
don't have much to do except wait on Ma. She is just the same. I am not homesick but
sometimes think of home and what nice times they will have but I think after all I will
have a very nice time of it. It seems rather quiet since we left the noise of the city and I
feel very lazy, we have no sewing to do and I do not care to knit.

October 17
Today we are fairly out to sea. It was a fine afternoon and a nice breeze. I have been
on deck a good deal today and had a fine romp with the dog. I do not feel a bit seasick
though she has not rolled any, but I used to have a sickening feeling as soon as we got
to sea which is all over with now but I expect to get a little sick when there comes
much wind. We have plenty of music, one of the men has a fiddle and I hear him play-
ing it now. We are about eighty miles from the light-house. The wind has freshened
some this evening. I sleep on the lounge that Pa bought when we were in Philadelphia.
Ma is about the same. She is not frightened yet.

Crossing the mid-Atlantic, the small sailing ship meets a mix of weather: rolling, pitching, and becalmed. Amelia does not refer to her previous voyages, but it
is apparent from her attention to the weather and the use her father makes of her,
that Amelia has been to sea before. Amelia keeps up her diary calmly:

October 23
It is blowing pretty hard today and the vessel is rolling very much. Ma is getting fright-
ened. The wind is blowing harder this afternoon and evening. It is raining very hard.

October 24
Blowing very hard and rolling very bad, this afternoon it is a gale and the water is
coming in the cabin, the carpet is all wet, Ma is frightened. Everything is getting wet
and disagreeable. We are hove to tonight.

By November 1, they near the Azores where it is warmer and the seas calmer.

November 6
This morning we had a good fair wind, but it blew rather hard this afternoon and
evening. I wrote some today on a verse that I began Sunday. I wish I had something to
do. I suppose those at home are going to school now or just coming home. It gets night
here sooner than it does there. We were talking of home tonight. This evening it rains
and had some pretty heavy squalls. I cannot sleep tonight and Ma cannot either. I am
not frightened but Ma is dreadfully, Pa is, too, a little. I have read through the book
that the mate lent me.

Passing the Azores and nearing the coast of Portugal, little *Mina* bucks a suc-
cession of squalls, rolling heavily in the northerly winds. Between bouts of bad
weather there are pleasant, warm moonlit nights. Amelia has run out of books to
read and takes up the concertina, which her father and the steward both play.
Near Cape St. Vincent there is more heavy weather; they are in danger of being
blown downwind on a lee shore, the seafarer's greatest peril.

November 14
Strong gales, hove to at 2 p.m. Ma is very much frightened. Wrung out some of the
clothes that I washed out yesterday because they were so dirty as I only had one pail of
hot water. It is beginning to blow very hard with heavy squalls and rain.

November 15
Terrible weather, the squalls are dreadful. I could not hear it much because the windows
were all shut up. The rain was pouring down in torrents. We are inside of Cape St. Vin-
cent and if we do not make the Strait we will run on shore. Pa got the sun today. Every-
body is on deck. Pa is dreadfully anxious. We were hove to at eleven o'clock tonight but
after a while went on again. It was blowing like everything when I fell asleep about two
o'clock, and Ma is half frightened to death. This must be the rainy season.

Sunday November 17
Lying in Gibraltar Harbor, wind blowing in squalls from the westward with heavy show-
ers. Would like to go on shore but there is too much wind and rain. The Rock is very high
and the town is built pretty close down to the water and looks as if it was a pretty nice
place. The mountains in Africa appear very high and look a great deal nearer than they

really are. We got some fresh meat, radishes, oranges, pomegranates and grapes today. They were nice. We are very comfortable on board but rather lonesome. This afternoon the mate and second mate got out the boat and went on shore, came off about dark in the evening. Pa played on the accordion and we sang some hymns.

Mina stays at anchor several days at Gibraltar, waiting for orders as to where they were to deliver their cargo. Equipped with some Shakespeare and some Lord Byron to read, and some apples and oranges to munch, Amelia settles down for the continuation of the voyage into the Mediterranean to Majorca. The ship's pig has grown to seventy pounds and so it is eaten. Barcelona is their destination, but at this time all North American ships are required to spend ten days in quarantine at Port Mahon. Amelia records the process of fumigation:

Friday 13
This is a very fine morning. The people that are in the vessels here in quarantine have to go on shore every third day and be smoked. We will have to go when we have been here three days. There are two men on board employed by the government, one stays on board the vessel and the other goes with Pa to see that he does not go on board of any vessel.

Monday 16
Went ashore this morning to be smoked. Pa thought at first that they would let us off, they let Ma off, however she had to go on deck to let the doctor see her. I did not go in when the others did, the Sandad, that is what they call the men that watches us, took me right in and right out again, the others had to be shut in. What little smoke I got was nasty. This afternoon, Pa and Ma and I went on shore, there is a garden in back of the smoke house. It has flowers in it in summer-time, but now there are none. We had not been on shore long until the English captain came on shore. He smuggled a bottle of cod liver oil to Pa. The Sandad was not near then, but he came after a little and said they were sitting too close together. They are very strict here. The American captain and his passenger, Mr. Hall, came on shore too. The Sandad gave Ma and me a bunch of flowers, he is a nice man. We came on board about four o'clock.

After being smoked again, the people of the *Mina* are cleared for Barcelona and leave, well supplied with apples and oranges and a live turkey for Christmas.

Tuesday 24 December
It is a fine day. I felt a little sick this morning but soon got over it. The wind is nearly fair. I have nothing much to do. I did not hang up my stockings tonight. I expect Santa Claus is about home now. The apples and oranges are almost eaten up. I wish I could hang up my stocking but Santa Claus cannot get over the Atlantic.

Wednesday 25 December
This morning nothing distinguished today from any other day, but we had a turkey for dinner and some delicious doughnuts. The turkey tasted very good. This afternoon I did nothing but read. I am twelve years old today. I expect they will have great times at home. It is almost calm some part of today, it has not been very cold. I expect they are having grand times home and plenty of sliding.

Mina struggles through contrary winds into Barcelona, a big port with many ships and plentiful fresh food. As is frequently the case, they anchor in the harbour rather than tie up at a pier. While their vessel is unloading, there is much visiting back and forth among the sailing ship captains and their families.

Sunday 29
This is a fine morning and I went up on deck as soon as I got up; the town looks pretty, as much as we can see. There is a mountain pretty close to the town, it looks very much like Gibraltar only it is not rock. We can only see the front of the town, the houses look pretty. They do not have much Sunday here I guess. Pa's broker got some fresh meat for dinner and a boat came alongside and we bought some oranges and apples. There are a good many vessels here loading and unloading. The American barque came alongside this afternoon and said he came in day before yesterday. We got some letters from home, I got one from Amy, one of the letters had some sweet clover in it. I have not been reading much today. There is a bell here that is just like the one in Havana and when it chimed it played the same tune.

January 1 1868
All our men have asked for a holiday and we are not working today. The weather is fine, but it is cold. Pa went on shore this morning and came on board at dinner time. He brought some figs and raisins and some little cakes. They were made out of eggs and sugar and flour and tasted delicious. I have begun to write my letters for home. I heard the bells ringing all night. They ring every hour. They are ringing chimes this morning and it sounds very nice. I am not doing anything today different from other days. There is an English vessel on each side of us, the crew all drunk in one and the mate, too. There was some nice music up in the town.

On this day, Edwin Holder writes in his personal log: "Discharging petroleum from Philadelphia. Wife sick. Daughter Amelia well. I wish wife was home."

January 5
This is a beautiful day, the sun shines very brightly and the air is pure and cold. There is a great ringing of bells on shore and the band playing. I believe there is no Protestant place of worship here. I would like to go ashore but ma is not able to go and I do not

like to go without her. There is not much regard paid to the Sabbath here, it is more
like a holiday. The English captain went to sea this morning. He came on board and
brought me a present of some preserved fruit and pickles. This afternoon an American
captain and passenger gave us a call. This evening is very fine, the bells are still ringing
and the music playing. I pity the bell ringers. I am reading the Bible through, I have got
over to Deuteronomy.

Amelia declines to go on shore with her father because her mother is not well
enough to go, but she is finally persuaded to go with him, and sees the great boul-
evards, the fountains, and her first elephant. Finally, Captain Holder has his vessel
towed to sea and sails for Italy.

Monday 13
We went out this morning, a steamboat towed us out. I was up on deck after we had
got out. I could see all the city. It is on a flat plain with mountains all around it. We
had intended to go to see the famous Montserrat but as Ma was not well enough, we
did not go. It is not far from Barcelona. I went down again and my head began to feel
a little dizzy. I have been lying on the lounge and reading. There is not much sea but
the vessel has a motion I am not used to. The wind is fair. We are going to Messina in
the island of Sicily.

Tuesday 14
The vessel is rolling very badly this morning and if I am not seasick, I am very near it.
I did not get up today, but nevertheless I said my lessons as usual. I read some and do
not feel very sick. My appetite has not failed. We are not out of fresh meat yet. The
wind is nearly fair and we are going along pretty fast.

Saturday 18
We have a fair wind and are going eight miles an hour. We are in sight of Sardinia
yet but soon will be out of sight of it. The day is beautiful and we almost forget it is
winter, there is just a nice breeze this afternoon. I have sewn some and am making a
Holland apron.

Amelia takes to reading the "Sailing Directions for the Mediterranean Sea," pro-
nouncing it quite interesting. They pass Sardinia and the volcanic Lipari Islands,
including Stromboli, and then sight Mount Etna.

The wind does not blow half as hard this morning as it did in the night and it blew
very hard. We are going in to the mainland and are pretty nearly up to the Straits of
Messina. The land is very high and one mountain with its top covered with snow is

*away up in the clouds. I was frightened almost when I first saw it. The snow on top
reminds me of home. I have been looking at it with my glasses very much.*

*1 pm. In the Straits of Messina, I have been looking at the land with my opera
glasses, I can hardly describe it. Along the shore there is a flat plain and behind it is the
high land. The olive trees rise on the hills and look like terraces. There are no houses
among the trees, it looks beautiful. We took a pilot to take us up to Messina. I see three
or four little towns on the Italian side among which is Scylla, a very dangerous place
for vessels on account of the sea and tide setting them on it. It is in the Straits. We cannot go up to Messina till the tide turns. The Italian side is steep mountains and hills.
The tide is now fair, it is almost calm in here, there is a long point which we have to
pass called Faro Point, it is like a breakwater. There is a town on it, chiefly fishermen
and pilots. We are going along pretty fast, my eyes ache looking at the country. There
are some pretty houses. Ma has been on deck most of the afternoon.*

They tie up alongside a schooner in Messina, a port that sees a lot of visiting.
Amelia cleans the cabin, taking out the dirty carpet and scrubbing the deck. While
Mina has the ballast unloaded, there being no cargo from Barcelona, a number of
visitors stop by: a minister, a doctor with medicine for Hannah, the attending
waterman with flowers, various captains' wives on social calls, and in the evenings,
the captains. An English Captain Appledore, is a good friend and comes frequently.
Amelia records the social scene:

Saturday, February 1 [1869]
*This is a fine day. Mrs. Wilson came here this morning and staid till eleven o'clock.
She went away and came back in about a quarter of an hour, Mrs. Howes was with
her. She is the lady that was with her before and Captain Howes. They staid a little
while this afternoon. The minister came and staid to tea. The English captain was
here. I have not done much today. Several American vessels came in this afternoon.
This is a beautiful evening. I was on deck a little while. The steward is playing his accordion and it sounds very nice. The moon is very bright.*

Sunday 2
*Pa went with the English captain to where the minister preaches. The schooner inside
of us hauled out and we went next the wharf. The captain and his wife and little boy
that were here the first time came this afternoon. They had expected to go to sea two
days ago but something prevented them. The English captain, whose name is Capt.
Appledore, and Pa and I went out for a walk while they were here with Ma. We went
on the main street which is a very nice street, with hardly a bit of dirt on it. The streets
are paved with stone all the way over. There are a great many beggars in this town
and I saw a great many friars. By the time I got on board I was very tired. They staid
to tea and we had a nice time.*

Captain Holder and Amelia pay a return call on Captain and Mrs. Appledore in their ship *Annie Grant* the next day. Amelia is impressed with the fine mahogany finish in the main cabin of the English vessel and is presented with a gift of a goldfinch in a cage. Later she meets two captains' daughters. The goldfinch does not survive the change of scene, dying within two weeks and Amelia's father buys her a canary as a replacement.

On February 16, Captain Holder moves out of Messina Harbour in a heavy rain to anchor before sailing back toward the west. Amelia does not record what cargo they pick up. The next day they head out to sea. Winds are contrary and they are driven back to Messina. Amelia's father falls ill with headaches, so the mate takes the ship into port where Amelia nurses her father, placing wet cloths on his head She describes him as "flighty." They start off again, passing Sardinia and Majorca on the way to Gibraltar, making good progress. Approaching Gibraltar, Captain Holder is up and well enough in the fine weather to teach Amelia to steer the brigantine. On Monday, March 9, they are in Gibraltar Harbor again. Hannah Holder has had choking spells and a doctor is brought aboard to treat her. They sail on along the coast of Africa to pick up the steady northeast trade winds that will carry them across the Atlantic.

Tuesday 17
This is a fine day, the sea is not so high and we are in the trades. Pa and I were reading Pilgrims' Progress this afternoon. I have been on deck and sewing some.

Sunday 22
Very fine weather, fair wind all last night with one little shower. This morning the wind came around to westward for a little while then fell calm. Sun very hot. We are going along slowly. I was steering some this morning. We have all the windows in the cabin open and are quite comfortable. Ma is a little better than when in Gibraltar, but not able to sit up yet.

Friday 27
Going at the rate of five miles per hour. Ma is not so well today. I have been washing a little and sewing some. I am anxious to get home although I should enjoy myself very well if Ma was well.

Saturday [March] 11
The wind is ahead today, it is not blowing hard, but there is a pretty bad sea. We are on the edge of the Gulf Stream. There are two vessels in sight. We were very much surprised about half-past five to see a boat astern, a man came on board and said he came from one of the vessels. He wanted some provisions. They were from Shields bound for New York, they had been ninety days at sea.

Monday 13
The wind is blowing very hard today and on shore. We are about sixty miles off Cape
Hatterass. The vessel is rolling very much, it rolled ma out of the berth. I have been ly-
ing down most all day. It is pretty cold.

Cape Henlopen, at the entrance to Delaware Bay, is sighted on April 15 and a
pilot is picked up. Two days later *Mina* is tied up in Philadelphia, ending a voyage
of just six months. Amelia sadly reports that the canary has died and that her
mother is not as well as when they first sailed. The air was fresh, but, except for
the occasional tropical fruit, the nutrition was terrible and the life stressful.

Undated entry
I have not written in this journal for almost a week. Ma has had two very bad turns
and has a very weak turn now. The first she had was in the night, we all thought she
was dying. We sent for Captain Crosby. His ship is at the same wharf as ours. She got
over that, but had another in a day or two.
*   There is a Captain King here that Pa knew before, with his wife and daughter.*
They were on board before Ma had any bad spells. They came on board the next day
after she was so bad and staid to dinner. Captain Crosby introduced us to a Mrs.
Chadwick, a friend of his that keeps a boarding house. She is a very nice lady, she has
a little girl ten years old.
*   On Friday Pa and she and I went out for a walk while Mrs. Chadwick staid with*
Ma. On Sunday in the afternoon Pa and I went to church and Mrs. Chadwick staid
again. When we came back Ma was very bad though not quite as bad as she was a lit-
tle while before we came in. We had the same doctor that we had when we were here
before, Dr. McLellan, brother of General McLellan. Mrs. Chadwick stayed all night.
The people here that we know are all very kind to us. The owner of the cargo brought
down some preserved strawberries and jelly and Mrs. Chadwick gave Ma some peach
jelly and custard and made her some flaxseed with lemon and loaf sugar, and some
mutton broth, and in return Pa gave her a pair of kid gloves, a bottle of wine and some
oranges. I have been on shore two or three times with Pa and Luly, Mrs. Chadwick's
little girl. We found old friends that we knew when we were here before.

Thus Amelia abruptly ends her journal of the first voyage. Her mother Hannah
Holder returns home to Holderville on the St. John River in New Brunswick, and
dies of tuberculosis about two days later. Edwin Holder continues to make his
annual winter voyages, taking with him for company one or two of his children.
The eldest, Thomas, is put to work learning seamanship. Amelia continues her
practice of journal-writing on later trips as well.
    On the second voyage, to Buenos Aires in 1868, Amelia is accompanied by her
sister Agnes, who is ten years old. Captain Holder now commands a larger (but

still relatively small) vessel, the 316-ton barque *Hannah H.* Amelia records an encounter with a hurricane in the Gulf Stream on the way home, which she witnesses, of course, from below decks:

We were bringing as passengers Mrs. and Mrs. Mahar from the Argentine where they had been farming, but finding the country unsettled they had decided to come back to the U.S.A. They were of Irish extraction. The hurricane began in the morning with a very low glass and squalls increasing in force all the time. All the sail was taken off or what was left was soon torn to pieces, while one of the sailors had his clothes blown off coming from aloft. The squalls continued to increase in force, sounding like thunder coming from the sky. Two men stood at the wheel while my father stood by calling to them, 'Keep her up! Keep her up!' meaning 'Keep her before the wind.'

We could hear them saying, 'There go the boats'. But fortunately, although washed adrift they did not go overboard. The hen coop was washed overboard. After a while as the wind increased they could keep her up no longer and she broached to and lay on her side. We thought the last moment had come then, but after going a certain distance she stopped and did not roll any farther. After a while the squalls began to abate a little, each one not quite as hard as the last. We could hear the mate and my father shouting to each other, for it was only by shouting that one could make themselves heard, that they had better set a staysail.

Mr. Kerr, the mate, comes and talks to us for a few minutes. He has an axe strapped to his waist ready to cut away the masts if he has to. He was in a hurricane before and they cut away the masts.

As we huddled in our room, Mrs. Mahar, who was a devout Catholic, kept repeating her prayers and saying to us, 'Say your prayers, girls, say your prayers.' At last she whispered something to her husband. He started for their room, reaching it with great difficulty as it was on the lee side and got what he wanted, a bottle of holy water, that he threw up against the side where the wind was blowing. It was soon after this that the wind began to abate and I suppose they always believed it was the holy water that saved them. The hurricane lasted six hours.

They return to the smaller *Mina* for the third voyage, leaving Saint John in November of 1869. Along with a load of deals to Buenos Aires, *Mina* carries Amelia, Thomas, and younger brother Edwin (Eddie), who is seven or eight years old. There is no doubt Captain Holder enjoys having his children with him; he plays games with them and teaches them aspects of sailing. The boys are expected to contribute seriously to the working of the ship. Thomas, who is old enough at eighteen to be a member of the crew and understudy the officers, very likely lives in the fo'c'stle with the other seamen. Amelia is Eddie's schoolteacher. *Mina* departs Saint John on November 13, 1869. Amelia writes a month later:

Saturday, December 11 [1869]
I have not written in this journal for a long time. We have had very fine weather so
far. We came across the Calms of Cancer without any calms and got the Trade Winds
in Latitude 31 degrees. They blew pretty hard and sometimes there were some heavy
squalls. Pa takes the wheel pretty often now on purpose so that I can come up on deck
and skip; I skip a good deal now. Pa pierced my ears yesterday. Pa and I take sights
now. I take the time by the chronometer while he is taking the sun and I am learning
to work them up.
    It is calm today, or if there is a light breeze, sometimes it is ahead. Eddie caught a
fish this morning. We do not know what kind it is, it is striped something like the pilot
fish which is a small fish that goes ahead of the shark to guide him. If anything is
thrown overboard he will go and smell it before the shark will eat it. We saw a shark
right close to the vessel this afternoon. There were a great many little fish ahead of it.
A little while after there was a whale right close to the side of the vessel. I was almost
frightened it looked so close. We tried to catch some of the little fish but could not.

Tuesday 14
It is calm almost all of today. There were a great many fish around this forenoon of a
great many kinds. There were some dolphins, they look lovely in the water, green and
gold and all colors, and there were a great many browns. We caught two aft, They
were of different kinds, The last one was a lovely one. We have not gone much this 24
hours and what we have gone is not on our course. We are making northing instead of
southing. The barometer has fallen very suddenly this afternoon. It is quite calm now
and is cloudy.
    There has been a shower since I last wrote, with some wind. This evening the wind
is fair and has the appearance of the trades. We are going along with all sail set.

Thursday 16
We want to go east now so that we can weather St. Roque. We have had bad trades, I
hope we will not have a very long voyage, there seems a great prospect of it now. I
worked the sights up today alone. Tommy is learning to work them up too. He can
take the sun at noon. I washed some today. The sea is smooth. Eddie saw a nautilus
today and was very much surprised at it, and asked what boat that was. It looks lovely
when the sun is shining on it, then it is all colors. It looks very much like a little boat.

Sunday 19
There is still a good wind. Pa thinks we are about 12 degrees, 09 minutes. He cannot tell
till he gets the sun at noon. The mate is sick and cannot leave his room. We find we are
in Latitude 11 degrees, 59 minutes at noon and are getting more easting too. We will soon
be up to Maury's navigation track if the wind stands. Sunday is a lonesome day at sea.
There are no meeting houses or churches to go to and we have to amuse ourselves as best

we can. I have been sewing a little and reading much of all my stock of books. I have read them all through and now I have to go back to the old ones I have read before. I have been reading Shakespeare, it is a long time since I have read in it. The moon is shining and the sky is clear. The moonlight is always lovely on the sea.

Monday 20
We are up to Maury's Track today. There is more wind than there was yesterday and the sea looks so blue and I think, how can anybody be sick at sea, It seems so exhilarating to see it and feel the fresh breeze in your face that comes off no swamp or smoky city, but from the salt sea. I have been sewing a good deal today. I have not been on deck much. I was up on deck this evening to see the peculiar kind of phosphorescent lights. I have seen it when the sea looked on fire, but tonight they were distinct lights like little lanterns. Pa said he never saw any like it.

Thursday 23
Had a squall this morning about breakfast time, it was pretty hard, it was thundering, too. The sun is not out. Pa has to find where the vessel is by dead reckoning and he is teaching Tommy and me. Navigation is a great study, I like to learn it very much. Eddie is almost a sailor. He whips ropes and has climbed up to the foretop twice. Eddie and I will hang up our stockings tomorrow.

Saturday, December 25 Christmas Day
This is a fine day. Eddie got a letter from home in his stocking. Santa Claus brought it. I am fourteen years old today. Pa put my earings in yesterday. They went in very easy. This afternoon it is very still. Pa is sleeping on the lounge and Eddie is in the bed and I am thinking of home. I suppose they are at church or meeting now. When I think of Aggie, I almost wish she was here or I there. I think more of her because we have been together so long. I have been reading in this book about the time we were together in the Mediterranean.

Mina passes along close to the coast of Brazil, closer than seamen like to pass as it is a dangerous lee shore to be blown against. They pass close enough to Pernambuco to see the unique fishing catamarans and the coast seven miles away. Amelia is more lonesome, thinking of Aggie's company and that of the Mahars on a previous voyage, when time passed more quickly. While their father is on the wheel, she and Eddie heave the log to determine their speed and decide the ship is going four miles an hour. It grows colder as they proceed south and Amelia thinks of those at home sleigh-riding and skating. She does not go on deck much. In the evenings she plays the concertina.

Tuesday 18
The wind is fair this morning and a good breeze, there is a little sea on. I have not been on deck this forenoon, I have been sewing a good deal and heard Eddie's lessons. Eddie has made a boat and I made some signal flags and the boat is towing astern. I have not worked up a sight for so long I am afraid I will get out of practice. This evening there is quite a sea on and sometimes the vessel gives a great roll and then I can hear the things in the cabin clattering across the room and dishes clashing together.

January 25
We have been lying in Montevideo two days. I had so much to see I did not get time to write. We had a good run up the river and got in here Sunday morning. We anchored pretty far out from the town, it was very hot. Monday we ran closer to the town and that afternoon pa took Eddie and me ashore. I have been up to the town with Mrs. Vroom. It looks much like Buenos Aires. This evening it is blowing a Pampero. It blows very hard.

Amelia's journal ends here abruptly. She writes similar diaries for three more voyages in family vessels, accompanied always by one or more of her siblings. The fourth voyage, again in *Hannah H.*, begins in November 1870, in West St. John. Amelia's younger sister Ada goes along for the first time. They depart to encounter a rough November at sea:

Montevideo Harbor, Uruguay late in the nineteenth century. Upon arriving in such major ports, captains' wives looked eagerly for familiar vessels, usually finding friends and female society among the vessels anchored there.

November 12, 1870
We left St. John today at half past one. I was over to town all the forenoon. It is rain-
ing now, the wind blowing quite strong, it has been raining all day. Ada is not seasick
yet, she is a little dizzy. This is her first night at sea, she is not homesick either. I hear
the old familiar sounds again, the swinging about of doors that are not hooked, and Pa
on deck walking about and giving orders. Mr. Holden came out as far as the island
with us and his son came out too. I like his son very much, he seems so sociable. Pa is
staying on deck all the time and Ada wants to know if he never comes down.

Sunday at Sea, 20th day of November
We have had an awful time since we left St. John. We have not had one whole fine
day, it has been blowing harder today than it has been before, but this evening it is
finer. It has not been much of a Sunday to us. It came in squalls and just before dinner
we had one terrific squall. Ever since we left St. John Ada and I have either sat on the
lounge and held on or laid in the bed and held on. One night we undressed ourselves
and that was the only time. We have had some water in the cabin.

The first night of the gale we lost all of our cranberry apple sauce. It was at the foot
of the lounge in two jars and I had some of my new books there also. When the vessel
gave a heavy lurch to leeward, away went our cranberry apple sauce and boots and
stockings and books went with it. It was an awful mess to clean up the next day. One
of my new books had to be thrown overboard and I regretted this more than I did the
cranberry apple sauce, I think. But the poor steward felt very badly about it for we lost
every bit of it and he had bought it and put it in Pa's charge.

The weather was very strange, it would blow a gale for a day and night, then the
glass would rise and the wind abate and our hopes would go up and we would be re-
joicing when the wind would begin to blow again as hard as ever. Today I thought we
would never get out of the gales and I was getting quite discouraged when the water be-
gan coming in the washroom through a hole in the side of the vessel. Ada and I went to
work drying it up and work we did as far as we could until the mate bored a hole in
the deck and it ran down in the hold. I felt a great deal better after that.

This afternoon the vessel gave two or three very heavy lurches and I caught hold of
the side of the bed and Ada the head of the lounge. The water jug first turned and
poured water on the bed and then turned around again and poured water on the foot
of the lounge, then jumped out of its place, flew at Ada and hit her on the forehead
when I caught it and put it on the only vacant corner of the bed. The corners of the
bed are full of a mixture of everything: in one corner are tumblers and spy glasses and
boots and books, in another are plum preserves and in another are bottles, slates and
sheets of music. Monday is a fine day and we are up on deck enjoying ourselves.

In 1867, at age eleven, Susan Amelia
Holder went to sea to care for her invalid
mother. Photographed in Montevideo
aged about thirteen. She went on five
more voyages with her father, keeping
him company and caring for various
brothers and sisters, finally quitting the
sea at seventeen.

Miss Amelia Holder at eighteen at the
end of her sea-going days.

Emily Gay Harris as a child with her
father (left) and mother. Emily was born
at sea and stayed with her father,
Captain T. H. Harris, until she was
seventeen, long after her mother died and
was buried at sea. Emily's father
employed a tutor aboard for her schooling.

Banjo playing by Emily Gay Harris, like
all musicianship, would be welcome
aboard the barque Levaka of Windsor,
Nova Scotia in 1884. She went on to
study music and art at a finishing school
in Philadelphia.

Christmas at Sea on Board the Brigantine Mina *in the Year of Our Lord 1870*
We were divided in opinion whether Santa Claus would visit us south of The Line.
Ada thought he would, but I did not think he could come so far, but we hung up our
stockings just to see if he would come or not. We jumped up as soon as we woke up
and got our stockings and there, sure enough, Santa Claus had filled them quite full.
Ada never believed in Santa Claus before, but now she does. This is my birthday, too,
and I am fifteen. I begin to feel quite old. We spent a very nice Christmas. We had
roast chicken and stewed chicken and chicken soup for dinner. They killed three chick-
ens and the men had chicken forward. Pa and the mate had some brandy after dinner
and the mate's toast was, 'A very Merry Christmas!' and Pa's was, 'Many Merry
Christmases.' And so ended our celebrations.

Amelia's sixth recorded voyage ends at Sandy Hook, New York, April 1, 1873.
She spends her eighteenth birthday back home at Holderville, where she is desolate over the departure of a sailor she admires, who leaves on a voyage to the
"heathen" South Seas. In a diary fragment from January 1874, she writes: "My
heart is broke. He's sailed to Typee [Fiji]… I suppose I must give him up now, so
farewell my dreams and hopes and let us plow on in the dreary sameness of this
life." Amelia last saw this sailor two years before, in March 1872. She made a
winter voyage to Montevideo that year. He might have been a member of her
father's crew on the trip. But hope rises again on April 9; her diary reports, "Great
news! He is in St. John. Pa saw him. To think he is so near." But there is ice and
high water in the river, making communication between them difficult. No more
is heard of this romance.

In 1875 the family leaves the farm on the river and moves down the river to
Saint John. The era of the farmer-shipbuilder-master has closed. Amelia Holder
marries Benjamin Henderson in July of 1886 at the age of thirty-three. She dies
at eighty-one in 1936 at Holderville.

X

THE NAVIGATORS

SEVERAL CANADIAN WOMEN HAVE TO TAKE OVER NAVIGATION AND DIREC-
TION OF THEIR HUSBANDS' VESSELS, SUCCESSFULLY COMPLETING LONG VOY-
AGES. WOMEN RUN THE EARLY NAVIGATION SCHOOLS.

Plotting the ship's position and progress across an ocean hourly on a chart is fascinating work. It is no wonder that naviga tion should arouse the interest of a captain's wife with time on her hands. A few women, like the Americans Mary Patten, Honor Earle, and Caroline Mayhew, achieve some fame in their time for their navigational skills. Similar cases in Canada, of which there are several, have failed to receive notice beyond their home ports.

Conducting a sailing ship across the seas in the nineteenth century required a practical knowledge of the art of harnessing winds and currents, an ability to handle the hard-bitten crews and the maintenance of the ship, and a head for navigation. Before Loran, which determined position using radio signals, and today's precise position readouts from satellites, the ability to navigate was critical to finding one's way over the trackless sea. Schooling in the seafaring ports, as elsewhere, was rather limited. Good seamen became competent mates without being able to read or write. Those with a few years of schooling, able to make calculations, and read logarithmic tables for fixing the ship's position from the sun and stars became the masters. To be caught far at sea without a navigator constituted a desperate situation, and with only two navigators aboard at the start of most voyages, sailing without a navigator was always a possibility. Navigation was something slightly magical to the seamen in the fo'c'stle, for whom even reading and writing were often a mystery. Most masters did not have a great deal of formal education either, but they usually had enough to enable them to learn the keys to navigation without considerable difficulty. Of course, intuition was an element of successful navigation.

Evolved throughout the centuries by mathematicians, astronomers, and daring navigators, the traditional art of navigation consists of two elements: calculating the ship's position and dead reckoning. In the first, the navigator calculates the ship's actual position on the globe in latitude and longitude by measuring with a sextant the inclination of the sun above the horizon at noon and similarly by measuring the relative positions of the stars at night. The second element, dead reckoning, calculates where the winds and currents have taken the vessel since the last fix by the directions and speeds of travel as they occurred. Dead reckoning is necessary in bad weather. Today, at the beginning of the twenty-first century, a ship's precise position can be found at any time by glancing at a satellite readout on the wheelhouse bulkhead. Ship's officers still use their sextants, but only for practice.

In the nineteenth century, navigation was usually taught by a friendly captain or mate, but there were schools ashore. The wife of the captain of Henry Pratt not only taught navigation to apprentice Sam Samuels, but later she also ran a navigation school. Courses were taught in some of the ports of the Maritime provinces, and one of the most reputable schools was run by Miss Eliza Frame, a schoolteacher from Maitland, Nova Scotia. Living on a seafarer's coast, Miss Frame quite likely picked up her skills from family members. Duke's Academy in Martha's Vineyard is reputed to have offered a course in navigation for women as early as 1840, probably a result of the high concentration of whaling ships in Martha's Vineyard at the time and navigators' penchant for leaving wives and daughters to chase whales.

Teenaged Amelia Holder, along with her brothers, practiced navigation in the family atmosphere of her father's vessel. She took sights, calculated position, used the log, and steered. She loved the sea, but nowhere in her diaries does she give any hint of wanting to take up sailing as a career. Women seem to have used navigation as a way of passing time at sea. Whether it interested them in any long-standing and serious way is difficult to know.

The whaling vessels tend to be crewed to a large extent by family and hometown friends. Women sometimes contributed to the voyage by taking watches and steering when the crew were away in the boats chasing whales, though they are often considered too bossy by the crew. Vessels effectually in the control of women gain reputations among seamen as "hen frigates." Mark Twain mocked one whaling wife for strutting about on shore spouting sea lingo. He was, of course, a veteran Mississippi River pilot himself. Eliza Williams' whaler carries four mates. Only one could navigate and the others, chosen for their abilities as whaler catchers, can't even read. The vessel is dependent upon the captain and one mate for finding their way out of sight of land. Eliza, her young son Willie, and daughter Mary learn how to make dead reckoning and how to cast the log to determine speed. Whether they might have found the way to a port for their ship without their father never had to be tested.

Janey Congden Crowe, sister of Ida Congden Crowe, was one woman at sea who studied the navigation of her ship seriously and, when tested, passed with cool skill. On one occasion when her ship *Selkirk* was in Hong Kong, there was a fracas on board and a sailor drowned. Captain Crowe and his mate were strict disciplinarians, and once ashore the crew laid charges of cruelty against them. British law could be severe with officers found to have maltreated their crews: the mate was found guilty and sentenced to a two-year term, while Captain Crowe was sent to jail for a month. Thus *Selkirk* was left with no master or mate and, because under charter to sail at once or lose a lucrative, time-based cargo contract, the ship had to sail immediately for Manila to load sugar. The remaining group reached the decision that the second mate would handle the ship as first mate, the bo'sun would act as second mate, while Janey Crowe would navigate as unofficial master. Janey proceeded to lay out daily courses that the mate loyally followed out across the South China Sea. Each noon she shot the sun with her sextant and worked with her logarithmic tables to establish their position, and she calculated by dead reckoning using the log, current charts, and the China Sea Sailing Directions. She unofficially but confidently brought *Selkirk* straight into Manila Bay after an uneventful voyage. Captain Crowe rejoined his ship after being exonerated by a higher court. Janey died on a later voyage and was buried at Manila, a long way from her old home of Great Village, Nova Scotia.

HELEN (SMITH) GRANT

The daughter of a local shipbuilder, Helen Smith of Maitland, Nova Scotia, was teaching school in 1873 when the dashing young Captain William Grant came to town to take command of the newly built barque *George*. In the months it took to place the spars and rigging on his ship, Captain Grant, who had his master's papers at the tender young age of twenty-two, and Helen Smith courted. When he was ready to sail they were married and set out on their wedding trip, which took them first up the St Lawrence River to Montreal, then south to Montevideo, around Cape Horn to Valparaiso and back around up the Atlantic to Antwerp. In fact, Helen Grant spent the next thirteen years at sea, coming ashore for only one period of time to have her two children, boys who knew no other home but the ship during their childhood.

Helen Grant loved the life at sea. Her strength was mathematics and, equipped with a good education, she plunged into the intricacies of navigation, charts, currents, sailing and rigging, as well as ship's business and contracts. It was not all learning and fun: terrifying Atlantic storms damaged their vessel *Thomas E. Kenny* in 1879. One storm lasted six days, with mountainous seas washing the mate and a seaman overboard, smashing the boats, and flushing everything out of the galley and storeroom. The grain cargo shifted and the main and mizzen masts had to be cut away to save the ship from capsizing. Finally, with a Portuguese brig standing by, Captain Grant decided to abandon ship. Before jumping into a fishing dory that was pitching wildly alongside, Helen Grant made a last calculation of the *Kenny's* position for the official record. Her great fear during the protracted storm was that the entire crew, on deck desperately fighting the elements, would all be swept overboard, leaving her alone with her two young sons in the cabin below.

Helen Grant describes the leap into the Portuguese dory:

A heavy sea was running and it was impossible to bring the boat alongside. They waited for a chance to back up, and when they did so I jumped. I was dressed in a heavy cashmere frock with a train and pleated frills, soaked to the knees and clinging like a leaden weight. But fortunately, I was young and quick on my feet so I landed safely in the dory. The older boy came next. He was only four. I heard his father calling for a loose rope, the end of which was tied around the child, who after a few moments of suspense was tossed into the outstretched arms of a sailor in the boat. Then came the baby, and we were all taken aboard the Brunette. After many trips in the dory, my husband, the last to leave our beautiful ship, came on board the brig and we bade goodbye to our wrecked home.

The Grants are back aboard *George* in 1883 on a voyage to the Orient. Captain Grant becomes very ill en route, and he is diagnosed with appendicitis and peritonitis in Shanghai. He is critically ill and in hospital for weeks. Before he fully recovers, he determinedly sets sail on the return voyage to Montreal, concerned about the cost of the delay to his voyage. Far at sea, he weakens and suffers a complete relapse. For the next five months, *George's* master lies helpless and delirious, hovering between life and death. Helen faithfully nurses him and looks after her two children. With the aid of the mates, who take over his watch on deck, she manages the crew of seventeen, takes the sights, and plots their courses across the Indian Ocean, around the Cape of Good Hope, and across the Atlantic to Montreal. Why don't they put in at an intermediate port? Perhaps Captain Grant's dangerous condition becomes reasonably stable and is weighed against the probability of the family being left stranded in a remote foreign port. The whole responsibility is on Helen Grant's shoulders. No-one else can navigate and her husband can not help. After their safe return, Helen Grant modestly gives all the credit for this outstanding performance to her husband for having been such a thorough teacher. Captain Grant recovers and the couple eventually settles in Victoria, British Columbia, in a house they build with a view of the sea, and decorated with furnishings and souvenirs from across the world. But the Grants are not finished with the sea; they invest in the sealing industry with William managing a fleet and Helen owning a sealing vessel. She lives until age ninety.

As late as 1897, scurvy strikes on the British ship *T.F.Oakes*. The navigators are put out of action, the mate dies, and the captain falls desperately ill. The captain's wife, having mastered navigation, is also a good helmsman. She takes command

and sails the ship to port. Her role in bringing the ship to safety is recognized by the underwriters, and she receives the Lloyds' Silver Medal. In contrast to cases of women saving the day through their navigational abilities is the story of the British vessel *Aberfoyle*. After losing his mate, who is washed overboard in a storm in the Southern Ocean, and losing his wife, who has died at the last port, the captain drinks himself to death. He leaves his two little daughters and the rest of the crew lost on the vast sea. Fortunately another ship comes along that provides an officer to bring *Aberfoyle* to port.

There could have been any number of captain's wives who demonstrated an interest in navigation, steering, and other aspects of running a sailing ship. No doubt many are in a class with the American Lucy Smith, who wrote in her log as an aside, "I have taken the sun twice today, made the latitude the same as George and longitude within two miles. George says that it is as near alike as two persons get the altitudes." That was satisfaction enough for her.

BESSIE HALL

Wives and daughters of sea captains who foster an interest and gain competence in navigation and ship-handling in the age of sail usually do so only after going to sea to accompany the captain. A noteworthy exception is Elizabeth "Bessie" Hall of Granville, Nova Scotia, whose father is Captain Joseph Hall, and whose mother Priscilla declines to go to sea. Thus Bessie spends her childhood on land. Nevertheless, she grows up keenly interested in everything nautical. It is not until 1856, when Bessie is seventeen, that she is considered mature enough to accompany her father on a voyage. Over the next four years Bessie keeps her father company at sea. She turns out to be a popular social asset in her father's dealings with agents and officials in the ports they visit. But Bessie takes a greater interest in the running of the ship. By the age of twenty, she has been tutored by her father daily for three years in the use of the sextant, plotting courses, keeping the log, standing watch, and handling sail; she is an all-round competent mariner. She is fascinated with the plotting of courses and with making the ship follow them across the ocean. Captain Hall is pleased with her interest and aptitude.

Late in 1869, father and daughter sail from Liverpool in the 1444-ton ship *Rothesay* on a charter to New Orleans and back. The westbound passage is uneventful, but troubles begin at New Orleans when they suffer a long delay of over two months. They are waiting upon an American shipper to pay for their cotton cargo run. When the cargo ship finally arrives, Captain Hall is in a hurry to transport it to its destination, Liverpool. He leaves with a somewhat depleted crew; there is only the captain, first mate, Bessie, the cook, a seventy-two-year-old carpenter, and six seamen when they tow down one hundred miles of the Mississippi to open sea.

Four days out the mate falls ill with smallpox. Captain Hall puts him in isolation in his own cabin to be tended by a seaman who has had smallpox, and moves with his daughter into the carpenter's shop on deck. A precaution of the time is to dispose of all produce and domestic animals so all fruits, vegetables, and the cat go overboard.

Thirteen days out, fighting the turbulent squalls of the Gulf Stream, Captain Hall himself falls ill and goes below to join the mate in the temporary sickbay. Bessie is left in temporary control. She has to summon her father on deck to help when *Rothesay* is taken aback, floundering in the freshening gale. He manages to right things by reducing sail to two topsails, but, dizzy and ill, he asks Bessie to take command for the continuation of the voyage. She agrees and her father names the old carpenter mate. The seamen, however, have doubts about Bessie's fitness for the task and consider whether they should proceed into Saint John, *Rothesay's* home port. But few seamen can handle the ship in the tricky Bay of Fundy currents, so they decide to proceed. Finding another ship from which to borrow an officer seems unlikely: who will take on an undermanned, plague-ridden vessel? The best course, they decide, is to continue with Bessie Hall as master. They accept her firm assertion that she can take *Rothesay* to Liverpool. Storms rage all the way to the Grand Banks while Bessie performs all the duties of captain, standing a six-hour night watch plied with black coffee.

The leaden skies of the North Atlantic prove to be the new captain's greatest problem, for though she is competent in celestial navigation, she knows little of dead reckoning. In a later narrative she says:

There the distance run, the leeway, currents, cross-currents, and heaven knows what had to be taken into account. I had to study it all with the help of the 'Epitome, A Summary of Nautical Practices'. Believe me, I found it hard enough, but I made a bluff at it and put our supposed position down each day on the chart and in the logbook.

On the first clear day when she is able to reckon by shooting the sun, Bessie is relieved to find they are not far off course. But reckoning by sextant is also difficult; to get a sight on the heaving horizon, she has to climb on top of the spare spars lashed to the bulwarks alongside the forward house—a feat not generally taught to young ladies in 1870. The stormy weather finally clears and the ship moves sluggishly under storm sails across the rest of the Atlantic Ocean to the Irish coast. With only five sailors, Bessie does not dare raise more sail. A pilot brings them safely into the port of Liverpool and to anchor. Bessie Hall has successfully completed a 4800-mile trip in adverse weather with minimal crew, taking only nineteen days more than the average for such a run.

After difficulties with quarantine inspection, the overdue *Rothesay* finally docks. The mate is carried off on a shutter, and Captain Hall is weak but recovering. Bessie, still in the sailor's clothes she has adopted, steps ashore to the cheers of her crew. The insurance brokers, grateful for the safe arrival of a valuable cargo, plan a dinner in Bessie's honour, and think to present her with a gold watch engraved with the details of her feat. This proposal is never carried out, though, as the ship has been docked illegally (without proper quarantine clearance) and so cannot receive any publicity. And so Bessie Hall's grand achievement remains almost unknown, living on only in the legends of the seafaring world. Bessie makes one more voyage, to the Falkland Islands, then retires from the sea, like the others, leaving no record of her regrets about the impossibility of becoming a legitimate career sailor.

Logs and Diaries

A log kept by a daughter of Captain Robert Cochrane and his wife Hannah of St Martins, New Brunswick details life aboard the ship *Alabama* on a voyage from Newport, Wales, towards Jamaica and Apalachicola, in the United States, and back to Liverpool. At seventeen, Folly Cochrane is apparently suffering from teenage boredom and a lack of peers. Interspersed among reports on the weather, the ship's course, and the ship's position, which imitate the style of official logs, are Folly's personal observations. She starts with an entry for October:

I am very lonely today. I should like to be on shore some place to go to meeting. This weather is very hot. (Temp.90 degrees).

October, 25 [1860]
Gentle breezes and fine weather. People variously employed. Father is asleep on the poop and I am going to work at fine shirts. I should like to be home a little while and see how they all are. I am tired of salt grub and would like to see something fresh.

Further entries carry personal opinions such as: "Flying fish for breakfast. Boobie tastes good. I have been employed painting the front of the poop. Sunday is bad enough at home, but it is worse at sea…We are lying over a good deal and I can't go on deck, so I've got to stop where I am. I should like a cup of mother's good tea and a slice of homemade bread for my supper. The ship has been charging about very much and has robbed me of my sofa twice."

Naturally the daily writing of events aboard ship by captains and their family members varies in content. But the official log was a legal requirement and was to record vital information on events involving the ship's passage and on personnel. Occasionally the log was written by one of the women aboard, usually the captain's wife or daughter, but to record what interested them in their daily lives they turned to their own journals. Consider the difference between a personal journal and a ship's log in the examples of Emma Spicer and her husband Dewis of the sailing barque *E.J. Spicer*. The Spicers were prominent owners and masters from Spencer's Island, Nova Scotia. Jacob and Mary Spicer had four master mariner sons, Dewis being one of them, and two daughters who married captains.

Leaving Rotterdam in 1880 on a voyage from Liverpool towards New York, Emma and Dewis write in their respective logs:

[Emma]
> *Aug. 22, 1880*
> *This day fine weather and fresh breeze from North East. I was busy all the morning putting away all the pictures and getting ready for sea. At 11 am we unmoored from the dock and went off, steam tug Nellie pulling down the river. At 5 pm steam tug and pilot left and we are out to sea again. I tried to press some of my clothes, but turned very seasick and had to give it up.*

[Dewis]
> *Fine weather and fresh breeze from NE. Got papers in morning. 11 am we unmoored and weighed anchor and proceeded in tow of steam tug Nellie. River pilot left at Maas Sluis. Got sea pilot and steam tug left off. 6 pm N Rur head bore SS by E. distance 7 miles. Wind north.*

[Emma]
> *Aug. 24, 1880*
> *This day hazy weather and fresh breeze. I am feeling better today and put away some of my clothes and did the rest of the ironing. We are going down Channel very nicely and I hope the wind will keep fair and that we may have a quick passage.*

[Dewis]
> *Dull weather and fresh breeze of ENE. 5 am sighted lights West by S. 9 am Dover Pier bore North. 10 am off Dungeness NW. Noon Dungeness bore ENE. This day contains 12 hours and ends at noon.* [He has shifted to logbook time wherein the days start and end at noon when the daily position is calculated.]

On a voyage from Liverpool towards New York, Emma and Dewis write:

[Emma]
> *Feb. 19, 1882*
> *Comes in a strong breeze of wind and snow—the first snow storm of any account that I ever saw at sea but it looks like home today with the snow drifting about and it is cold so it makes our seaboys look whizzled up. Most of them have scarcely any clothes. We pass the time away reading and singing.*

[Dewis]

Comes on light breezes backing to west. 1:30 tacked ship; 6 pm strong breeze, stowed light sails. 8 pm stowed topgall. sails. Wind SW by S; 10 pm Wind ended early shifted WNW, 11 pm tacked ship WNW with sleet and rain; 6 am commenced to snow and continued snowing very thick the remainder of the day; 8 am set main top gall. sail. Noon thick snow storms.

Lat. about 45°-24' N

Long. 47°-36' W

[Emma]

Monday, February 20, 1882

Cloudy weather and cold it looks very wintry. Have head winds and are making noth-ing today. I do hope we will get a chance soon. Dew is getting discouraged, but we might as well laugh as cry for we can't do anything unless we have free winds. I knit a mitten for Dew today and set up the other one. Vessel in sight this evening. All is well.

[Dewis]

Comes in with clearing weather. 2 pm ceased snowing but kept cloudy and cold winds brisk NW. 4 pm wind west with hard squalls; 11 pm stowed upper topsail and spanker main sail etc. wore ship. Strong breeze with hard squalls; 2 pm jibstay carried away; 8 am wore ship. Noon set upper topsails etc. light baffling winds, got jib stay spliced and jib back; very cold weather.

Lat 44°-22' N

Long 47°-36' W

Emma Spicer and her new husband Captain Dewis Spicer in full figure for a portrait taken in the main cabin of the Nova Scotian ship George T.Hay.

The detail and human interest in the women's journals are the better source for a picture of family life on a sailing ship. However, Emma Spicer was subject to seasickness at the on-set of stormy weather and although she did perform many of her "house-hold duties" in bad weather, she often did not continue her practice of diary writing at such times.

XI
FAMILY LIFE AT SEA

A YOUNG WOMAN FROM YARMOUTH WRITES TO HER FATHER ABOUT HER EARLY SEAFARING LIFE IN THE WOODEN SHIPS. HER DAUGHTER REMINISCES ABOUT A CHILD'S LIFE AND DOMESTICITY AT SEA.

A detailed record of life at sea kept by Grace and Kathryn Ladd of Yarmouth, Nova Scotia, leaves us a fine seafaring travelogue and, in particular, a record of how well—and precisely what— they ate. Their accounts show how a determined approach could ensure a healthy and interesting cuisine on long voyages, despite a lack of refrigeration and modern packaging. The basic diet aboard sailing ships in the age before refrigeration consisted of salt meat and fish, pea soup, and biscuit or hardtack. The British Board of Trade laid out a skimpy minimum required diet for seamen, and many merchant ship owners were happy to comply with the base provisioning that government standards demanded. The debilitating effects and death caused by the lack of vitamin C are part of the history of the naval and merchant services. But even after the cause and cure for scurvy were found, penurious owners were reluctant, even though it was in their own interest, to take the measures that would ensure a healthy diet for their crew. It is hard to believe that seamen could survive months of hard work and the cold, wet quarters on such a diet, but on the whole they did.

Shipmasters could have made stops at ports along the way for fresh food, but most did not want to take the time from their schedules or incur the costs involved in stopping. However, brief stops at sea in the Asian archipelagos conveniently brought out native boats with fresh fruit and vegetables for trade. Some masters were corrupt enough to short change their crews on food and pocket the savings. Such inequalities were rare on Maritime ships because the captain's relatives and neighbors often made up a good part of his crew.

Reasonable owners and honest, wiser masters kept their seamen fit by providing better cuisine, even on long voyages. In the nineteenth century, the practice of keeping livestock on board provided crews with some fresh meat. The most practical animals to keep were chickens and pigs. Laying hens provided eggs, a great treat if the weather was not too severe, and the occasional roast. Small pigs were fed scraps until they were big enough to be slaughtered, at which time a roast pork pig-out lasting a few days was held. This feast was followed by head cheese, sausages, and blood pudding. With some imagination, in the 1890s operators like the Ladds managed to eat relatively nourishing meals. Captain Ladd was not reluctant to stop for fresh food, especially if it meant stopping only for an hour or two off an island to attract bumboat traders.

Grace (Brown) Ladd's Letters

Grace Ladd left a record, covering almost twelve years, of her life at sea in the form of long letters to her father at home in Yarmouth. These "sea-letters" were written and added to intermittently until her ship arrived at a port where the letters could be mailed. Grace's letters say little about the ship's business, such as what cargo was being carried; however, Grace was keenly interested in the world around her. Kathryn, Grace's daughter, describes her mother as an untiring tourist. Grace spends a period sailing in a traditional, Nova Scotia built square-rigger,

Full-rigged ship Morning Light, *built in Meteghan, Nova Scotia for Yarmouth-area owners in 1878. A comfortable vessel of 1240 tons, it was the honeymoon home for Grace Brown Ladd on a six-month voyage to Shanghai.*

considered a beauty among vessels but already ten years old by the time Grace Ladd first sets sail.

Grace Brown and Fred Ladd were married in Yarmouth on May 20, 1886. Their wedding trip took them by steamer to Saint John, then by train to Boston and New York, where they joined his ship to sail on May 29 for far-off Shanghai. This full-rigged ship was *Morning Light*, a fairly large wooden vessel at 1240 tons, built in 1878 at Meteghan, Nova Scotia, for a group of Yarmouth owners. *Morning Light* would be the last of the great globe-girdling, wooden square-riggers sailing out of Yarmouth. Grace's letters home from *Morning Light* to her father leave a valuable picture of life at sea.

Grace's first letter home was written at Latitude 39°, 40' S and Longitude 70°, 48' W, deep in the South Atlantic between Argentina and South Africa. It shows a new bride adapting well to a new environment with the help of an attentive husband. Perhaps to ease her introduction to life at sea, a stewardess has been signed on with the crew for the voyage. Grace regularly starts her letters, "My Dear Papa" and signs them, " Yours Affectionately, Grace F. Ladd."

14 August, 1886

No doubt by this time you will think we are well around Cape of Good Hope. Instead we have not fairly started out and are about ninety miles from Gough's Island much east of it. Fred wanted to sight Tristan da Cunha, but we passed it in the night. I was sorry as I have almost forgotten how land looks. We have had splendid weather ever since we came out, not one storm and only a few squalls. By splendid weather I mean for me. Poor Fred is almost discouraged. Wherever there was a calm we have had it. Perhaps we would get a fair wind for a day, but if we did, head winds would blow for a week. However, since yesterday morning we have had strong fair winds; I think they will last.

During the first week I felt dizzy whenever we would get a breeze but since then have been perfectly well, have not had a sick day. Everything seems to agree with me. The weather was awfully hot but just before we crossed the equator, the thermometer standing between 80-88 degrees for over a week. Fred had a cover made for the after skylight so the sun could not get in. Then we had an awning all over the poop. Mr. Crocker, the second mate, made me a fine canvas hammock with twine fringe all round. I used to lie in that nearly all day and read. Evenings Fred and I would walk up and down the house. It took us about quarter of an hour to walk a mile; the house is forty feet long. One cannot take much exercise aboard ship. I have a small pair of dumb-bells I try and use every day, but forget it often.

Have had three wash days. The first time it took me all day. Everything seemed so strange and I had such a large washing. I have two tubs, a wash bench with board. Mama would have laughed if she could have seen me. I rinsed the clothes in the bath tub. Fred rang them all out for me and hung them up. Since then I have managed better, get them all washed and dry before dinner. The stewardess would do the washing for me, but I like to do it. She does the sheets. We have sighted a number of vessels and spoken some. Day before yesterday six were right round us, all speaking each other and getting their times. Before that we had not seen a sail for a number of weeks. Just after we left New York we sighted a Norwegian barque, spoke her and found she was out two days longer than we from New York and bound towards Shanghai too. On board her I could see the sailors quire distinctly through the glasses you gave Fred.

We have caught lots of birds with a piece of pork on a hook, the steward stewed some cape pigeons. They were very nice, very like wild duck, only the meat was much darker. One day we had seven molly hawks tied up under the bridge. The steward fried the liver of three for tea, but I could not make up my mind to eat them. Fred said they were splendid, could not tell the difference from bullock's liver. They are great looking birds, about seven feet from tip to tip. An albatross has been flying round, but it wants something more tempting than pork to catch it.

About two weeks ago Fred called me on deck to see some whales. They passed right by us. One went off with my hat—or Fred's. I ran up in my bare head, he gave me his hat as I ran to the stern to see them better. Away it went, it was the only thing we have lost yet. It was more provoking than losing a hat over the bridge.

Photo taken in Calcutta for "carte de visite" of Grace (Brown) Ladd in the 1880s. Grace Brown married at twenty-one, taking a long, six-month honeymoon voyage to Shanghai and staying at sea with her husband for an exceptional twenty-five years.

Captain Frederick Ladd went to sea at seventeen, was a master and married at twenty-seven. He and his wife Grace were sociable when in port and made an effort to retain their connections at home in Yarmouth.

27 August
Ever since I wrote last we have had fair winds. Fred was up all last night, it looked very stormy but passed off and today is beautiful. It does not seem possible we have been out three months tomorrow, three months since I have seen land, but I expect we will see too much of it before long up among the islands.

Three months out, without seeing land, Morning Light completes a great run from near the island of Tristan da Cunha, through Sunda Strait to the island-studded East Indies. The vacant ocean gives way to straits full of islands and native canoe traffic, many of them out to barter local produce and souvenirs for manufactured goods from passing ships. Fruit, coconuts, sponges, turtles, shells, mats and parrots went for tobacco, knives, iron wire.

29 Sept
Well, we are almost up among the islands, early this morning Fred sighted Fly Island, a small island south of Sandalwood. After breakfast I saw Black Point on Sandalwood quite plainly, but there is not much satisfaction in seeing land at a distance of 15 or 16 miles. Fred says 120 days is too long to be at sea without seeing anything.

One day we were just about sixty miles from Australia, it was perfectly calm. I was sitting at the stern of the ship reading. On looking up, I saw Fred out rowing about in a boat having a fine time all by himself. You can imagine my surprise. They had put the boat over the side so quietly I had not heard the least noise. However, they soon got the ladder over for me and we had a splendid row for about an hour. While we were out a whale blew about a quarter mile from us. I enjoyed the row very much, but it is not like rowing in the ponds where trees are on all sides. The ship was the only thing we could see and had a good view of her under full sail. Fred has been getting his firearms put in good order preparatory for the savages, but trusts we won't have occasion to use them, but I will write more when we get safely through.

Morning Light passes slowly up the Banda Sea, east of Celebes, Indonesia. Grace admires the scenery, green hills and, at night, the light of fires along the nearby shores. Boats come out to barter fruit and chickens for tobacco and iron goods.

They were very friendly, shook hands with us, one called himself Captain Paul. He was the captain and could speak about six English words. Another fellow was all tattooed, there was not a bare spot on him. They have long bushy hair and are darker than our Indians. In one of the boats there was a little boy. They brought him on deck and let him run about. They must be used to trading with passing ships. They were like monkeys, going up and down the ropes and seeming pleased with their bargains. We were glad when they left us, they made an awful noise all talking together, and so loud.

Further in towards the China Sea, the Ladds meet more boats, peopled with natives whose poverty is obvious. Here they make an unusual purchase; from the natives of Anna Island, Grace is endeared to a young boy, who they buy for four pounds. The wild youth is cleaned up, clothed, and taught the routines of ship-board life. Grace expresses no apology about her purchase of "Johnnie" and shows no sense of responsibility for his tragic outcome. Given the times, she probably thought (ironically) his life could only be bettered in "civilization."

Nov. 22
Safe at last, anchored fourteen miles from Shanghai at a place called Woosung. Fred is going up to Shanghai with the tug so I have only a few minutes to write. Just think, last Wednesday morning we were about ten miles from the lightship, sailed about all day trying to get a pilot for the river. Well, toward noon it began to blow, the glass falling fast. At night it was a fearful gale. A steamer passed us bound in, promised to send us a pilot. We had to put way out to sea. It was something terrible, thought the masts would blow out of the ship, sea coming over everything. Filled the cabin, kept the stewardess and me wiping up salt water all day. The plants were looking splendid, but they got a salt water bath. However, it lasted only twenty-four hours.

We have been very fortunate, have had no sickness among the sailors and have been perfectly well ourselves, lost nothing and had no storm except the one we had the other day.

Fred will bring me letters this afternoon. You can imagine how anxious I am to hear from home, but the time has passed quickly and pleasantly. I hope you will get this before Christmas, which I hope will be a pleasant one for all.

Grace Ladd enjoys the exotic charms of the great port of Shanghai, her honeymoon destination. But back aboard ship, a flower garden in the main cabin under the two skylights offers a touch of home and a touch of land. Just as a heavy hail squall is thundering on the deck above, Grace writes:

My flowers in the skylight never looked better. I have watered them with warm water and the cabin is always warm. Mama would never recognize the geraniums. The ivy is just getting settled and I notice fresh shoots coming out all over. I wish you could see a rose I have. It has been on board the ship two years. Fred got it in Java; it is a large tree now with one full blown rose, three large buds and two green ones.

Grace also collects a variety of plant and flower seeds from around the world, planting them to see what will shoot up. She sends some to her father and trades seeds with interested friends in different countries. (The sequoia proves a favourite in many ports.) In contrast to the exotic ports it visits in the eastern and the southern hemispheres, in 1888 *Morning Light* voyages to Scandinavian ports. Grace writes from the Norwegian port of Christiansand on April 9, 1888, there having been a long gap in the correspondence since she and her husband were home in Yarmouth in the summer of 1887. The dates of the letters waiting there for her suggest that she has had a long voyage. It is their last voyage in *Morning Light*.

Ship Morning Light, Christiansand
We got our mail last eve. I received four letters from you, 29th Feb., 6th, 7th and 14th March, then lots of papers—they will last us for some time. We hope the ice will be out of the Sound (Oresund) the last of this week at the latest. With a fair wind Landskrona is hardly a day's sail from here. Christiansand is the third place in size in Norway, our ship is lying three miles below the town.

By water it is three miles to Christiansand and four by land. We row up some days and drive back. We have found the people very hospitable. Several have asked us to spend the day with them. We return the compliment. They always seem to enjoy a day on board the Morning Light very much. Fred feels very proud to have the ship praised and I am duly proud to have the cabin praised and we certainly are very comfortable and cosy. The harbour master says it is the finest ship ever in the harbour and there is no house as nice.

Fred and I have had a great time snowshoeing and coasting. We are about five minutes row from the shore. Any of the farmers are pleased to lend us shoes or sleds. The snowshoes are made of thin hardwood turned up at the toes, four feet long with a strap across the middle for the foot. They are very awkward at first. One has to take a pole to keep from slipping down the hills. However, I think we get on very well now and it is good exercise. We always come on board ship with a good appetite. We get fresh milk every morning. I tell Fred he had better fill the tanks with milk, it is so cheap, one cent a quart.

They have such a funny fashion of thanking you for any hospitality you show them but especially after eating or drinking. They shake hands, make a courtesy (the women and children) and thank you. The children thank their mother, the gentlemen lift their hats to each other when they pass (perfect strangers) even young boys. When we go ashore we meet a lot of little girls. I get Fred to take off his hat and I bow, to see them courtesy one after another. It looks so odd.

They leave Christiansand on the south coast of Norway, sailing down the Kattegat to the narrow Oresund between Denmark and Sweden. Unlike most of these diaries, letters, and accounts, Grace Ladd's diary does not often mention what cargo the ship is carrying.

Landskrona, Sweden, 20 April, 1888
We arrived here safely this morning early. Have had head winds and thick weather ever since we left Christiansand. Fred has not had an hour's sleep therefore he is nearly tired out, but he won't take time to rest even now and is ashore busy about something. There was one letter from you awaiting us here besides a number of papers. By this

time no doubt know we are chartered for Cardiff to load coal for Capetown. It will be a pleasant voyage. Although Landskrona is only two degrees further south than Christiansand it is much warmer, not a bit of snow to be seen and the grass is turning green, but ice is still in the Sound drifting about with the wind and currents. The Baltic is still unnavigable.

From our deck we can see Copenhagen, Elsinor and Helsenborg. A steamer leaves here for Copenhagen twice a day going in one hour. I am looking forward to that trip with much pleasure. Tuesday Fred is going to Helsenborg to see about getting the ship coppered. There is a very old castle there which we will go through. Fred and I have planned long walks. When he can't go, I shall go alone. I will find out whether it be true, that in Norway they feed cows on fish.

All [the crew] left the ship last night except the mate and steward. They were a happy lot of sailors. A great many of them are going right home. All are Swedes and Norwegians. They were singing "Homeward Bound" as they went over the side, the first time they have been on shore for ten months.

22 May
Last week the exhibition in Copenhagen opened. I enjoyed it very much, We stayed two days, it was quite enough. We saw the Royal Family, the king opened the exhibition. I think I stood it better than Fred. He is lame yet. I shall be glad to get in England where we can hear English spoken. Very few people here speak English. We only know four. Most all speak German.

Cardiff, 8 June
We had a pleasant trip coming up the English Channel, went the whole length of the channel in 24 hours, passing by the land it was evening when we passed Dover. It was a very pretty sight, the town all lighted up. Just back the cliffs are very high. On the top is a castle used for barracks, this one a flame of light. The Isle of Wight we passed the next morning, every thing looked so fresh and green, it must be a beautiful place I think.

In mid-July after a long wait for a coaling berth, the Ladds are finally loading at Penarth, near Cardiff, the most famous of the coal-exporting centres. The high quality Welsh coal is a staple cargo for the sailing ships, prized the world over, but it is disliked by masters for its dust, which dirties ships that are normally kept sparkling clean. On the invitation of a Captain George, they take a trip to Bristol, where they make many friends. There are many Yarmouth ships in Cardiff and one of their masters is of the well-known seafaring Cann family from Yarmouth. The Ladds run into members of the Cann family all over the world. Once the ship is loaded, Grace rolls up the carpets and puts away all the movables to make the cabins ready for sea. They set sail for Capetown.

Although Grace does not think Capetown itself very attractive, she finds the town surrounding it splendid for long hikes and garden viewing.

Capetown, 16 Oct. 1888
Every day we go somewhere. The flowers are beautiful, the wild ones I mean, all kinds and colours and so fragrant. Wednesday morning Fred was up at daylight to go on board a coolie ship which came in here yesterday for fresh stores. He has been telling me all about it. This ship is taking these coolies home from Demerara where they have served their ten years and made their small fortunes. There were 667 men, women and children aboard. I hope to get out to an ostrich farm before we leave.

Table Bay, 28 Oct. 1888
The captain of the tugboat came off for Fred at six this morning so that he could settle up what he had not time for yesterday, so I suppose we shall be away by noon. It is beginning to blow very hard. I am afraid it will be very rough outside. Captain G. Cann was aboard last evening and stayed until twelve o'clock. He is looking very well, quite fat.

In late December of 1888, Grace expresses her disappointment with Calcutta, about whose attractions she had high expectations. They have to fight their way up the difficult Bay of Bengal after crossing from Capetown.

We had a nice passage, beautiful weather until we reached the Bay, where we had it stormy enough to make up for the rest, nothing but heavy squalls one after the other and we just escaped a hurricane. The glass was very low and we took down our royal yards, but we had just the tail end of it, quite enough for me. We were fourteen days beating about in the bay.

I am much disappointed in Calcutta, although there is much to see it does not come up to my expectations. We have visited some of the temples. Today we went to one, they would not allow us to go near the goddess who has a tongue about half a yard long of gold. In the place they were offering up sacrifices—kids, pools of blood were about everywhere. Then we saw some horrible looking men. They believe they are very good, they leave home and friends and are continually praying. They cover themselves in ashes, their hair is all matted and long. They are frightful looking. Yesterday we saw where they bury their dead. It is like a large court by the side of the river. They make fires of wood on which they place the body. They had just finished burning one and another was there ready to be burned. I didn't enjoy that very much, but I made Fred take me there. All these things are worth seeing.

Tuesday evening we went to hear Bishop Thorburn preach, but I do not think missionaries have done much good in Calcutta. Christmas Day was very different from the one I spent last year. I thought of you all. I could imagine what you all were doing. Christmas morning with us was Christmas Eve with you so I had to think back. It was the first Christmas Day that Fred has spent in port in years. I am sure he enjoyed it.

I am so glad to hear we are going to Boston. I shall expect all the family to come over and pay us a visit. We can stow away as many as can come. I want you to see how we live. Mamma has promised so I depend on her.

The family reunion may have taken place as hoped in Boston, or Grace and Fred may have gone to Yarmouth. The voyage from Calcutta would have been at least 105 days. In any case there is a period without letters from Grace to her father. The next letter is dated October 24, 1889, from Dunedin, New Zealand, and describes a rough passage from the eastern seaboard, likely New York:

After a rough and stormy passage we arrived safely yesterday morning. It is now 4 p.m. and we are all fast at Dunedin wharf. I think I wrote you I intended writing a little every Tuesday so that I would have a long letter all ready to send on arriving. The first few Tuesdays I did, but the letter was so monotonous I gave it up. I do not think our Lat. and Long. Barometer and distance would be interesting to you. We had a good run to the equator, crossed it fifty-five days out on the 2nd of August. We passed a ship homeward bound very near, Fred kept off to speak him. We supposed the captain thought we wanted something as he kept off too. Wasn't that contemptible? However, we hoisted our number. He must have been able to read it, but did not answer and we were not sorry to lose sight of him. We signalized one other vessel, a bark bound to the River Plata. We have sighted lots of sails way in the distance looking about like flies on the horizon. The days have all passed smoothly away, the crew peaceable and willing. The first mate, Mr. Vickery, and steward first class men, the others passable, except the carpenter who was never on a ship before and does not know how to do ship's carpentering at all.

We used the last of our potatoes the day we entered the Indian Ocean. I often thought of the nice vegetables you were all enjoying. Our stormy weather commenced about the 8th of September in Lat.37.1, Long.23.45. (West of Tristan da Cunha). From that time until we passed the latitude of Tasmania we had a gale of wind every twenty-four hours. It was terrible and frightfully cold, the salt water freezing two inches in the buckets. The poor sailors—I was sorry for them. One good thing—we are very light so the decks were not wet. The cabin fire was kept burning night and day. I hope we will never come on this voyage again. Fred says he won't, but he will forget all about it I am afraid. On the 25th of September we passed about four miles to the northward of the Crozet Group, Lat. 45.56 S, Lon. 50.21 E. I made Fred promise to call me as soon as they were visible, which he did about five o'clock in the morning, but it was so cold I saw all I wanted to of them through the window. On these islands provisions are placed in a cave for shipwrecked crews, but it is a dreary looking place, snow on the mountains and nothing growing except a few shrubs.

We sighted the first land of New Zealand about four o'clock Saturday afternoon, 19th of October, Penegut Point. Tuesday morning we were through Faveau Straits (inside Stewart Island at the southern tip). I sat up all night, it was delightful, not a cloud in the sky and the stars shining so brightly. Towards morning some old friends came up over the horizon. In some parts of the strait it was very narrow. Until daylight I could not see very well except the high mountains on both sides. At five o'clock we passed the bluffs where we signalized our presence. By this time it was quite light. The country looked brown and cold.

We had a fine breeze all day, at four o'clock were within thirty miles of Dunedin when it commenced to blow. At six were obliged to lay to. The gale lasted thirty hours. It was heart-breaking, the sea and the current carrying to the northward two or three miles an hour. On Monday a heavy sea struck us on the port beam, carrying away fifty feet of rail and 28 stanchions. It swept over the whole ship. I thought she had struck a rock and was so thankful it was what it was I could not feel so sorry, but it was too bad after sailing so far without losing even a rope, that it should happen.

We got within twelve miles of our port when I went to bed on Tuesday evening. At one in the morning, Fred came down to tell me he saw a light. He thought it was a pilot coming off. I was up and dressed in a few minutes and on deck just as the welcome pilot was coming up the ladder. The tow up to Dunedin was pleasant. It is spring here now.

Grace admires the spring flowers and vegetables on walks in Dunedin, but, cosy in her main cabin in the ship during a rain, admires equally her ocean-going greenhouse:

Just now there is a heavy hail squall passing. My flowers never looked better in the skylight. I have watered them with warm water and the cabin has always been warm. Mamma would not recognize the geraniums. The plant Ron gave me is thrifty enough, but not in blossom. I shall put it in a larger pot. The ivy is just getting settled. I notice fresh shoots coming out all over. I wish you could see the rose I have. It has been aboard the ship two years. Fred got it in Java. It is a large tree now and healthy with one full blown rose, three large buds and two green ones.

This garden swings in pots suspended from two modest-sized skylights mounted in the deck overhead. Grace enthusiastically pursues her interest in collecting and exchanging exotic seeds from the flora of these distinctive habitats.

An enjoyable time seeing New Zealand with various new-found friends helps make up for the arduous voyage across the Southern Ocean. Grace remarks on the fact that the charming city of Dunedin has been built in only fifty years and that, previous to Dunedin, there had been no white men there. The Ladds also tour the cities of Wellington and Auckland and the surrounding countryside and take horseback rides in the

*hills, before departing for London, where they are due on February 6, 1890. She ex-
pects they will re-cross the Pacific, and pass through the Straits of Magellan, stopping at
Rio and Madiera on the way.*

There is a break from shipboard life in 1890 when Fred and Grace Ladd go
ashore to live in Liverpool during the captain's customary supervision of the fitting of a new ship. The investors of Yarmouth still have hopes for profitability in
the sailing ship, despite the general decline in the face of steamship competition.
The wooden ships of Atlantic Canada can no longer compete in world trade so
owners have to go to Britain to have steel vessels built. The new ship's name is
Belmont, a moderately large barque at 1415 tons.

Grace uses this time out to bear a son, Forrest. When the new ship is ready in
1891 she goes right back to life at sea with her husband, likely sailing out to New
York in the new vessel, but possibly stopping in Yarmouth for the local sharehold-
ers to see their ship, and to leave the baby with family. Forrest joins his parents
aboard *Belmont* the next year and Grace's letters home recount her son's adventures and clever sayings as he learns to talk.

Kay Ladd's Story

Grace Ladd's daughter, Kathryn Ladd, who went to sea as a child in the latter
days of the square-riggers, leaves a sketch that concentrates on family life aboard
ship. Kathryn, who referred to herself as "K," was at sea until she was thirteen; she
records her story later in her life, simply and seemingly without embellishment.

*My mother went to sea for 25 years out of my father's forty. He had gone ten years be-
fore he married her. My father was 27 and my mother was 21 when they married. On
their first voyage they went to Shanghai. The trip lasted six months and they ran out of
food. He wasn't used to having food for a lady. The rough sailors had hardtack and
salt beef, salt cod. But so did we. That's what we lived on - salt cod, salt pork, herring,
salt mackerel and a few cases of bully beef, which I suppose was considered fresh meat.
We had it once a week. I liked the salt fish better than I liked the fresh meat.*

*But this first time, my mother was a bride and they ran out of everything except for
a little bully beef and hard tack, and they ran out of water. The trip was very long, so
they caught rain water.*

*Coming up the Solomon Islands on the coast on the way to China they had to go by
various islands. In those days they were not charted. The chart would say 'island—unknown'. There could have been cannibals. So they came to this island and one canoe
pulled out. They were poor looking natives and father allowed only two of them to
come on board. The sailors were all ready for them with sticks and so on. And these
men came aboard and with them came a little boy. Mother was dying to have him, she
thought that would be so much fun. They ended up buying the little boy for four*

pounds of tobacco.

He didn't know anything. When he saw stairs he started down head first on hands and knees. Of course, he had no manners either. He had to be taught. He was given a bunk forward with the ship's carpenter who had to teach him manners. He was a very smart little boy. Mother gave him lessons and taught him to read and write and one day in his scribbler she saw all these Chinese characters. She asked him, 'How did you learn to write Chinese?' He answered, 'Oh, cook teachee me Chinese, for I teachee cook English.' He was about seven or eight years old. He came from a very poor island.

Many ships were attacked by natives and overcome and one never heard from them again. The boy was terrified of these natives. They used to raid his island and take people away to eat them. In Shanghai the boy caught a cold and on their way around Cape Good Hope he got worse. When they reached New York he was quite sick. He was also very homesick. They took him to the hospital. He wanted a coconut very badly. Captain Ladd combed New York and eventually found one. The boy died of TB, hugging his coconut.

My parents had three children. Their first baby died and is buried on the island of St. Helena. My brother, twelve years older than I, was born in England. Father's new ship was being built in Scotland and my father was there overseeing the process. My mother was in England, too. An aunt lived there, her husband a sea captain also. Mother took a house near her, at Ainslie, just outside Liverpool. My brother Forrest was born there. I was born right here in Yarmouth.

When my parents were first married they went all around the world, but then the steamers came and these could go around the Cape so much more quickly. They also later went through the Panama Canal, so that left our sailing ships just going up and down the coast to places like Buenos Aires and to Capetown. My brother had gone around Cape Horn when he was young. He went with our parents when he was small for a few years, but when I came along, we went only to Buenos Aires.

My childhood was different. I didn't lead the kind of life that most children lead. I had bronchitis, which was caused by an allergy, but they didn't know then about allergies. We found that on board ship I did not get ill, so when I was 18 months old, my mother took me to sea and I didn't get home until I was about five or six. Even then I had such an awful croup that they took me back to sea. There was plenty of fresh air and no dust. I am allergic to feathers.

On board there was not a great deal to do. In the mornings I would have my lessons, as soon as I was old enough to remember. I don't remember what I did as a very small child, but around six or seven I had spelling, reading, writing, history and geography. Mother taught me those every morning. We had no blackboard so mother wrote on a big mirror with soap. I could never see the words very well, so I never learned to spell.

At eleven o'clock, I would go up to my father and he would give me arithmetic. As I got a little older, I remember I was twelve, and was supposed to be doing decimals. My father looked at the book and after two days he called it perfect foolishness and pro-

ceeded to teach me navigation instead. I had my own charts he gave me and I charted my own course. I had to draw in the course wherever we went down to South America. We went way across to the Canary Islands in order to catch the fair winds and then we came back. We made sort of a triangle and then to Buenos Aires. On the way back we came straight up the coast of South America. I remember one trip took about seven months. We had a lot of bad winds. It was nearly ninety days going down, but we came back in fifty-six days.

The after cabin sitting room was very comfortable. It had a fireplace, beautiful panelling, even a piano. I took a few lessons when we were at home and was supposed to practice at sea, but the piano got out of tune. We kept chickens and a pig on board. I helped the sailors scrub the deck and clean the brass. My father didn't want me to help, but he allowed me to do it. I was only allowed to work with two of the older sailors. I could never understand why, but I suppose the others were kind of rough. I was very much the spoiled darling. The cabin boy brought up tubs of water and mother washed just the sheets and our personal clothes. We used to hang it up on deck to dry on a fine day. We washed on a day after a rain when there was lots of fresh water.

My brother went to sea when he was small, but my father wanted him to go to school so he could go to college and wouldn't have to go to sea. Nevertheless, he came on one trip with me. I was supposed to be delicate and they used to put salt water in a big pork barrel so I could take a bath every day in warm salt water. My brother was bored on that trip and he talked the cook into putting the pig in the barrel while I was taking my bath. The pig didn't like it any more than I did. I called my father. I remember very well, because he would rescue me. But, when he came on deck, he disappeared again quickly, to come back with the camera to take a picture.

Our dog came from Argentina. When I was a baby, we went up by Montevideo and the pilot came on board. It takes two or three days to sail up to Buenos Aires and the pilot guides the ship through the huge river with its flats and sandbars. The pilot was Argentinian and they loved children. He said the bambina should have a dog and he had a lovely puppy, just the thing for a baby. So they sent the cook with a big basket. He didn't come back for a long time. Hours later he appeared, dragging this tall six-months old dog on a string, flea-bitten, dirty, never washed in its life. We called him Pilot and he became a great pet. He was also a good watchdog, the vessel was never robbed as so many others were.

Shipboard life was lonely, extremely lonely. I had no friends. However, Bue-

The fine British-built steel barque Belmont was the first home for Katherine Ladd in company with her parents. She lived happily at sea until the age of thirteen, when her parents retired.

nos Aires was beautiful. I enjoyed going there. I had friends there, but on board, on stormy days, we just stayed in bed. My mother stayed in her bed and I in mine. My bed was a stateroom bed, up high with dresser drawers underneath. I used to climb up on the settee and there was a big high board so I wouldn't fall out. Sometimes it would be three days that we'd be in bed. When one of these storms came up, the only thing I could do was look out the porthole. And my mother never felt well when these big storms came up. She wasn't scared, but didn't feel well because the ship pitched. I was a good sailor, it didn't bother me at all, but I had no one to talk to. I don't know how we got our meals, the cabin boy must have come in with food on trays for us.

Kay Ladd, in her father's boots, at home on the poop of the barque Belmont at sea, heeling on a port tack. Children were part of a civilizing element aboard ship.

Grace Ladd with children Kay and Forrest on capstan of Belmont while in port. Small children and crew enjoyed one another's company, although they were restricted by the limits of their respective territories in the ship.

Grace and Kay Ladd, cat and dog, on the stern of Belmont at sea, a helmsman at the wheel. The Ladds had a camera and left these relatively rare family pictures.

The ship's pig joins Kay in her bath at her brother's instigation. A seaman fetches more seawater from overside.

Aside from that nothing happened. My father would come down every so often to look at me, to cheer me up and then he'd go to mother to talk and then go back up on deck. During these stormy times he never slept at all. He just stayed on deck and never left, even when the first mate or second mate were in charge on the watches. It was very scary. The vessel would roll a lot, you'd be up, you'd roll way over to starboard and then you'd look up and see the sky and then she'd roll back again and you'd be looking down and see her racing through the foam and terrific waves. The waves would be so high I could barely see out of the window. That might go on for three days. The weather always kept one in suspense. Other than that it was monotonous and very lonely.

Christmas was quite different aboard ship. We took days to get ready for it. Of course, life had to go on with the galley and so on, so we had to make the cake one day and something else another in getting ready and I helped with the citron. Mostly eating it when I was supposed to cut it up for the cake. I have never been able to eat citron since, I ate so much. We also made lots of molasses candy. My father would come down and he'd pull it. He was a great taffy puller so it became white and as hard as could be. Then we'd have long twisted pieces, cut it up and do it up in waxed paper.

The ship had a slop chest, which was really kind of a store for the crew. When the seamen came on at a port, they'd perhaps come aboard with just their shirts and trou-

A Hong Kong studio portrait of Forrest Ladd in oilskins. He was early put into school ashore so he would not have to grow up to be a seaman. His parents considered leaving him for several years at an English school in Uruguay.

Kay Ladd went to sea with her parents as a small child and stayed until she was thirteen. This photograph shows her aboard Belmont with her dog "Pilot," acquired in Buenos Aires.

sers they had on. These sailors were kind of shiftless, most of them. Some of them were all right, but most of them were just the dregs of humanity. They would come on board without the right kind of clothes for cold weather. Father kept this slop chest store: they could buy warm trousers, warm shoes and socks from it. He also had lots of dark brier pipes. Most of them chewed tobacco. I would wrap up a pipe and a plug of tobacco and the candy. We put it in the basket and on Christmas Day, I would go around and give it to them as a present.

If we had a turkey, we would have it then. If not there might be a goose, or we might just have chickens for Christmas dinner instead. The turkey would be just for the family and the officers. One time they gave the sailors chicken for Christmas dinner because they had lots of chickens, but a delegation of sailors arrived to see my father and they said that the ship's articles said they were allowed so much salt beef and they did not have to eat chicken. Father was perplexed, but apparently chicken did not stick to a man's ribs. Of course, if there was a pig slaughtered, they would all have fresh pork with the rest of us. We took only one pig each trip and as soon as it got fat enough, they would kill it. The sailors didn't mind having fresh pork once in a while.

Mother was sort of Victorian and very strict with me, but my father spoiled the life out of me and I could have anything. He would do anything I wanted. We were great pals. I used to go with him in Buenos Aires when I was a small child. When I got older, he would take me to the billiard parlor where all the captains went. I would just

Captain Frederick Ladd (left) on a visit with Captain and Mrs. Dick Lee and their daughter Marjorie aboard the Lee's vessel, Pass of Balmaha.

sit there and watch them play cards. The last time we went to Buenos Aires he would not take me. I was too old. It wasn't really a girl's place. Mother tried to interest me in going with her to look at the shops, but I didn't want to look at shops, I wanted to go with father. When I was small, my mother dressed me beautifully. She bought all my clothes from a child's shop in New York called Beth's.

Life on board ship never seemed the least remarkable. As far as I was concerned it was the most natural way of living. My mother was not afraid of anything, including storms at sea. I wasn't scared because mother would say "Don't be silly, K." I was brought up with the idea of being fearless. My father was so wonderful that I didn't feel I had to worry about the storm. He would take care of it. My only phobia is feathers.

My father owned part of the vessel (Belmont) and an American firm owned part. The vessel was built in Scotland on the Clyde and registered here in Yarmouth. Quite a few local people had shares in it. It was built in 1891 and that was a time when sailing ships did not earn a great deal of money. So the people all wanted to sell off their shares. My father and the company bought them out. Then the war came, ships were scarce as hen's teeth and they needed the sailing ships for carrying cargo. So the vessel began making money hand over fist. After the war they sold her. I stopped going to sea at the beginning of the first world war and my father retired. Sea captains retired early. They needed a lot of stamina. Sometimes my father was up for 72 hours without sleeping. An older man could not stand it. I had gone to Buenos Aires seven times when he retired. I was then twelve or thirteen.

On my last trip, when we came up north my father dumped my mother and me off in Barbados and we stayed there two weeks. He went on up the coast. It was January weather and after two weeks my mother and I took a steamer up the coast to New York. We went to the hotel as soon as we got in and Mother contacted the shipping agents and they said father's ship had been sighted and she would be in that evening, and sure enough, father arrived on the scene and there was great excitement.

My father had been to sea for forty years, so he had another captain take over. We then came back to Nova Scotia.

Back home, "K" never married: she taught piano and lived in the old family home until an old age.

XII
WINDJAMMER YEARS

MORE LETTERS HOME FROM SEA AND PORTS OF THE WORLD, AND MORE
SEAFARING MENUS BY GRACE LADD IN A LATER, STATE-OF-THE-ART
STEEL WINDJAMMER.

The letters of Grace Ladd in this chapter are from her life in her new home, the new steel, square-rigged sailing ship *Belmont*. In *Belmont*, the creak of timbers is replaced by the clang of steel scupper ports. More sophisticated facilities and sail-handling gear alter the sailing experience. Like other dwindling Canadian-built, wooden vessels and their owner firms, the Ladds' old ship, *Morning Light*, is unable to compete. *Belmont*, on the other hand, is state-of-the-art for sailing ships and represents their final era when they are popularly known as windjammers.

The latter part of 1891 sees Grace and Fred rounding Cape Horn in their new *Belmont* on the way to Portland, Oregon from Liverpool via New York. They have contrary winds that stall progress, though Grace says their new vessel proves to be a splendid performer. Grace's brother Arthur apparently has much respect, gained from personal experience, for the trials of rounding the Horn. Though it cannot be mailed until they reach port, Grace writes her mother on Christmas Day from a position a few hundred miles off the California coast:

I suppose you are wondering how we are and where the Belmont is today. Ten days ago we had run our distance down so that one-hundred-and-fourteen miles a day would have taken us to Portland yesterday, and today we were going to wire you of our arrival and wish you a merry Christmas. But the best laid plans of men gang aft a'gley. A strong wind came straight from the northeast and until yesterday we had nothing but light winds. When they have been strong they have been head winds, and been, 'calm wherever there has been a calm for the past forty years'.

Fred says, 'Tell Arthur how I wonder at him allowing his sister to come around
Cape Horn without one word of warning.' We were off there three weeks and the
Belmont proved herself a duck. I shall never feel a bit afraid in her after such a test. I
often used to think of Arthur when I saw the men pulling on the frozen braces and
thrashing their arms to keep warm. Our grate burned splendidly all through the cold
weather and a stove in each fo'c'stle kept the sailors warm.

Later in the voyage, she writes: "Since last night at twelve o'clock we have
come 200 miles. The Belmont has proved with plenty of wind she can sail; one
day we made 330 miles, the biggest run yet, and she did it so easily. Well, you
can imagine when that day I made four pies and was sewing all afternoon, my
machine on the table."

The crew, however, is not much to the Ladds' liking: the mate is apparently
useless and retreats when put under pressure and the cook and stewardess are
dirty, extravagant, and slow to learn. Only a young stowaway, John, who is brought
aft from the fo'c'stle to help in the cabin, proves to be a fast learner, having previously been a cabin boy in a Norwegian ship.

The Christmas meal demonstrates how well they eat without refrigeration on
a long voyage, and stands in stark comparison to the miserly fare sanctioned by
the owners and captains for so long. In *Belmont*, as in most of the British, Bluenose
vessels, there are usually one or two young relations or family friends serving as
seamen or apprentices in the fo'c'sle; they eat what the seamen eat, but on a special
occasion such as Christmas, they are invited aft.

Christmas is celebrated for the *Belmont* at Lat. 37°30' N Long. 136°40' W (off
California). For breakfast they serve steamed Boston brown bread, fried bacon,
tea, and coffee. Dinner is mulligatawny soup, beefsteak pie with cranberry sauce,
boiled ham, stewed canned corn, gingerbread pudding, orange sauce, and lime juice.
For tea they eat macaroni and cheese, cream biscuit, guava jelly, and, of course, tea.

The menu was limited by the fact that the potatoes ran out before they were
around the Horn. Grace tells her mother:

I fortunately had saved a net of onions, so we still have a taste once in a while of some-
thing green. There were five in the net this morning when I went to get two for the pie
I made. I told Fred it was hard to realize five onions could ever make one feel so
happy. It is the last voyage we will ever make without plenty of onions and potatoes.
Both will keep in nets and since I have found out how well they keep, I have made
twenty-four nets, four will hold a bushel.

The following Christmas, *Belmont* tosses about in ballast far into the southern
Indian Ocean, near remote Amsterdam and St. Paul Islands. Forrest, now aboard,
nevertheless is found by Santa Claus and Captain Ladd turns his ship off the seas

to make the ride easier during Christmas dinner. The seamen are invited aft to see the Christmas tree, have a cigar, and a drink of rum or ginger beer. This year a turkey that has thrived despite rough weather has been fattened up. The pigs often kept by the Ladds stand up well to sea life, sometimes being given the run of the deck and becoming pets. Hens in particular are valued for the fresh eggs they supply if the weather is fair.

The Ladds continue perambulating about the world, visiting principally their home port of New York; the northwest American ports of Astoria, Portland, and Tacoma; the oriental ports of Shanghai and Hong Kong; Newcastle, Australia; and Manila and Buenos Aires. With long loading times they made side trips as tourists. Grace tells in detail of a visit to Canton in the summer of 1895:

I do not think I have ever told any of you about our trip to Canton, which we all enjoyed except Forrest, who says it was too much for him, meaning horse manure, dirt, etc. We left Hong Kong one Sunday evening in a fine large steamer, with six-hundred Chinese passengers so had lots of attention from the waiters on the lookout for fees. The captain, an Irishman, told us just how to see the most of Canton in a day. We anchored for two hours in the river on our way up so as not to reach Canton before daylight. There are no lights on the river except the lights of a few stray junks. We had dinner and went to bed soon after so as to be ready for a long day. These steamers all carry an armed guard, Portuguese. At daylight we were surrounded by hundreds of boats, all kinds. Flower boats beautifully decorated with all kinds of flowers, sampans, all anxious for passengers from the steamer.

While I was watching the boats Fred had engaged a guide, and we were at anchor, just outside the wall over which we could see the tiled roofs. About fifty policemen were on the wharf on the lookout for thieves. Such a noise I never heard before, of tongues. We got our breakfast on the boat and had a lunch put up so as not to lose time by having to come back for it. Our guide looked out for this and engaged our chairs, four. Forrest and I using one with four coolies, Fred one, Sydney one and the guide one. The chairs were comfortable and the little trot the coolies kept up rather pleasant. Passing through the narrow streets one could see everything in the shops as they have no front partitions. In a very few minutes without a guide we should have been lost. The buildings are so close together, with so many turnings and all look alike, no paint, not white, just dark gray; every now and then we would pass a store building with high walls and a large doorway. We visited many factories. The most interesting to see was the scene from which the willow pattern is taken, the willow still thriving, an unusual tree, now sacred. The bridge is removed but the stone arch is still there, quite a number of lotus plants grow in the water. The pagoda at the back still is a pretty picture. The English willow pattern is copied from the Chinese so that platter on the back of the sideboard in our dining room must be Chinese. If so, is valuable as it is not made now, the art is lost so the story goes. I could not buy a piece in Canton.

We saw the water clock. This clock was invented a great many years ago to give the time to Canton. For many years it was the only timepiece in China. We took our lunch in the top of a five story pagoda. While there the wife of a Chinese officer came to offer thanks to this god of war. She had the smallest feet I ever saw, could hardly walk, had a servant on either side of her. This pagoda was built on a hill about six-hundred feet above Canton. We got a fine view of the country outside the wall. Visited the viceroy's palace. When we got back to the ship had been just seven hours away, had not seen a single European. The steamer reached Hong Kong about three in the morning. Our sampan was waiting for us, we were glad to get back to the Belmont.

On their later world voyages there are, in the *Belmont's* crew, three young relatives identified only as Ralph, Stayley, and Ron, apparently nephews of Grace. She finds them good company and, although they are "crew," she takes an interest in their welfare. Stayley does not take to the sea or perform well, and so he leaves to work in the cotton mills as so many Maritimers did around 1900. Ron does well; he is good at math and loves the seafaring life, taking the watch on deck when the mate is ill for two weeks. Before long he moves aft to replace a departing second mate, where Fred teaches him navigation. Ron's rise in position, which occurs all on one voyage, is typical of the fashion in which officers got ahead in the Bluenose vessels. There will be no great prospect for Ron, however, unless he goes to steamships. Unfortunately, there are few berths left in sailing ships.

The letters cover nine world voyages taking up to fifteen months each away from New York, their ship's operational home port. Coming south from Tacoma, Puget Sound, in November of 1897 to round the tip of South America, *Belmont* goes as far west as Pitcairn Island to avoid unfavorable winds and currents before turning east. On this long haul Grace Ladd writes:

21st November
Fifty-nine days out and until we got in the Latitude of Pitcairn Island the weather had been perfect except two days good rain just before crossing the equator. Have not even a squall. We hoped to sight Pitcairn last Sunday the 14th but on Friday night it commenced to blow. Saturday at 4 p.m we were reduced to goose-winged lower topsails main and fore, and blowing a hurricane. It seemed to me I had never seen a worse storm, but I suppose the disappointment of having to give up a chat with the islanders was half. One tremendous sea came over, sweeping fore and aft. Forrest and I were sitting in the cabin under the after skylight, were drenched, the sea raised the weather skylight and came down full force, putting out the lights, etc. On deck they fared worse. It took all the rails off the bridge and threw one lifeboat to leeward, tore the chocks away, not hurting the boat. However three men washed against the rail, (Ron one of them.) I do not believe one of them even got a scratch. All day Saturday, Sunday and Monday it blew, with a heavy sea running. We used oil during the worst of it and all the time the

sailors were bending good sails. We did not think to get such a storm there. We were still in the Southeast Trades. Have only seen one sail and that a long way off, bound with us. We are all well after leaving the Sound. Ron was laid up for a few days with a bad sore throat. We applied linseed meal poultices which relieved him at once. Since then he has been perfectly well.

Grace helps her husband by taking on the role of doctor, and she, like most women at sea, could treat a simple fracture or wound with confidence. On one voyage they find they have a young man whose health is declining steadily from tuberculosis; he is segregated in a small room. On another occasion, Grace falls and breaks her arm. Fred diagnoses it as a clean break and it is easily set. On a later voyage, Grace reports a fall down the stairs by Forrest: "Forrest is anxious I should tell you he fell down our after steps leading to the cabin one day just after we left Hong Kong, cut the back of his head against the corner of the door. Fred had to shave his head and put a stitch in the cut. It must have hurt badly, but he did not whimper. My finest needle was number eight and he used my silk embroidery thread." Much more difficult to deal with are internal injuries and diseases. She reports, "We have been fortunate since leaving Rio not to have had any sickness except the carpenter. He is still in bed with congestion of the lung, typhus or some liver disease. It is hard to tell what the matter is. Anyway, he has been doctored for all three and is not getting a little better."

Sunday 28 Lat. S45.30, Long. W88 [off South Chile]
Fine weather all week, today has been beautiful. Tuesday we sighted the ship Erby *of Liverpool, from Victoria, B.C. with a load of salmon for London. Yesterday we killed our pig, dressed it weighed one-hundred-and-eight pounds, the largest one we have ever had. today had a fine spare rib for dinner, we had apple sauce, but squash had to take the place of turnips. Tomorrow I am going to make sausage meat and head cheese. We are sugar curing one 15 pound ham, more to experiment than anything else. If it is good we will cook it for Christmas. We were all weighed yesterday while the scales were out: Fred 207 pounds, Mr. Durkee 176, Ron 178, Forrest 60 and myself 138. I think we are all in good condition to go around the Horn. There is a new moon, this is a perfect night.*

Thursday 2 Dec. Lat. S50.1, Long. W97 [Maximum southerly point]
Today is my thirty-fifth birthday. I cannot realize it. The weather is still fine. Ron said tonight, 'If this is Cape Horn, I would like to be down here all the time.' I told him he had better say it easy, a gale can come up so quickly, but the sky looks fine and the barometer is high. I had good luck with my sausage meat and head cheese, have also made mincemeat and prepared fruit for the Christmas pudding. I use tinned apple and steak for mincemeat and when I make the pies I put little pieces of butter in to take the

place of suet. So you see I have been busy this week. Forrest has his lessons regularly, is getting on pretty well. He likes to talk about when we go home again, just as he used to about meeting Fred at the boat. He has written a letter to Santa Claus.

Sunday, 5 [Dec] Lat. S54.30, Long. W84 (coming around to Magellan Strait, eastern end.)
Weather still fine with strong westerly breeze. Forrest thought he would commence a letter today, but it was too rough for him. Yesterday I had to read all his letters over to him, he can almost read them himself. We have two fires going, the grate keeps the after cabin very comfortable in this weather, but in New York last winter Fred had to get a stove. Forrest is getting ready to go to bed. He doesn't see much fun in going to bed in broad daylight. Last night there was daylight in the sky all night long. The sun rises in the morning at 3.30, sets at 8.30.

Wednesday 8
Diego Ramirez Island bears S.W. by W about 20 miles. Passed about three miles on the north side of it at 7 p.m. We could see the land also to the north with the snow and the setting sun shining on it, a fine sight, but we have not the heart to enjoy anything, such a sad accident has happened.

Worrisome times at sea are inevitable for Grace Ladd and she learns to accept them. Seafaring families know well the high casualty rate among sailing ships. She is spared the horrors of strandings, shipwreck, and fire at sea, but there is a tragedy of a lesser sort: in the legendary Cape Horn weather off Diego Ramirez Island, a seaman falls from aloft into the sea, a sailor's greatest peril. Seamen were required to handle the numerous sails in all weather, and they sometimes fell from aloft to the deck or into the sea, both frequently fatal accidents. Because of the violent weather and the numbing cold of the sea, many ships simply sail on in such a situation rather than risk other men or the ship itself in the slight chance of a rescue. Grace refers us to Fred's journal recalling the incident in detail:

Monday, 6 December. Lat. 55.40' South, Long. 78.34' West (Near the eastern end of Magellan Strait).
At 6 p.m. blowing hard, as the starboard watch came on deck we hauled up the mainsail, all hands going aloft to make it fast. They furled it, all but the clews. Charlie Ritchie was the outside man on the yard. He was down on the footrope, sitting down, passing the gasket to the man inside of him holding the sail down. Somehow he lost his balance and slipped through the footrope and came down, hanging on the gasket. But it was a small rope and slipped through his hand so he fell into the sea.
As I saw him fall I rushed aft, calling to the man at the wheel to put it hard down. In the meantime I had thrown a lifebuoy; it fell about ten feet from him. He clutched

the log line, this slipped through his fingers. When he came to the log at the end it dragged him under. As he let go, the lifebuoy was close to him, in a few strokes he got it. We let go the upper halliards. I sent the boy and Otto Anderson aloft to watch him.

We took the covers off the gig, a splendid seaboat, and carried it across the deck cargo, throwing it over the rail. Mr. Durkee, the mate, and four men started from the ship. I gave them a tin of oil, the sea was very heavy and breaking badly, the boat would stand almost on end. After half an hour we lost sight of the boat. I wore the ship around at once, clewing sails up. Rain squalls shut in, blowing hard. As soon as I wore ship, I set the ensign, the signal agreed upon to recall the boat, but for an hour and a quarter we saw no sign of her.

I had given her up. One must go through this experience to realize how horrible is the feeling. Charles Collins was up in the crosstrees all this time trying to see the boat. At last he saw her right to windward as the squall cleared, steering for the ship. As they kept her right before the sea the boat would run as much as ten feet of herself right out of the water. They got under the lee of the ship and pulled alongside, the boat full of water, but no Charlie, he was gone poor fellow. Twice the water had been up to the thwarts as the sea broke over them. The oil saved them. It smoothed the water, kept the sea from breaking.

Poor Mr. Durkee. He said it was the hardest thing he ever had to do, to come back without him and he did not think it possible they could save themselves. They had lost sight of the ship in the squalls. When the men got back they were most exhausted, they were gone two hours. Never again would I risk a boat's crew in such a sea, it was only Providence that saved them.

Grace comments on the attempts to rescue the seaman Charlie:

I do not see how people can call sailors 'dogs'. If they could have seen the seas those brave men started out in with a small boat to try to save a man's life, I am sure they would never do so again. I did not go on deck until Fred said we had lost sight of the boat, but had hot fires and lots of hot water and blankets ready. It seemed so terrible, the sea was so dreadful. We have had nothing like it since we left, except in the hurricane, and not since have had exceptionally fine weather.

11 Dec
Fred's birthday, thirty-nine-years-old. We feel such a change in the climate, so much warmer. We can see plainly a small island thirty miles south of the Falklands. Thursday at 2 a.m. (broad daylight) passed eight miles south of Cape Horn, spoke the English ship Travancore from San Francisco for Queenstown out sixty days. On the ninth we had six ships in sight, all coming east. Yesterday, the tenth, the four-master Corinnea signaled and asked if Captain Ladd would take some mail for them. Of course we were pleased to do so. It was a lovely morning. We were just about thirty miles south of Staten Island, almost calm, nine ships in sight. At 6 a.m. Captain

McMillan and his passenger Mr. McGrady were alongside. It was pleasant meeting them again. They stayed with us about an hour, would not wait for breakfast, so we gave them hot chocolate. They brought us a piece of sparerib and were so disappointed when they found we had just killed a pig. Their steward had not made any sausage meat so I gave them about two pounds, also some mincemeat and books. Soon after he left us we got a breeze and separated as we wanted to go west of Falkland, but the wind headed us so we had to come east. I am glad we are headed for the river (Plate) as we would have made a very long passage home.

Christmas Evening Lat. S.40.30, Long. 55.20. (off Mar del Plata, Argentina)
We have thought of you all at home today and hoped you were having a very happy Christmas. Notwithstanding head winds and rain squalls, we have all enjoyed ourselves, although we have almost given up ever getting in. We are in a trap here. We have a strong current against us running three miles an hour, as that is all the Belmont can sail now, she is so dirty. The outlook is poor, this last week we have only neared our port 94 miles. I just heard the man at the wheel say she would not steer, so tomorrow we will lose some of that. Last evening Ron represented Santa Claus (Forrest's faith in him is as great as ever). The makeup was splendid. A sailor had made a fine large costume, with long new manilla rope wig and beard which was combed out. We were afraid Forrest would recognize Ron by his eyes, but we kept the light turned down on account of it hurting them. He changed his voice and acted it out splendidly; it was really fun for us all. We had ginger beer and sandwiches for him and again Santa was delighted with the tree we had ready for him to trim later. We had already put on the popcorn, tinsel and bags of nuts.

We invited all the sailors in to see the tree and gave them a cigar. The steward gave any who wanted a strong drink and for the others ginger beer. They had a good dinner. They were supposed to have a holiday instead of which they were hauling yards since 7 a.m. Ron had dinner with us, which we all decided could not have been better had we been in port. A beefsteak pie took the place of turkey.

30 Dec.
We ought to get in soon now, are only thirty miles from Buenos Aires, but have been stuck four times already in the silt: we are drawing more water than there is in the river. We came to anchor last evening in Montevideo Roads, could see the city plainly and all the ships at anchor. In a short time a pilot came off in a tug. Since then have been trying to get up here. It is a beastly place to get to. The poor sailors are completely tired out. Ron knows what real hard work is, but he has done well and our mail will make us forget everything tomorrow. I have written Arth and Flo. I know they are so anxious to hear of Ron and it would be so much longer to have to wait to hear from you. Fred and Forrest and Ron join in love to all.

Belmont crosses the River Plate, really a huge silt-laden estuary, to Colonia, a small port on the Uruguayan side, to load a cargo for Europe. As usual, Grace does not say what the cargo is. Her father is connected with the owners and probably knows anyway. It could have been tinned beef, hides, bones, or hay.

Colonia, Uruguay, 9 March, 1898
This is such a funny little place with about two-thousand inhabitants. Our vessel is moored half a mile from the town. We came over here on the 25th of February and for a week were the only ship. We get very little news here, there are no English people living in the town. Fred met a young Englishman the other day who came along to help Fred with his Spanish, said his name was Nino. He lived out in the country ("camp" they call it)—would bring his sisters in to see me and would like us to come and see them. We have a sail in our boat. There is nearly always a breeze so we enjoy boating. Forrest does the steering, he has not yet learned to swim well.

Half a mile below the town there is a nice farm. We land on the beach with our boat and get such lovely vegetables. One day we bought a turkey alive, the only one they had. We get milk every day and fresh eggs.

We met so many Yarmouth people there it seems that I must have been at home a few months ago instead of over a year. I was never in a port where so many captains had their wives. It was pleasant, every evening we met on some ship to play cards or if there was a piano, music. Ron was always called on to sing when they met here and was invited out with us several times.

We are all well, will be loaded in about two weeks. Go to Queenstown for orders. I shall write lots of letters on my way to make up for lost time here. All join in love.

Colonia, 19 March 1898
There is a man-o-war here now, the Beagle. The officers have been aboard. Fred, Forrest and Capt. Lovitt returned the call. They sent us fourteen partridge. They were a great treat. The American consul has invited Fred and I out to breakfast with some of the officers Wednesday morning. We will not be able to go as we are several miles out into deeper water to finish taking our cargo. It is not safe to come so far in a small boat. these pamperos blow up so quickly.

We have met several nice English families. The Eastons, mother and two daughters keep a boarding school. They have a very nice place and the children belong to ranchmen who live many miles inland. We think it would be a nice place to leave Forrest for a few years. These children all have their own ponies and learn to ride with a sheepskin, not a saddle. The Eastons came off one afternoon and a pampero came up so quickly they had to stay all night. There were six of them, three were seasick. It was very amusing, the Eastons were in great distress about their school. The children had a holiday, of course.

We expect to get away this week if the weather keeps fine. I will write again and send back by pilot. With love to all from all.

This is the last letter in the collection until May 12, 1899, when Grace starts a new letter as *Belmont* beats down the Australian coast from Shanghai to Newcastle. But Fred must finish the letter because Grace falls and breaks her right arm before being able to finish it herself. In October, *Belmont* and the Ladds arrive in Manila from Newcastle with coal. In Manila the Americans are mopping up after their invasion of the Philippines. From their anchorage Grace can see sporadic fighting and bombardment going on all around the bay.

The mails are irregular, nearly all coming by transports which are arriving every day. They anchor near us, the men sent on shore in lighters towed in. Sometimes they are kept on board two or three days, they have no places for them on shore. poor fellows, they are sick of the American army long before they get to Manila. Imagine, the Americans have had Manila for over a year, the bay is only twenty miles in content, yet they are fighting on all three sides of it. We hear the bombarding daily. At night we can see the burning villages. It looks as if this fighting may go on for years. It does not interfere with us at all except prevents us from getting a cargo. We are not able to get vegetables of any kind and the beef is very poor. Fortunately an English ship is here with a load of ice and frozen mutton. We are able to get some of these.

If the weather keeps fine shall be discharged in about ten days. Fred is going to put in a full set of sand ballast. We cannot form the least idea where we will go to load. You will probably know before we do. If the Pacific Coast, Fred has made up his mind to go home with me for a year, so I hope it will be there, but it will be better for the ship if it is Hong Kong or Singapore. Just now we feel pretty dusty with coal. It is dreadful, we are obliged to shut everything up and it is so hot. There is one consolation, there is not a happy looking captain here. They console one another going and coming in the launch. Some ships have been here one-hundred days.

The Ladds have decided to take a leave from the sea for a year when they reach Astoria, Washington, as orders come for them to proceed there rather than to Europe. Grace sells her piano in Manila and ships some belongings to New York.

Hong Kong, 10 November '99
We imagine how surprised you will be when you hear we are in Hong Kong. It is a surprise to ourselves. After leaving Manila we worked up close under the land to the north end of Luzon. As we opened up the Babuyan Channel got the full force of the northeast monsoon. The vessel could not work at all, neither tack nor wear. She drifted to leeward like a crab, would not sail at all. We felt pretty blue, I can tell you, the only other way was around Australia, fifteen thousand miles. Measured the distance to Hong Kong, found it two-hundred-and-ninety miles, concluded the only thing to do was come here and dock. From the time we squared our yards until we had arranged for the dry dock was just about forty-eight hours.

This is the last of the letters from Grace Ladd to her father covering her travels in *Belmont*. They stop briefly in Hong Kong in pleasant November weather while *Belmont's* bottom is cleaned, which increases her speed and allows a prompt passage across the Pacific to Astoria. Early in 1900, Grace is home in Yarmouth. Her letters to her father end in 1899 when the Ladds return home for a rest. Their daughter Kathryn arrives on the scene in 1903 or 1904 and her diaries tell of the next era. Kathryn describes their return to sea in *Belmont* in the South American trade—North America to the River Plate, which after the turn of the century is the last resort for Canadian square-rigged sailing ships. The dominant trade was American lumber to the Caribbean and Argentina. As a child, "K" makes seven voyages with her parents on this run and her description in the previous chapter is the only record we have of this period.

The Ladds finally leave *Belmont* and the sea at the outbreak of World War One. Unlike many long-time sailing families, they have kept a permanent home in Yarmouth, spending an active retirement in their home community and with friends they have maintained contact with. Grace Ladd comes across as a resilient individual, keen on seeing the world and meeting people, and ably supported by a competent and organized husband. Her letters home never dwell upon the problems of obtaining profitable charters in the declining years of sailing ships; she leaves such worries to the captains and owners, and details as whether the ship carries coal, sugar, lumber, grain, case oil, or ballast to the captain's log.

XIII
CORA HILTON'S WEDDING TRIP

Cora (Williams) Hilton, a bright, articulate woman, describes with humour her first ocean voyage for her family back home. Cora Hilton has been described by her daughter Margaret as bright-eyed and bright-faced, energetic, and an eager talker. She had long auburn hair, and was not very tall, but she stood up straight and bounced slightly when she walked. She was passionately interested in other people, wholesome, not intellectual and not particularly gifted, though she had a fine singing voice.

On March 16, 1898, Cora Williams and Captain Arthur Hilton were married. After their wedding in Yarmouth, the Hiltons proceed to New York via train and coastal steamer. As in the case of so many masters, Arthur times his marriage with his appointment to command in order to take advantage of the privilege of having his wife with him at sea. He will move up from mate to succeed his Uncle Bradford as master of the barque *Abyssinia*. To the newlyweds' surprise, however, Captain Bradford Hilton has decided to take just one more voyage and his daughter Marjorie has arrived to accompany him. Arthur will still be mate, but Cora must return home. She takes it in good humour and enjoys having a two-week solo honeymoon in New York while awaiting *Abyssinia's* departure. Nova Scotian seamen always had friends and relatives in New York and Marjorie helps Mrs. Hilton find her way around.

Eighteen months later, Bradford changes his mind again after arriving in South Shields, England; he quits the ship and turns the command over to Arthur. A message arrives in Yarmouth for Cora to join the new captain in Mobile, Alabama. As was common, they live in a boarding house, the Gales', in the southern port while their ship is loaded with a cargo of savoury southern pine.

Cora starts writing home to her mother and her younger sister Edna during this stay in Alabama.

Mobile, Oct. 10, 1899
My dear Edna
We are with the Gales. We came out last evening in time for supper—a good one, too—waffles and fried chicken. They are two very Southern dishes. Some of the ship-ping people sent their buggy down to the vessel for Arthur to drive me up to town in. The walk is not so very long, but near the railroads and an unpleasant part of the city and the dust was a good many inches deep. While he took the carriage to the office, I went into a drugstore and had a soda. Then we came out on the street railway, a ride of about three miles.

We have a large square room downstairs—the walls are just clapboarded and painted, no plastering in the house. The dining room and kitchen are away from the main part, though the same veranda goes around both. There is a herd of twenty three cows and nearly a half dozen horses. The family are very friendly and not much for dressing up about the house. I am "Miss Cora" and Arthur is "Arth"; Mrs. Gale is "Linnie" to everybody. There are three daughters and two sons and a deaf, elderly aunt who is always reading novels. They have two pet hens who wander at times in the kitchen, a dog, three cats and funny names for most of them. There are several negro servants, too.

Mobile
October 19, 1899
Tuesday morning after Jack Gale had delivered his milk he took me to ride on what they call the Shell Road. It runs along the bay under beautiful trees and is made of oyster shells. It is fine and hard and white and really, the only decent road I've been on so far. Arthur came home early yesterday and took me out there again with one of Jack's teams and today Jack is going to drive me somewhere else, so I shall see some of the country.

Sunday we went in the morning to a very homelike Methodist church with Mr. Bright, the grocer that Arthur does business with. We went afterward to dinner with him and had

Cora Hilton reclines in a hammock in fine weather at sea aboard Abyssinia. She took lessons in photography from a professional photographer in Yarmouth.

a very pleasant afternoon. His wife was very kind and we had quite an elaborate dinner, served in the best of style. I sang some for them and then we went to visit two cemeteries. I shall feel quite sorry to leave the people here at the house for they have taken me right in. They are very outspoken and different in some ways from homefolks but their hearts are all right and Cora is fine.

The streets are in a dreadful state from the work being done. I never saw such deep dust in my life, and so very fine. There is one quite fine street of residences and other nice houses scattered about, but the city looks rather ordinary, though odd to me because the architecture is so different from any I've seen before.

Bark Abyssinia
Nov. 4, 1899
My dear Mother
The vessel has been here in the mud now for a whole week and still the wind is the wrong way. But everybody predicts a pleasant voyage for us, as the hurricane season is past and there is likely to be plenty of wind and little calm weather. It bothers Arthur to be kept waiting so long, but it is something he cannot possibly help.

On Wednesday morning when we were leaving the Gales', we started out and were on board the tug which was to bring us to the vessel when the boarding master appeared. He said that two of three sailors he was to bring had skipped out. We had to go back as Arthur could not go down without them, and you can imagine how queer I felt going back to the house! They had a good laugh. I felt quite bad when I said goodbye to them that morning, for they were all so good to me.

The next morning we started again. We did not get on board the tug, for Arthur said he wanted to be where he could get after the tow-boat people, so back I went again. Friday morning we left for the third time and came all right. I did not bother to say goodbye the last time as twice is exhausting enough!

Arthur is going to send five dollars to you for Christmas and the same to his own parents. I want you to use it all for yourself and Daddy—get something pretty that you want.

Off Fort Morgan
Nov 7, 1899
Dearest Edna
At last we are out of the mud, thirty miles from Mobile and if our first mate was not sick and one of the sailors had not skipped out, we would be spreading our sails in the Gulf. The weather has been very fine, only the wind blew steadily from the north and as the channel down the mouth is shallow at any time, it is more than ever so with such a wind. The tugs have shoved us down here in little more than eighteen feet of water and the vessel draws twenty-two feet. So she has run along in the soft mud—four feet deep in it.

It has made it quite lively having the tugs coming down every day and working on her. One old captain and I grew quite chummy and he brought me a pet—a tiny alligator. Imagine me with such a thing! Well, we can easily get rid of it anytime we don't want him. He is about eight inches long and very tame and gentle but I'm not very much in love with him. He lives in a pasteboard box and eats crumbs and a little water.

Last night we came about fifteen miles and with all the signals to the tugs—first to go "hard aport", then "hard a starboard", then to "stop" and "back" and the straining and groaning of the towing cables, I did not sleep very well. But there were only two times that I heard any swearing.

Perhaps you would like our menu for one day

Breakfast: buckwheat pancakes, hot salmon and biscuit, hot potatoes, hot coffee.

Dinner: pea soup, baked fish with parsley, roast meat, sweet or Irish potatoes, salad, cranberry pie, bread and tea.

We do not often have fish and meat both, but you see we do not fare too badly.

Your loving sister Cora

Abyssinia has been heavily loaded and has settled its keel into the muddy bottom of the river. By blowing water out of Mobile Bay, the north wind adds to their difficulty in getting out. With the aid of tugs and dragging its keel, the ship gets away to sea with a full-paying load, a profitable gamble. Cora's younger sister, Edna, is sixteen and, in addition to receiving sisterly advice, she receives drawings, for example, of the chair Cora sits in the most. Cora fights off seasickness on this first voyage and never mentions it again.

Bark Abyssinia
Nov. 13, 1899
My dear Family
The walls of our little parlour are gently moving up and down. We either walk uphill or down in going from one side of the room to the other. We are very comfortable, though. We left Mobile Bay after dinner on Friday and have been travelling at the terrific rate of about three miles an hour ever since.

Today is Sunday. This easy rate of travel suits me very well, for I feel no inclination to be seasick. Coming out over the bar there was a good swell and it gave me a disagreeable headache, but no lumps in my throat. I did full justice to my supper.

Father would have enjoyed the performance of getting the sails up. So far I had not seen Arthur much in his commanding capacity, but when he got into his shoes somewhere and with his voice spoke from them in such stern tones, he seemed quite different to me. The mate is getting around all right now. He says he is a professional growler.

Today being Sunday Arthur and I are dressed up—I have on a clean shirtwaist and he has a tie on. Yesterday I did not feel very well so I read almost all day, lying on the sofa under the skylight and in the lounging canvas chair on deck. This morning sev-

eral of the sailors had their faces washed, celebrating Sunday. I think it must be their first wash in a week.

You should hear Arthur and me warbling together—of course we stick to hymns today, but other days we rake up all the old college songs we can remember and the little alligator comes out to hear. He went promenading last night out in the forward cabin and nearly got stepped on. He seems to like to wander at night and sleep through the day.

I have seen lots of porpoise and a school of flying fish went by this morning—they were not near as large as porpoise and some of them jumped four or five feet high, I should think. The splashing of the water and the shine of there bodies was very pretty. I see lots of odd jellyfish, too.

It is hard to realize that we are a long way from land, sailing in the Gulf of Mexico. So far we have gone so quietly I have not heard much talking in the rigging or splashing of the waves along the vessel's sides, but there is plenty of time for any and every kind of experience between here and Buenos Aires.

Nov. 21
A week is more than gone and so is the alligator—overboard, he did not thrive—and so is most all that I have eaten!

On Monday I did our washing assisted by Arthur and had it rolled up that afternoon, ready to iron on Tuesday. Iron on Tuesday I did not, though, for I felt very much upset and all this last week I have spent most of the time on my back. I have got up and dressed and been out on deck every day, though.

We have been pitching into a head sea and my head and stomach rebelled against getting used to it. But yesterday I took dinner and supper at the table and now am coming round very well, though I do not feel very energetic yet. I was not violently sick but felt decidedly uncomfortable all the time that I was not asleep. Arthur has waited on me, dressed and undressed me, braided my hair and trotted in my little toast, fixing me as comfortably as anybody could. It has been tedious to Arthur as well as to me, this tacking back and forth against head winds. It's such slow work. We had a shadowy glimpse of Cuba in the distance two or three times.

Arthur had to block my bed up and when they tacked in the night he would have to take out and put in blocks to keep me from sliding out. He has taken the little room Marjorie had as he has to be up quite often in the night and I am not to be disturbed. We have read "Martin Chuzzlewit" together this week and I have read, too, Francis Burnett's "His Grace of Osmonde." We have the sequel, to—"A Lady of Quality". I'd like Edna to read them. It is almost a month since we have had home news.

Saturday morning I had flying fish for my breakfast and it was real good. It is small and something like a smelt, not many bones and the meat white and sweet. Two of them flew on deck and the mate gave them to the steward to cook for me. The mate is having another attack of fever and chills and will persist in crawling out on deck. He has the idea that Arthur thinks he is shamming sick. He told me after the first attack that he was never intended to be sick as he could not bear to stay in bed, but it would be much more sensible if he would.

When I come home you need not be surprised to see me promenading on the side of the roof, for the ship lays over so that walking seems almost impossible. There are three loose pieces of furniture here in the aftercabin and first they go sliding to one side and then at the next tack, to the other. It is quite funny sometimes - they seem alive. I tried playing the organ one morning with one foot braced against the easy chair, blowing with the other, but it was rather a strained position.

I have not commenced to study navigation yet, but I watch her position on the chart and it does look such a long way to go that at this rate it must take a long while.

Monday was not fine so we did the washing Tuesday. That is, Arthur did it nearly all. I did the heavy looking on. This week we have had a mixture of weather but we got the clothes dry and ironed on Wednesday. It is precious little ironing that I do. I heat the irons on the oil stove in the bathroom.

I have a sketch of the chair that I have spent so much time in and Arthur and I have been reading some Tennyson and "Betsy Bobbit", one of Samantha Allen's books. Sundays we read those books of Sheldon's that Mother Hilton sent to Arthur.

Yesterday I had felt a little uncomfortable and after three in the afternoon I got some nuts and Arthur and I braced ourselves on the floor and ate nuts for a while. Then I took some exercise by sliding across the cabin on my heels and did a few calisthenics braced against the wall. A few minutes after I had to run quick to lose the nuts and part of my dinner. Arthur rolled on the bed laughing at me. He says I am seasick the funniest way. Well, I laughed myself and half an hour afterwards ate my supper.

These last two and three evenings I have been watching the phosphorus in the waves as they break under the vessel's sides. The foam looks so beautiful with starlike lights breaking all through it. We have had some beautiful sunsets, too.

This week we have had large steamers pass very near us. The one two nights ago came altogether too close and Arthur had to stop the vessel. It sounded quite exciting and she really had no business to run right across our vessel's bows. We laid over so that when I went to hang up my nightgown yesterday morning I found myself walking right up the wall!

So far we have had all sail on almost all the time. The mate, poor old man, has been sick about half the time since we left so Arthur has double duty to perform. We are in the same time zone as you tonight. Arthur and I have had our sing. I practice days when I can sit at the organ and no one is asleep. Very often I close my eyes and realize that I cannot possibly get to you and that so much could happen without my knowing anything about it. But we won't worry, for what's the use of that?

Monday Dec. 11 1899
Well, we have crawled across as near Africa as we have to and since yesterday after-

noon have been going south. I find it very interesting to watch the charts and the day's sailing from one noon to another. If Edna cares to, she can look up the way we take. Come from Mobile out of the Gulf by Florida, then north as far as North Carolina - we were about five hundred miles from Yarmouth one day—then go east halfway and more, I think, to Africa, then south. It seems such a roundabout way to me, but I am beginning to understand something about the tracks in the ocean, which are like well-known roads. Though I am not studying navigation I take down the time from the chronometers for Arthur.

The mate has been sick again for a week. He has been so careless, going out just after getting over a chill, that he has not been able to shake the fever. He is improving, but is very thin and weak and does not come out of his room at all. He is too old anyhow to be going to sea—nearly sixty.

Arthur called me up to see the vessel go. There was a fine breeze and she made a lot of foam around her bows. We have had all kinds of weather this last week. Saturday it poured all day and towards night was very disagreeable. There was a tremendous swell on. After I went to bed one or two seas came in and some water rushed right down the companionway that is our front stairs. The door was open. Arthur was lying on the sofa and he jumped up and soon had the water mopped up. It did not come into the cabin.

I have not lost a meal this week. Even a head sea and wind does not affect me. Today we have had rain again.

I have studied French, drawn a little, painted a little, played and sung, had a nap after dinner and Arthur read some to me. We have been reading Trilby for light literature this week. We read Sheldon's books, the ones his mother sent Arthur, on Sunday.

I make tea nearly every afternoon for Arthur. I don't eat between meals and I drink milk and water. I don't eat much meat. I like the steward's hash, and beans, peas and corn you know I like. Oh, we have a very good variety, well-served. I have got Arthur's mending about done, though it is likely there will be some every week. I should like a "hunk of totolate tate wif fossin" on it. Your loaf of fruit cake is all gone and we are on the other, which is a little dry.

Very lovingly, Cora L. W. Hilton

Bark Abyssinia
Sunday Dec. 14, 1899.
Dear, dear all of you,
And I wish you were all here at this very minute, though where you would all stow at night time is the question. We are having a quiet day, reading most of the time. We are laying over pretty well, which is nothing unusual. I am getting used to it, but you would find it rather difficult to do much walking. I walk on the after deck—the weather side between the house and the rail—so whichever way she sways I am easily braced and I remind myself of some caged animal, pacing back and forth. It is not easy for me to take exercise enough, but I do considerable walking.

We have had contrary winds now for nine days. We want to go south—instead, we are making north east, much to Arthur's disgust. It really seems as if we must make a long voyage. It is worse for Arthur than anybody else, but I think of you—I know if we do not arrive in good time you will get a little worried and I hate to have that happen. Arthur says it is some consolation to have me here through the tedious days and really I am very contented. We have good times together. It is a good thing that I am not one of the homesick kind and I am thankful not to be so.

This week we could not wash until Friday. We have real big washings for so small a family, but I don't dread wash day a bit, especially when there is plenty of water to use. We caught a lot this week. Yesterday we had one of our rare days when a chair would stay in the middle of the floor if you put it there without sliding. I really enjoyed doing the ironing.

I am getting brown and burned, but I don't look bad yet—it is impossible not to get tanned, though I wear my sunbonnet. Imagine yourself wearing a lawn sunbonnet in December!

Our old mate is on his feet once more, though we almost feared at one time that he would not pull through.

Monday evening

Again the mate is in bed with another chill and Arthur is tramping about overhead in the rain. I have been up, too, but my feet got wet, so I have come down and dried off. We thought this morning that it would be fine all day, so we did our washing. It got plenty of sun and wind but some will have to go out again, as it had to be brought in before it was dry. I washed the cushion covers and the curtains we have over the lounge at sea. They were sadly in need of it. This afternoon I made a new case for one of the cushions and studied the verb "aimer."

There are several stories on board that Marjorie left. I have read one—that is, enough to understand it, but I have not a dictionary, so shall wait until we can get one before attempting the others. We are going to study Spanish so we will have a little knowledge of it before we get to Buenos Aires. Arthur knows quite a bit now. It is considered an easy language but if I get French and Spanish mixed, it will be funny. I am reading a book on English painters by Ruskin which is quite interesting. We vary these high-sounding employments by a fight every now and then. I don't object as the exercise is good for me!

We have a fair wind now for which we are thankful. There are none of the usual feelings as far as gift-receiving and giving goes, except that Flo remembered me with a parcel. I don't know yet what it is.

Dec. 24

Well, we are now in the tropics and going up and down lazily in the swells. They make the sails flap back and forth and the rigging groan and creak. I have dressed up in my old brown silk-waist for Arthur's benefit; he admires it very much.

We have had a splendid run this week, doing over a thousand miles. In one twenty-four hours we sailed over two hundred miles. It was grand to watch her go! She left such a fine wake, all a pale blue-green and quite a change from the ordinary leaden color of the water. There was so much foam along the sides! She laid over very much but nobody seemed to mind. But we could not stand still in the cabin—it was all sliding or climbing.

It was on Tuesday that the wind commenced to blow strong from the north east and by Wednesday the waves were up pretty well. About the middle of the forenoon I went down into my bedroom and suddenly I heard a rushing sound. Turning round, I saw a large stream of water pouring in the port just a little to one side of the head of the bed. Before I could get up to close it, another dose came in and Arthur came rushing down expecting to see me flooded out, I think. It is quite funny to have the ocean pouring into your bedroom, but there was not much after all and we soon got our mattress aired and dried and the springs cleaned and away back under the bed where some cleaning was needed, anyway. There was nothing wet but the bedclothes, fortunately. I went up on deck shortly afterwards to try and walk, though that was a little difficult, for I was first on my ear (almost) and then bracing with both hands—walking with hands and feet, you see!

It was rather awe-inspiring to watch the way the waves broke, almost as they might on a beach but so much higher. An extra big one climbed and broke against the side so high that quite a stream fell on the deck and I got the benefit of some heavy salt foam. For just a few minutes I was one of the "salt of the earth", for it went inside my rugby coat collar and ran down my neck, front and back. I was neither hurt nor scared, though the man at the wheel made a pitying noise as I went down below, but he grinned, too—my head did look funny all wet. We ought to be having a steady breeze now for we are in the trade wind regions. But Arthur thinks from the barometer (which is his little god) that the wind is farther north. The big swell tells us there must have been wind somewhere.

I am doing Edna's 'sleeping Cupid' and I have a pretty good idea of the "four conjugations." We have been reading aloud Dumas' "Taking the Bastille." I wish we had the "Tale of Two Cities" here to compare with it.

The steward killed the hen this morning for tomorrow's dinner. We are to have it fricasseed, I believe, and mince pie for breakfast. We'll have some nuts to crack, so you see, as far as our stomachs are concerned, we might be envied by a good many. I would like to think I could have Mother's mince pie, though, and more than anything, just the pleasure of looking at you.

Of course we wonder all about you and yet it is not much good, for I suppose I shall know it all in time, this being my first experience of being out of reach of post offices. Arthur and I are both in good health, both getting fat. How different your Sunday must have been from ours! I suppose this morning Mr. Braithwaite preached a Christmas sermon and I do wonder if the chimes sang an anthem or just the Christmas hymns, which are certainly better than most anthems.

One day two weeks ago as I was walking—it was a quiet day with a long swell—I saw the boy at the wheel suddenly fly into the air and land on the other side of it with a thud. It made me weak all over, but he was up like a flash and in his place again and he laughed—could not seem to get over the fun of it. As soon as I saw he was not hurt it struck me funny, too, he looked so lively swung end-up in the air. That is something (picture drawn of boy flying over wheel) the way he went. He did not get caught a second time.

We are quite happy this last day of the old year, for after a really disheartening week, we have as beautiful weather as heart could desire, though Arthur would like more breeze to make up for lost time. Still, if this could only hold I think he would not complain. We have just dawdled along the last seven days with almost a calm and what little breeze there was, a contrary one. I dreaded to have Arthur make his calculations—he usually puts her on the chart before dinner and when it is so discouraging the meal is rather funereal. After dinner he is pretty sure to be more cheerful, though it may be in rather a desperate way. He looks just fine today in a white suit. He shaves only once a week and toward the latter end looks a little rough, so Sunday is a special day in every way. Just at present he is on the floor munching nuts and raisins, assisted by a very handsome fruit knife and nut pick combination which we discovered was Flo's Christmas gift to us.

We have just been spooning—oh yes, we have a dose of that every day and flourish very well on it! We get up early mornings now and step into our tub of salt water and have a rub down. The weather is so warm that the chill feels good.

While I think of it, I want to tell Edna to try very hard and wash her hair every week. Mine was full of dandruff when I came on board but my scalp is almost clear of it now. I use very little soap, but quite a lot of rubbing with my fingers. I don't see why washing your head should be injurious any more than washing the face and I want Edna's hair to keep growing and be always as beautiful as it is now.

Schools of large and small fish have been going past the last day or so and the sailors caught two or three the other day. The one we had tasted very nice indeed but no one knew the name of it.

Yesterday afternoon I held the wheel for a few minutes and came to the conclusion that steering was quite a particular job. I think the ship's course would be funny under my hands, so fashion, [wavy line drawn] though Arthur says I brought a fair wind. It is so warm now that I want to dress as lightly as possible and we do not need even a sheet over us at night. I do my walking just after breakfast, before and after supper.

Our old mate still has severe ague chills and fevers every few days. He thinks perhaps he will not live long. I do hope he will not die with us.

Yesterday I finished Edna's Cupid and he is now sleeping quietly, pinned up on the wall. I shall try and do several nice crayon drawings to have in case I want to make any gifts in port of that kind.

We had a lovely Christmas day away off here in the Atlantic, the warmest one I ever spent, surely. The dinner was fine and we had Flo's little gift to make us remember that part of the day. I wonder what you all had and what Margaret had from Joe. Perhaps you are writing me all about it this very day.

I just heard the second mate calling "Victor." He is a tall Norwegian, just a young fellow, and he is always missing. He is the only sailor I ever hear called for and we smile now whenever we hear his name called. We have all old sails up now - so many patches! I am going to sketch some of them.

The rats are more than thick and they won't be caught. They serenade us every night and I watched one trying to get out of the port at the foot of my bed yesterday morning. I have not yet had them run over me.

Sunday afternoon just a little after two o'clock, January 7
We are at last "over the line" and glad enough, too. Arthur says we shall be out at least thirty days yet. Pretty soon now I shall let myself look forward to the letters awaiting me. There is scarcely a day passes but we see one or more sailing ships, but we have only been near enough to speak to the little French vessel I think I wrote you of. I had hoped a little that we would meet Herbert's vessel, the Arizona, but of course we were not very likely to do so. We are in very warm weather, though they tell me it will get warmer yet. I have not suffered much so far. It makes the perspiration run, though.

We said goodbye to potatoes this week but I don't care, for I'm not so very fond of them. They lasted longer than Arthur expected—he will miss them.

My week's work is not worth telling of and now I must finish making Arthur's cup of tea as the water is boiled. He does not take it as a regular thing and I do not take any at all. I do wish the drinking water was colder and an ice-cream would set me right up.

Arthur has to be mate and captain as Mr. Alkin is very weak. He is a little better than he was the first of the week, but he is only a shadow and does not come out to the table yet. Arthur and I are usually just by ourselves, you see. He works quite hard some days, but he has not had to lose much sleep. He seems fated to do double duty.

We often wish we had Edna here and Arthur says, tell her to be a good girl and someday if all goes well, she shall have a ride with us. I think the first time we come near enough home we will try to have her come. We could have such fine times together! Anyway, it will not hurt to build our little castles in the air and it would be a good thing for her.

Monday 11 am Jan 15
Well, my people of the North, we of the South have had an ideal week. The water has been a glorious blue, we have sailed a straight course and the breeze has made us fairly comfortable. We are almost under the sun now and I am wearing the same clothes that I do at home in summer and do not very often feel them burdensome. That is because I am not working hard, probably. I did start to dress with as little as possible, but

Arthur suggested that as I would have to dress to go about in port, it might be as well to use myself to it—a very wise idea.

Last Monday you should have seen me perspiring while doing the washing! It ran down over my eyes and cheeks and neck in streams, but that made the heat easier to stand. I must give you a sample list of our weekly wash: sheets and pillowcase, sometimes two. Arthur's suit of underclothes and mine. Two or three pairs stockings. Half a dozen towels. Nightgown and pajamas. Shirtwaist or cotton dress. Two negligee shirts for Arthur and some part of a white suit. Sundry small articles.

So you see, there is one day in the week that I earn my salt. The ironing: pillowcases, negligees, shirtwaist and white suit. A very small part of the wash!

You will not have to wait now more than a month before you hear of our arrival.

We are reading Alton Locke together and I am reading "Peveril of the Peak." The mate seems quite well again.

Well, this week has gone and we hope that another Sunday will find us at or very near our destination. We are now on our eleventh week, quite a long voyage for my first, but it does not seem long as I look back on it. You will no doubt be thinking now about me and wondering how my first experience of regaining the land after being so long "rocked in the cradle of the deep" will affect me. It seems to me that it will be more than delightful.

Today the weather is very calm and raining and so I have to stay below, which I do not like. I think I must be getting fat and feel as well as can be—I'm brown enough! It will be hotter on land than it is here, though. The breeze this week has kept us very comfortable. We have had perfect weather and if all going to sea was so pleasant, everybody would want to live part of their time at sea. We are likely, though, to have it more changeable now until we get in.

I have about finished my picture, "The Shepherdess" and now I am wondering who will get it.

One of the sailors caught a beautiful fish yesterday—it is called "albacore" and weighed about fifteen pounds. We had it fried for supper—some of it, that is. It was very nice, too, though not equal to halibut.

I am beginning to look forward to drinking real cow's milk and eating strawberries—how does that sound? I expect Margaret and Edna would scarcely like, on these cold winter mornings at home, to jump into the bathtub half full of cold water and lie down and splash around as I do, but you see, it is summer here.

Jan. 30

Well, we are about sixty miles from Buenos Aires and if the Lord sends us a fair wind will be there tomorrow. It will be so delightful to arrive safely there! Arthur is so anxious about his damaged mainmast that he has been very serious so I shall be glad for his sake, too.

We have had very calm weather coming up the river, which has made it a tedious trip. There is plenty of water in this river but sometimes a strong wind blows it out. It is so spread over in some places that we are likely to stick unless the wind blows the right way.

I have opposite to me at table an old Italian pilot—he eats much and noisily. But I don't mind that—I shall write next on land, I hope.

Lovingly, C.L.W.H.

In due course, *Abyssinia* arrives in Buenos Aires, anchoring among other sailing ships in the old port that lies in a small river mouth called La Boca. Cora has an active time here, joining a group of other sailing women on outings while the pine is unloaded, the cracked mainmast replaced, and a cargo of grain loaded for Delagoa Bay, Port Elizabeth, South Africa. The Boer War was proving a boon to shipping.

From Buenos Aires to South Africa, the next run will be all the way to New-castle, Australia. As it becomes apparent that a new member is soon to join the family, Cora leaves the ship at Delagoa and returns home by steamer. Early in 1901, *Abyssinia* reaches Manila when the cable arrives, "Child born, mother and child both doing well." Frustrated at not being given a clue as to whether it is a boy or a girl and mindful of the cost of intercontinental cables, Captain Hilton sends a one-word message "Which?" The answer returns: "Girl." The girl is Marion, the first of the three Hilton daughters. The ship makes a particularly slow passage to London with a cargo of heavy Australian timber, worrying Cora who has come with the baby to join it. The family sails on in their seaborne home, *Abyssinia*.

Arthur Hilton commands *Abyssinia* over some 100,000 sea miles before the ship, still in good condition, is sold to an Italian buyer. The Hiltons arrive home in June 1904, to a great welcome by both families. There is a happy summer off, during which Margaret Emily is born. That autumn, Arthur Hilton goes back to sea, for the first time in command of a steamship because there is now little demand for deep-sea masters in sail.

XIV
FROM SAIL TO STEAM

CORA AND ARTHUR HILTON, COMBINING TWO OLD SEAFARING FAMILIES, TELL
OF THEIR LIFE BRIDGING THE TWO ERAS OF SEAFARING: SAIL AND STEAM.

A s the twentieth century arrives, the steam ship rapidly replaces
the sailing ship, effectively ending the era of family life at sea.
Voyages become shorter and more regular; the new breed of
owners is less sympathetic to the idea of the ship as a home. East coast Canadian
masters who have enjoyed the company of their families aboard retire at an accel-
erated rate, while the few who make the transition to steam move over to British
companies. One major Canadian ship operator successfully makes the change to
steam—William Thomson & Company of Saint John, New Brunswick builds up
a fleet of fifteen steam freighters in tramp service around the turn of the century.
One of Thompson's senior captains continues to take his wife and daughters to
sea with him, a rare exception at a time when the home-built Maritime square-
riggers are gone.

The sea-going daughters of Arthur and Cora Hilton of Yarmouth, Nova Scotia,
have preserved the seafaring letters and diaries of their parents. The family story illus-
trates the end of an illustrious line of seafarers and the end of an era in which Yarmouth throve as a sailing centre.

Among the numerous multi-generational seafaring families from the Yarmouth
area were the Williamses and the Hiltons, who came together in the marriage of
Arthur Hilton and Cora Williams. The Williams family traced their line back to
1617, when the first Williams arrived in Plymouth, Massachusetts in the ship
Fortune. Arthur Hilton was a fifth generation sea captain as was his brother Herbert;
both were the sons of Captain Stilson R. Hilton and Marion (Hilton) Hilton,
and the nephews of Captain Bradford Hilton. All sailed the seas for the prominent Yarmouth owners William Law & Company.

At the age of seventy-nine, Arthur Hilton recorded for his three daughters memoirs of his life as a child at sea with his parents and, in turn, his own rise in the profession.

My father, following the family tradition, was a shipmaster and, in the custom of the time, took his family to sea with him as often as was convenient. Consequently, my very early childhood memories are of playing around Chebogue and on ship's decks and in ships cabins and travelling with my mother and brother and sister to far places of the earth.

The first ship of my father's that I remember was the Annie M. Law. She was built in 1875 and he sailed her until 1879. Some of that time I must have been at sea. I can faintly remember the family arriving home from a long voyage and not having a key to the house. I was told to go over to my grandmother's and get it. On the way I met a little girl who asked me, "What little boy are you?" I countered with the question, "What little girl are you?" It turned out that she was my sister Julia coming with the key, so we joined forces and returned together.

The year 1879 I remember quite well as that was the year father left the Annie Law to come home and be ready to take out the new ship that was being built for him, the William Law. He was home several months that time and I remember my mother had quite a few parties, chiefly brother captains and their wives. We children used to love to hear the captains talk and would sneak to the head of the stairs after we were supposed to be in bed to hear them. Great stories there were of storms and shipwreck and other high adventure.

I remember being bitterly disappointed at being left at home on the day the new ship was launched. Father had hired a horse and carriage for the trip to Tusket, but so many others wanted to go that there was no room for me. I have always felt sore about it since it would have meant a lot to me and they could have crowded in a kid of eight somewhere. Well, the ship was duly launched and towed around to Yarmouth where she was rigged. When she was all ready she sailed for New York with a full crew and my mother, brother Herbert and myself on board.

The William Law was a fine looking ship, first class for her time and father was very proud of her. The accommodations for the master and his family were quite roomy and comfortable. There was the forward cabin (dining room), after cabin, and off that to starboard, the captain's room and a smaller stateroom where whatever children were brought along were put, and on the port side an office and a bathroom. An after companionway (from the deck) was provided for the captain's use and another entrance from the main deck was used by everyone else. The cabins were handsomely decorated and painted out in white enamel and, with the furniture, it looked very homelike. Off the forward cabins were storerooms and the staterooms for the officers. The rest of the ship's company were housed in the forward house in which there were also the galley and carpenter shop. Everything was shipshape and tidy, with a place for everything.

I can remember the day we sailed from Yarmouth though it is seventy-four years ago. The departure of a new ship was quite an event in the life of the town and a big crowd of people had gathered to witness it. A tug took a line from our bow and we slowly left the wharf and followed the channel out by Cape Forchu. As soon as we were clear of the cape the sails were set and she must have presented the watchers with a handsome picture with everything set. It was a fine fall day with just enough wind to keep the sails full. We were three days getting to New York where we were to load a full cargo of grain for, I think, Antwerp.

The crew consisted of twenty-three men all told. The first mate, Mr. Kinney, was an elderly man who had been a master and lost his ship and had to accept demotion. He was a thoroughly competent officer, but bad tempered and glum. The second mate, Mr. Elliot, had never been more than a second mate nor expected to be. He was a fine sailor man and good tempered and jolly. The Bos'n was my Uncle Amos, my father's brother. He went to sea for some years, mostly with his brothers, but never got above second mate. His ambition was to get a little money and farm his father's old place. The steward, John Troop, was quite a character. He was first class in his job and always got more than the usual pay. He had been with father in the Annie M. Law and left her to go in the new ship with his old captain. He was very good to us children and when he served afternoon tea to our elders he would cut a thick slice of new bread, anoint it generously with butter then spread it with good Demerara molasses for us. I have never tasted anything so good since.

During the years he commanded the William Law father took mother to sea with him most of the time and usually one or two of us children. Julia, being the oldest, was mostly left at home on account of her schooling, but we boys, in the early years were taught by our mother when away. Every morning after breakfast we got our books out and worked away at lessons. When we would come home and resume school we generally seemed to be able to take our place with our age groups. When I was about twelve it was decided that I ought to stay home and attend school regularly. From then on I went to school, first at Chebogue and later at Yarmouth where we moved when I was fourteen. There were always plenty of books to read. I remember reading all of Dickens at a very young age, and with our reading and the things we saw and heard in our travels, our early education was probably as well looked after as the most of our contemporaries.

During the years we children went to sea we must have met a lot of bad weather and experienced some severe storms, but they do not seem to have made much impression on us. We felt we were in a very sound ship that could take care of herself in any kind of weather provided there was sea room. I remember some anxious times when near the land in thick weather. We had no radio or radar in those days and had to depend a lot on dead reckoning.

We children were sternly required to keep quiet in the vicinity of the officers' rooms when they might be asleep during the day, but in the dog watches we were allowed a little more noise. We were supposed to stay aft and play around the poop deck, but there were always so many more interesting things going on forward that it was hard to keep away from them. I used particularly to like to go in the carpenter shop and watch *the carpenter at work. I also liked to watch the sailors at work and picked up a lot of knowledge about their work that was useful to me later.*

I don't remember that we were ever bored or tired of life at sea though it seems on looking back rather a dull life for children. We always clamoured to be taken away and then were sad when we left home. Although there was no refrigeration in those days and not so many varieties of canned food to be had I can't remember that we found the food very monotonous. One thing, in my early days we always sailed in the North Atlantic and did not make very long voyages. My father usually had a very good steward. I think John Troop sailed with him six or seven years. He finally left because he married a second young wife and wanted to take her to sea with him as stewardess. Father was afraid it might not work out well and refused to take her.

We were supposed to work at our lessons every week day, but when something special was going on, like meeting other vessels, or entering or leaving port, lessons often went by the board. When in port, there was always so much going on that lessons did not fare too well either. We used to be taken ashore on shopping or sightseeing expeditions. Usually there were other ships in port with whom we were acquainted and there would be visiting back and forth with quite frequent parties. I think, on the whole, we enjoyed life nearly as much as most children.

I left school for good at sixteen and worked for a couple of years in a woodworking factory in Yarmouth. At eighteen I had made up my mind to make the sea my profession and signed on as carpenter in the ship Asia.

William Law is lost on the shores of Cape Breton on a voyage when Captain Stilson Hilton is on sick leave and to get a ship he likes, he leaves the Yarmouth owners to work for Taylor Brothers. The Taylors run a Saint John firm, all of whose ships' names began with the letter "A." Captain Hilton takes command of *Asia*, a fine, full-rigged ship of 1398 tons. Sailing with his father, sometimes his mother too, and with his uncle Captain Bradford Hilton, Arthur makes his way up the ladder as an officer. His voyages take him to remote ports like Calcutta and Shanghai. Fortunately his mother is with him when he contracts typhoid fever on a trip to Padang, Java. She nurses him back to health.

In September 1896, after a couple months of study, Arthur receives his master's certificate. Staying with the same shipping company means waiting for a command; in the meantime, he sails as mate in the barque *Abyssinia*. In March of 1898 he takes time off to go home, where he marries Cora Williams. He writes:

We were married March 16th, 1898, and went on to New York together where my ship was loading for another South American voyage. We had two weeks together there before the ship sailed and your mother left me and had a lovely time finishing her honeymoon by herself, visiting various relatives in New England before returning home.

Cora's husband sails off on the usual tramping runs about the world as mate to his Uncle Bradford in *Abyssinia*. In July of the next year, while in South Shields on the Tyne and readying for departure towards Mobile, Alabama, Bradford decides to retire, leaving Arthur to take over in his first command. For Arthur, not yet twenty-eight, life looks quite rosy: as master, he has the privilege of taking his wife to sea, so he asks her to join him in Mobile.

We duly arrived at Mobile and began loading our cargo. I had written your mother to come on and join me there, and as soon as she heard of my arrival she came along. We were in port about a month and met a few people so it wasn't too dull for her. Finally we sailed on our long trip and your mother proceeded to get very sick. I nursed her the best I knew but she could not eat and kept getting thinner and paler till she had me frightened. Finally, however, she got over it and was never seriously seasick again.

GLIMPSES OF LIFE UNDER SAIL BY CORA WILLIAMS HILTON

Cora Hilton has left us her picture of family life in a square-rigged sailing ship at the end of the nineteenth century, the twilight of Nova Scotia's great age of sail. Comforts and food have improved by the 1890s.

We reached our house aboard ship by the after gangway which led to our cabin, a good-sized room, lighted by a port and skylight overhead. This also lighted the messroom.

There was a well-equipped bathroom just at the foot of and to one side of the gang-way. Our stateroom, with two ports, opened off the main cabin, and a smaller one opened out of the captain's room for any member of the family, a child or maybe a sister making a voyage with us. Our large stateroom had a bed fastened firmly to the wall. There was a good chest and places for clothes.

In the cabin there was a large desk under the skylight where the charts were spread. A large easy chair stood beside that: there were other chairs and a small cabinet organ. We liked to sing. All furniture was, of course, made fast to the floor. We could have some pictures and ornaments around in port, but when ready to sail, we stowed away anything that could be rolled around or

Marion Hilton learning to walk on a deck in constant motion assisted by her father, Captain Arthur Hilton.

broken. The rooms were painted in white and gold. The messroom was forward of the sa-loon and off it were rooms for the first mate and steward and the steward's pantry. The messroom table had benches on either side. In rough weather the mess table had fiddles, wooden squares fastened on the table to keep our dishes from sliding away, spilling soup or whatever, and even then you tipped your plate to suit the roll of the ship.

We woke mornings to the noise of the sailors washing the decks—the ship had to be kept clean. The steward then came to our room with early coffee, in good stout ship's ware—we kept our special china to use in port—and strong enough to float a log, as the saying goes.

After breakfast in the messroom—cereal, toast and coffee—it was up on deck, the captain to take the sun and find out how far we have travelled, the missus and child to watch the sea and birds, the small ones mother Carey's chickens, and the large albatross riding the waves. There was sewing, always mending. We read and wrote letters. The ocean highways were not crowded, but now and then we could see another ship and try to recognize the line or where she might be bound.

The captain's wife had her hands full if there was a small child to watch. Children are like little monkeys, running and climbing everywhere. The open stanchions through which a small child might so easily slip were a constant danger and we certainly did not lack for exercise. We tried tying one small daughter with a good length of rope to the binnacle light, but she simply wound herself up, then sat and howled—no tying up for her. But we never lost one overboard! With a lively wind the seas sometimes came

Marion Hilton and dog "Fiddle" against a backdrop of a mass of billowing sails aboard Abyssinia.

Marion Hilton tries out binoculars on the deck of Abyssinia at sea. These early amateur photographs were only possible in fine weather.

washing aboard and ran down the after gangway leading into our cabin. Then the steward would come along to mop us up.

A fine day in the tropics, running with a good breeze. The so-called trade winds, the ship heeling gently, the lovely blue of the sea under a sunny sky and the waves curling over with a bit of lacy foam left little to be desired. On such days there was likely to be an old sailor sitting up on top of the house with his palm and needle sewing on a new sail. The captain was an expert at drafting and cutting the canvas sails. In light weather the older sails were used and when hit by a sudden squall, blew to pieces. A new sail had to be bent on so there had always to be a new "suit of clothes" in the lockers. I have a picture in my mind of a small daughter telling all of a long story to an elderly mate, sitting side by side up on the bridge on a fine afternoon and I can almost see the ears of the man at the wheel trying to hear that tale. (Comment from Phyllis, the daughter in question, 'I remember that. Peterkin and then Little Hare, while he whittled and made me a toy. I think it was a windmill sort of thing.')

In fine weather the outside called so we took whatever sewing or mending we were doing, and books and playthings, and only went below when the bell rang for dinner. A lot of contentment at sea depends on the cook. When we had a poor cook, even with a good salt sea appetite, meals were, alas, nothing to look forward to, but if we had a good cook we could welcome the sound of the dinner bell. In those days there was no ice chest, not so many good things came in cans. There was very little variety. The pea soup, the first course, was usually good. There were no nice jellied desserts in hot weather. Instead there would be dried apple pie, raisin plum duff, a boiled affair, or a gray mixture called a bread pudding. These seemed to be the favorites with cooks. I occasionally had the ingredients brought to the messroom to make a cake or a special dessert and we took packages of dates and tinned cookies to help when the meals were too unappetizing. We had one steward who hatched some chickens. He had sand in a basin, a tiny lamp under it, an old cap over the sand— all this in his room. The chicks hatched and grew. Later we had a fowl dinner, but then we got into bad weather and they all had to be killed or washed overboard. They seemed to be a tough variety so the old Portuguse steward told me he would have to "allomode" the last one.

Afternoon tea was a must, a very pleasant interval, whether we were in fine weather or practically on our

Edna Williams, sister of Cora Hilton, who was sent to sea to forget an unsuitable man, entertains Marion Hilton in the saloon of Abyssinia.

beam ends when, beside keeping our own balance, we had to balance our cups, quite an exercise. Afternoons, maybe a nap and again on deck. there was a very comfortable canvas chaise longue. The captain had a hammock. Oh! just like yachting. Later, supper was probably hash, maybe real biscuits for a treat, and canned fruit.

After supper, it was on deck again with the night skies to watch as we walked back and forth, back and forth, on the poop deck. The ship's wake was often very beautiful in the moonlight, especially when, in the tropics, it gleamed with the opalescence of phosphorus. And so to rest.

We seemed always to have a ship's cat, maybe a big Tom tired of carousing ashore and hungry. I remember one day, shortly after leaving port, we were startled by a loud meow and there at the head of the gangway was a long-legged visitor looking hungrily at our dinner. You may be sure he got a good meal and earned his keep many times over by clearing the ship of rats, and being a pet. Cockroaches came aboard, too, but we soon got rid of them. In the tropics if it is not one kind of insect it is another, and they can make life miserable, indeed. Besides the ship's cat, we often had a dog, much enjoyed.

One thing we always watched was the barometer and our spirits rose or fell with that wonderful instrument. The chart and barometer were studied hour by hour. To follow the track of the ship, how many miles the past twenty-four hours, marking our distance on the chart, was the most interesting and important event always. On a sea voyage days lost were dollars lost. It could be very disappointing when the winds were too light, or we had to drive into a head wind, or when we were in the doldrums. These were most trying, the ship rolling on old seas, the sails slapping and banging and not making any headway. I believe some captains threw old shoes overboard at such times to bring a fair wind. We were much more likely to have trouble among the crew when they were not busy enough working ship. I had my heart in my mouth one fine day when there were ugly sounds and I heard the captain roar, "Drop that knife!" as he raced forward. One sailor had a grudge and out came a knife, but the voice of authority worked and no one was hurt. There were other occasions but no serious trouble. Men respond to decent treatment from captain and officers.

A stormy day when the ship was pitching in a head sea or wallowing and rolling as the wind directed we made the best of it below decks, just enduring until the weather cleared. We entertained ourselves with any games we could make up, and mostly just held on. It was astonishing how quickly after a few surprising bumps the children learned to balance and got their

Barque Abyssinia, one of the last big wooden vessels built and operated by Maritimers, seen in Hamburg riding light with neither cargo nor ballast aboard. Commanded for years by Arthur Hilton accompanied by wife Cora and one or two of their young daughters.

sea legs. Being seasick, finding it almost impossible to swallow, seeing everything that is loose swinging, and on looking through the ports seeing the waves rising and falling is misery, but once over, life again seems worth living. There is always excitement on reaching port—letters from home to be devoured and a new part of the world to see.

The Shift from Sail to Steam

Captain Hilton describes his move from a successful career in sail to the quite different world of steam ships, or simply "boats" as they were called then. Because of his good reputation, he is readily taken on by William Thomson & Company of Saint John, the only east coast ship owner to operate ocean-going steamers in any significant way. Cora is permitted to accompany her husband. Arthur recalls her arrival in his memoirs:

Following the sale of the Abyssinia and a few months vacation at home I joined the steamship Trebia as master at the port of New York on October 14th, 1904. Up to that time all my experience had been in sailing vessels and it was with considerable trepidation that I took over this new command. Naturally I tried not to let it be apparent. Later when I had the vessel's bow pointed across the Atlantic I felt more confidence. I was new to steamboat procedure, but quite at home when it came to navigation. As a young man at that time, thirty-three years of age, I felt proud of my ship and was determined to make a good record.

At Savannah (six months later) my wife joined me for the first time in that ship. In the olden times it used to be quite usual for captains to take their wives to sea with them, but in my time it was getting to be unusual. I was fortunate to be sailing for owners who did not object and during my whole career as master I was able to have my wife with me when it was convenient which, with a coming family, was not always. We had some good and some bad times together, and enjoyed seeing a lot of foreign parts together.

From the time of her husband's appointment to *Trebia*, Cora sails with him off and on, sometimes with one of the girls, usually the youngest, Phyllis, while the others live with their grandmother and attend school. Cora is aboard on one trans-Atlantic voyage when *Trebia* strikes an immense iceberg head on. Otherwise, they enjoy sight-seeing expeditions in Britain, Italy, and Germany. After four years, most of this fleet is laid up for lack of trade, but one vessel, *Leuctra* is retained with Arthur Hilton in command. He sails *Leuctra* for four years and then retires. Expecting to be relieved of his command for a rest in April 1912, in Rotterdam he books passage for home, but has to cancel as the relief captain is ill. He takes *Leuctra* on to Buenos Aires. The cancelled passage was aboard *Titanic*.

The Distaff View

Cora is one of the few east coast captains' wives to record her travels to sea in a steamship. She writes of one 1907 voyage in particular:

In April, 1905, I, with a small daughter, joined my husband in Savannah. He was then master of S.S. Trebia, *one of the Thomson brothers "Battle Line" of St. John, New Brunswick. The* Trebia *was a fine ship, sturdily built to battle with heavy weather and all the perils of the sea. With very fine living quarters she seemed like home to us. We made several voyages and in the spring of 1907 were at Hopewell Cape, New Brunswick, loading lumber for a port in the south of Ireland. Getting ready to enter a port is always interesting and so is leaving, with all the preparations of taking on fuel and supplies, making all shipshape and saying goodbye to friends. In the saloon the fine carpet is rolled up and stowed away, all furniture not built in is fastened to the floor of battleship linoleum. This was a summer voyage. The cargo of lumber, besides filling the holds, was piled high on deck. The more big sticks, the more money. We travelled about in runways between the well stowed piles. It was a good smelling, buoyant cargo and the ship rode above her Plimsoll marks.*

Once at sea the days usually passed quickly enough. We could speculate on how long the passage might be and just which port we might make. Doing one's washing could be quite diverting with the water first in one end of the bathtub and then in the other as the ship rolled. Ironing when there was a list meant holding the iron back and then dragging it back uphill. Keeping a small child amused, inventing games, and always keeping an eye on her when on deck filled many hours. Then there were dresses to make—no ready-mades, nylons or zippers—to say nothing of mending. We always had books, but no radio or TV.

At this time of year there was not much danger of heavy storms when with the pitching, if a head sea, or the rolling in a beam sea, life could be very difficult. We did not expect to meet any towering seas, an awesome sight, a black wall of water that would seem certain to break over us and sink the ship with its weight. It is surprising to feel the stern rise on the foot of such a wave and then to see it break, foaming and hissing along the sides. Banging into such a head of water was like striking a wall. The bow would dip and the stern rise, the ship would shudder with the racing of the screw. We weren't expecting heavy weather, but it was our bad luck to leave in thick fog. The fog was worse than bad weather for at that time there was no radar or ice-berg warning system—just the blaring of the whistle to say, "Keep away!" to any approaching vessel.

When near a coast, the lead was used and we would know we were very near land when the order, "Hard aport! Full steam astern!" rang out. Quite exciting as we realized that in the dark or fog a few more steamer lengths might put us ashore. Leaving our maritime port we steamed in dense fog for three days and nights. Making the coast of Newfoundland at night in the fog we once came close enough to see the black loom of the cliffs and hear the exciting cry from the bridge, "Full astern!" and the jangling bells from the engine room. It was close, but we were soon safely away. The night was warm and the sea quiet with a light wind from the south. The fog was still dense, giving no warning of the immense ghostly island of ice drifting silently to its dissolution in warmer waters. The captain, who had been without rest for some nights, knowing we were well away from the coast of Newfoundland, came below for some well earned sleep while our stout ship chugged ahead. About midnight we felt a heavy bump as the ship struck a wall of ice, bow on. I woke to see a streak of grey pyjamas flying for the bridge, and to hear the excited cries of the officers shouting orders, the crew getting the lifeboats ready in case of need. I ran across the saloon to pick up my daughter sitting wide-eyed and wondering in her berth, and dressed her and myself just in case we had to take to the boats. Our saloon, with a cheerful fire burning in the grate looked very homelike just then. I always kept a bag packed with some necessary things in case of need and had that at hand. About then the captain called down the speaking tube to say I'd better dress and sent the cabin boy, a nice lad, to be company for us.

The man on lookout and the first officer could just see the ice towering way above us, but the fog was so dense they could barely see half the ship's length [...] The captain had feared we might have run down a fishing schooner, and of course, was anxious that no lives should be lost. Anyway, we idled until daylight when damage could be assessed. Then the hole punched in the bow plates could be seen. The forepeak filled as the water poured in, but as the bulkheads held and no heavy storms were likely the captain decided to proceed. We carried a lot of extra water, but with our buoyant cargo and with the pumps going, we went slowly along.

Our donkey-man, whose bunk was very near where we struck slept trustingly through all that racket and commotion and was quite indignant when he came on deck in the morning, 'Why! I might have been killed!' How any mortal could sleep through that night I could not imagine. I often went up to look over the bow to watch the sea pouring in and out again as we rose on a wave. Well, we flagged Brow Head asking for our orders to proceed and the captain was glad to see the answering flags, "Go to Glasgow." Once there, [...] he broken plates were taken out and new ones put in.

There were days of rain in Glasgow as usual, but some lovely weather, too. Former Maritimers were more than kind to us and we visited back and forth. We had a trip to Edinburgh and one day our friends took us on a fine trip up and through Rothesay Bay among its lochs and kyles. We have many memories of this stay in Glasgow.

Retiring from the sea in 1912, the Hiltons settle in Yarmouth. The captain stays actively interested in marine matters, eventually serving as harbour master, shipping master, and port warden. In the late twenties he gives instruction in navigation in the Marine Navigation School at Yarmouth and later, is examiner of masters and mates. Among these mates is Molly Kool, the first female licensed master in North America.

XV
LAST DAYS OF SAIL

During the decline of the great square-rigger fleets, women occasionally boarded the last windjammers and schooners. In the era of powered vessels, women entered all sectors of the working world at sea as gender became less of a factor in employment after the mid-twentieth century.

Steamships reached a degree of size and reliability in the 1880s that greatly restricted the square-rigged sailing ship's ability to compete. But the windjammers had an advantage in bulk cargo, because they had little overhead expense during the long waiting and loading times in port. Other factors spelled the end for the wooden ships. First, they leaked after a few years of strain, which increased the insurance rates on their cargoes. Canadian ship owners had long succeeded with home-built wooden vessels, but only the British had the technology for steel ships. Owners like Troop & Son tried British-built steel ships, but the cost was high and they could not compete with the bigger, Liverpool-based lines except in a few special trade areas that frequently took them into remote and primitive ports. Such was the situation of the composite iron and steel barque *Troop* on a voyage to Indo-China in 1903.

Clara Fritz—A Schoolgirl's Sabbatical
Clara Fritz had always loved the sea. Not only her father, but also her uncle and her grandfather were masters. Grandfather Jacob Fritz had been commodore of the Troop & Son shipping line. Clara's family lived in Saint John, though her father's home port was now New York since most of the trade by the turn of the twentieth century was out of that port. On some voyages, Clara's mother and brother Eddie went along, but Clara accompanied her father much of the time from an early age. A younger sister, Madeleine, is not recorded as going on any

The Saint John iron and steel ship Troop carried Clara Fritz to Indo China on her schoolgirl sabbatical in the sunset years of the proud square-riggers.

Mrs. and Captain C.W. Salter at the wheel of Silver Leaf, a three-masted schooner of 1903, when these vessels had replaced the square-riggers in the specialized coastal trades as far as South America.

voyages. Clara's career at sea began before she was even old enough to go to school, when she was asked if she would like to accompany her father on a trip. "I don't think my family really expected me to go," she recalled. "They thought once I had seen New York I would go back home. But I was all for seeing the East, so I went along on the voyage." She never regretted that child's decision because some of her happiest hours were spent travelling down through the trade winds and up through the China Sea to the colorful port of Hong Kong.

To amuse and educate the children at sea, the Fritzes gave them books to read and encouraged them to question things they could not understand. Although the children did not realize it at the time, they were receiving a quality education—so good, in fact, that when Clara first goes to school at the age of eight, she is placed in the fifth grade.

In August of 1903, when Clara Fritz is sixteen years old, the *Daily Telegraph* of Saint John, New Brunswick carries a small item noting, "Captain E. J. Fritz left by train for New York today to take command of his ship, the *Troop*, which is to sail for China next week. He was accompanied by his daughter, Miss Clara, who will make the voyage with him. It is expected they will be away a year."

Estelle (Porter) Crosby and her husband Percy of Yarmouth comfortably at home in the main cabin of Sokoto, *1901, at that moment located in a Japanese port. The Edison cylinder phonograph on the table and all other loose objects would be put away when putting to sea. Bird cages hang at left.*

Clara knows from experience that this voyage will not be like travelling in a palatial passenger steamer, and, to add to the difficulty, she will be the only female aboard the ship. Perhaps she decides to go because she knows the chances for such an adventure decrease as the deep-sea sailing ships rapidly disappear. On the other hand, many captains going on long voyages appreciated family companionship and conversation after their wives had had enough of the sea, so perhaps it was her father's idea.

The big full-rigged ship *Troop*, the first Canadian-owned iron ship, had been built in 1884 in Dumbarton, Scotland. *Troop* is well equipped and turns out to be a highly successful trader about the shipping routes of the world as Troop & Son's first attempt to bridge the gap between locally-built wooden vessels and state-of-the-art steel construction. *Troop* was one of three iron and steel ships in their fleet of deteriorating wooden vessels.

Clara Fritz writes faithfully to her mother at home, and most of the letters that survive convey her feeling for life at sea in an era when some ships still travelled the world powered only by winds, tides, and currents. With ships at sea for months on end, letters are sent in bunches from each port and received in the same fashion, though in Clara's time, trans-oceanic cables are used for important business messages. The age of sail is fading, but there are still ships crossing the seas, often three or four months out of touch with the land. This is the case on Clara's last voyage.

A fine day at sea provides a chance for photography aboard the British barque Queen Elizabeth, *probably taken by longtime captain Eddie Fulton of Glenholme, Nova Scotia. Sailors watch from atop the forecastle.*

Clara writes first as *Troop* heads down the narrows of the Hudson River towards Sandy Hook, where the pilot leaves and, in keeping with long tradition,
takes any last-minute letters for mailing.

August 26, 1903
Dear Mama,
Last night I thought I should not be able to write again. But the pilot will post this line.
We have just had breakfast and I have written a very short note to Miss Knowlton.
The largest passenger steamer in the world just passed us. Papa called me up to see her.

Clara starts adjusting to life in a community of eighteen or twenty men who
live the simple, harsh life of seamen in sail. She belongs to the after-guard, comprised also of the captain, a couple of mates, and their steward. She is not permitted to go forward on deck as that is the crew's preserve. She must have been a
good sailor, accustomed to the rolling, pitching, and heeling of her home, having
spent her early years at sea.

Ship Troop 22 Sept. '03
Papa started a letter to you on Sunday. We have had bad weather since we left. For the
first three weeks it rained and the first week the storm was dreadful. Papa was sick for a
few days. He is better now. I haven't done anything. We did our first washing last Mon-
day and had great fun over it, neither of us knowing very well what to do. On Friday we
washed the white clothes we wore in port. I commenced my slippers yesterday.
I have not studied more than two hours since we left but I've read dozens of books.
Papa taught me how to play cribbage and we play every day. The carpenter made us a
new board and a set of checkers. I suppose Aunt Mary has gone up to St Martins. If
she has you will be very lonesome. I should love to hear from you. Madeleine is at
school I suppose. I hope she is well and Eddie. Our steward is not much good. He
never remembers anything. You must not worry about me for I am getting on all right.
I guess I must begin to study soon or I shall forget everything. Goodbye for now, with
much love to Eddie, Madeleine and yourself.

26 Sept. 1903
It is fine today and quite hot. All week we had quite a wind, but today it has fallen
away and it is quite calm. I finished the piece for one of my slippers last night. I
showed papa how to do it and he did some. I hope you are all well at home.
We are out over a month now. We have just had our afternoon tea and I came down
to write, but I can't find any thing to tell you. Papa says he will write tomorrow. Dear
mama, Papa says you will worry dreadfully about my being away but you must not for I
am getting along nicely and enjoying myself, although I should like to see you all.

18 Oct. 1903

It is some time since I wrote to you. We have not been getting along very quickly. We are out over fifty days and have just crossed the equator yesterday. I am getting on very well. I am sorry I did not bring something more to do. Reading gets tiresome. I made my slippers. The soles were a little too small, but they are all right and I finished my shawl. I knew I should be sorry when they were done.

There is a gap in the correspondence here, but some brief notations made elsewhere by Clara show progress over the next month. She leaves a record of the noon positions in latitude and longitude that confirm a normal route in search of reasonably good sailing. This follows a sort of zigzag down the two Atlantic oceans to find the best prevailing winds. On October 11, forty-six days out, *Troop* is in the doldrums, an area of confused weather, off Sierre Leone and south of the Cape Verdes, heading south. On this day Captain Fritz speaks with a passing ship that promises to report their progress on its arrival in Bahia. A week later, *Troop* crosses the equator.

October 25 finds them across the twentieth degree south parallel getting into cooler weather; they have covered a modest 1080 miles in the week. *Troop* is now near the remote island of Trinidad off the bulge of Brazil, well established as a course pylon for sailing ships. Here vessels heading for the Orient turn southeast, well below the latitude of the Cape of Good Hope, and fringe on the prevailing southern ocean westerlies. The next course point is Tristan da Cunha, then on November 15, well south of Capetown, Fritz heads more easterly, towards St. Paul and Amsterdam Islands in the mid-Indian Ocean. The westerly winds are helpful, though it is very cold through the rest of the month with hail and squalls.

6 Dec. 1903
Dear Mama,
We are today in latitude 38 south and longitude 85 east. Since Wednesday we have had very little wind. On Thurs-
day we saw St. Paul Island. We were in sight of it nearly all day. On the same day we saw two vessels. One of

Susan Fulton (behind capstan) and companion pose while taking advantage of good weather on deck of Queen Elizabeth.

them we were in company with for a couple of weeks at the equator and again for a few days after we left the trade winds. We had quite a breeze the last of last week and the first of this.

The steward thought we were having a little too much on Monday, for, just at noon, the biggest wave in the sea washed the deck and carried off the dinner he was bringing aft. We thought he was gone himself I guess. I don't know that he has gotten over his fright yet. I'm sure he'll never hear the end of it.

We have been very well since I last wrote. I hope you are the same. Things must be beginning to look like Christmas by this time. I hope you will enjoy it. I've been thinking of last Xmas. How pretty our little tree was and what a nice time we had. I hope you will have a tree this year, Madeleine enjoyed the last so much. I guess Santa will not find us this year. The best thing he could bring us would be, I think, a fair wind.

Christmas 1903
It has been dreadfully hot all week until today. Now it is just pleasant. We have been wondering what you are doing at home. I suppose you are asleep now, but it will soon be time to jump up and see what Santa has left. We had a very good Xmas dinner in spite of having no turkey. The cook is not much at fancy cooking, but he tried to show what he could do today and gave quite a spread. One thing he surprised us with was some potatoes. We thought we had finished them over two weeks ago, but I guess, he had a few stowed away for today. With love to all, wishing you a merry Xmas.

Of course, Christmas will be long over by the time the letter arrives in Saint John; the letters will be delivered in a bunch and read in consecutive order. Having crossed the Indian Ocean well south to get the best winds, Captain Fritz tackles one of the world's trickiest areas for navigation, the great mass of islands, straits and small seas of the East Indies. By January 10, 1904, Fritz has brought his ship up through the Lesser Sunda Islands of Indonesia and come out on the Pacific Ocean east of the Philippines, sailing up the coast and back westward around the northern tip of Luzon by the Balintang Channel. This roundabout route places him well on the prevailing currents along the twentieth parallel past Hainan Island to the coast of what was then French Indo-China (now Vietnam). Their destination is Tourane (now Da Nang). On January 27, their position is 19° North, 115° East, almost directly south of Hong Kong.

27 Jan 1904
On Sunday, it was so rough I could not write. The weather for the past week has been very unsettled. About every hour there has been a squall. We had one fine day last week and they began painting and oiled the deck, but toward night it came on to rain again and the wind and sea arose and since then it has been stormy.

We got through the Balintang Channel on Monday. We saw the island ahead about half past three in the afternoon and at dark (six o'clock) we were past it. Today we are in about 19°-40' north latitude and 115°-30' east longitude. Papa says you will be putting on black for us soon; we are out 153 days today, but we are getting quite near port now. We passed a steamer last night about one o'clock. They [captain and mates] could just see her lights.

They were not prepared for weather such as we have had and lost two sails and all their paint has been destroyed and decks have been so slippery with the oil that one could hardly move on them.

Finally, on January 31, after five months at sea in their little self-contained world, Troop and crew arrive at Tourane, in Indo-China. Clara pronounces it a splendid harbour.

Tourane, 3 Feb. 1904
We arrived on Sunday at six o'clock and were very much disappointed to find no letters. We had expected to get in on Saturday but we did not see any land until late in the afternoon. On Sunday morning the land was quite near and Papa thought by the peak it was Tourane, but when we got nearer we found it to be some islands away to the south. It was then almost ten o'clock and we almost despaired of getting in that day. However, it breezed up and we got anchored by dark. There was no pilot, but there was a steamer (the Progress) in and the captain came over. He is a German, sailing between Hong Kong, Haifong and Tourane. They left Monday, but will be back tomorrow. His wife was with him. He made us go over and have dinner that night because we could get nothing fresh until morning. On Monday we went ashore with him in his sampan.

The people here are all French. The captain interpreted for papa. The town is very small and scattered. The roads are very good. There is nothing much to see except the life of the natives and there is no need to say anything about that to you. There are marble mountains a short way from the town which I should like to go to see. Mrs. Brenner of the Progress was there the day before we came and said it was a lovely trip. It rained hard nearly all day yesterday. There was a lady came off with her husband and two little girls yesterday. She could speak no English and I no French so we had a hard time to understand each other. We went ashore at eleven and had lunch. Then papa had some business to do and as it was raining we remained in one of the offices until about five o'clock. Then a lady asked us into her house for afternoon tea and after that we went to dinner to Mr. Friard's, one of the Standard Oil agents. He had been on board in the morning and invited us. There were a few other guests, but only one could make an attempt at English.

On February 4, a tow down the river by the coastal steamer *Progress* is arranged and Captain Fritz sails his ship up the Gulf of Tonkin towards Haiphong, the port for Hanoi. How the women on non-passenger vessels treasure their encounters and companionship with one another is plain to see.

Ship Troop
12 Feb. 1904
We have got as far as the mouth of the river on which Haifong is situated, but it seems as if we are doomed to stay here. The "Progress" towed us out of Tourane last Saturday afternoon. On the morning of that day I was on board with Mrs. Bremer, and the chief engineer took those pictures of us which papa sent to you. They are not good for the sun was shining in our eyes. I stayed with her for dinner and then she came over for part of the afternoon with me. We were all going to have afternoon tea on board the Matilde (another steamer then in port) but papa found out on shore that he need not wait, so we got away about halfpast four.

The first day out there was no wind and it was dreadfully cold and damp and Sunday night we could still see Tourane light (visible thirty miles). The next day we had some wind, but a heavy head sea. Since then the weather has been fine. Tuesday we were off the coast of Hainan Island, Wednesday we passed Nightingale Island and about four o'clock sighted Norway Rocks, on the largest of which a lighthouse is placed. These are at the entrance to the Kwa Nam Treu River on which Haifong is. By dark we could see Hon Dau light which is farther north. Papa thought it better not to anchor until daylight, so he tacked ship and sailed the other way till one o'clock and then turned her again for the river.

It was not high water until 2 a.m. so they waited until afternoon and then crossed to the east and by five o'clock were again anchored to wait for wind and tide. We got no wind however until four in the morning. The pilots changed and the one we got couldn't speak a word of English. The tide had been on the ebb since two o'clock. At half-past eight we got to the bar and stuck there. If we had got but a ship's length farther we should have been in deep water again. There is only one tide in the day and it is not high water again until 3 a.m. so we had to make the best of a whole day stuck in the mud. At nine tonight there may be enough water to float us. We are certainly not suffering from the heat here. All the way up it was real cold.

Now I shall say good-bye, hoping to get many letters from you tomorrow, with much love.

Haiphong, Sunday 14 Feb. 1904
You are thinking that, since we had two towboats, which had only to take us about ten miles in six hours, we got to Haiphong that day, but it was not so easy. The tide was ebbing and when we got to the entrance of the canal the water was so low we had to anchor. But papa and I went to Haiphong in the launch. It is quite a large place. The streets are wide and wide pavements and it is real hot. After dinner we had to wait an hour and a half before any place was open, so we took rickshas and they took us to see

the market. It was the greatest looking place I ever saw. Then papa went to the office he does business at and afterwards we went to buy a few things we needed. We each got a hat. I wanted some kind of plain straw hat, but I couldn't get one, so I got one of the kind of stuff as papa's. It is a large white hat with a band of ribbon around it, and I got some combs for my hair.

Next week is China New Year so they will not be able to enter the ship or do anything. We cannot get any washing done for a whole week. We couldn't get any in Tourane either. Papa is hanging on with only two white shirts. On the way from Tourane I did up a suit of white underclothes and two shirtwaists. Just imagine me doing a white skirt, but I didn't do too bad for a beginning.

Dear Mama, I do hope you are better and you must not worry about me (except that I should love to see you all) I am having a very nice time. With much love, from your loving daughter Clara.

We bought quite a few things yesterday to take home and some dishes for the ship. We were on shore all day from nine in the morning till six at night. The company proposed a charter to papa yesterday. It was to load at Saigon for some place in Europe. But they have not received an answer yet to the terms papa sent and dear knows where we will go. They are to finish discharging on or before the 29th.

I really have not a thing to tell you, for we do about the same thing every day, just go ashore and around to the offices at which papa has business. One day we made a five minute call at the minister's. He was very nice. His wife is English, but she was not at home. We saw the church and he gave me some violets and some roses.

I hope you are well and that we shall get letters soon. We received a number of papers. Now, good-bye, with much love.

17 March 1904

I wrote to Aunt Mary early this morning and told her we were going to start at half-past eight this morning, but now it is seven at night and we are still anchored. Papa had a busy day yesterday. At seven o'clock the men came aboard to settle about the ballast. We got on shore at 9.30 and then he had to waste the whole morning at the tribunal over one of the sailors, who deserted and was brought back. They did not want to know much—only who he was, where he came from, etc., but they took until quarter to eleven and he could do nothing more until two. Then he had to hurry around to see how much money he needed before four o'clock when the bank closes.

He finished at the bank in time and at the Resident's by five, when he went to settle at Lyonnaise Co. and the butcher's and to get a bill of health. We thought that while he was doing this the ship was being cleared at the custom house, but found that it was left for this morning. It was seven by the time he finished, so we had dinner at the hotel and got on board by nine. Then papa had his accounts to make up. He was up until one o'clock. I helped him until twelve and then went to bed. I was so tired, for neither of us had slept more than a couple of hours the night before.

At last *Troop* gets away. They do not have an easy time getting through the delta mud banks and canal system to be transited in and out of Haiphong. Relatively inefficient facilities are a trial to sailing shipmasters, who are dependent upon them in close quarters when they can not sail.

> *Ship Troop*
> *21 March 1903*
> *Last Thursday morning I wrote what I thought would be my last letter from Haiphong and here it is Monday evening and we are just getting down the river now. On Friday morning the pilot and one launch came at five as they agreed, but the other boat was an hour late. We got started all right and got through the canal and we thought all danger over, in fact had just said so, when we noticed the mud being stirred up behind and in three minutes were fast aground. Then of course, we had to wait for another tide.*
>
> *It was high again next morning at six, but failed to float her. After dinner, papa and I and the pilot went back to Haiphong. They said it was useless to try to get her off until Monday at high tide, which would be at six at night. The tides here seem to go every way. Last Saturday the high water was at six in the morning and today (Mon.) high water was at six in the evening. We got a larger boat to come at four to-day. We stopped on shore Saturday night for it was very cold and would take a sampan two hours to bring us down. Sunday morning we started at seven and got off about half-past nine. It was very cold, papa felt it very much. He has not been well at all since, for he has worried the whole time. The boats came all right today, but there was only one small one fast when she floated herself.*
>
> *We are safe across the bar now and shall anchor near Hon Dau light until daylight. I hope you will get this, but do not know for I shall have to give it to a China man on one of the launches for the pilot is on the tug ahead. I hope you are all well. Papa will be well now he has nothing to worry about. He seems always to look on the dark side of things. Last night he declared nothing would ever bring the ship out of the mud and today she floated herself. Of course that gave him something more to worry over, for he had engaged a boat which was not used, but we got down all the quicker for having her. We shall be to sea tomorrow I hope and hope we shall have a good passage. I should love to see you all tonight, or at least know you are all well.*

Clara glosses over the hardships of the heavier weather on this voyage; she had had the most terrifying of sea experiences in a typhoon at the mere age of eight: "I came face to face with my first typhoon in the China Sea. I marvelled at the expert steering of my father's ship. It was a terrible typhoon and a great many ships were lost and never heard of again." At the other extreme, she remembers the strange sensation of being becalmed and feeling the occasional ocean swell come by: "It was an odd experience. The sea would be perfectly smooth, then you would see a line moving across the water and suddenly the ship heaved so much you thought it was going to turn over."

The casualty rate among sailing ships was still high at this late date in their era. The *Troop* itself meets a sudden end two years later, striking the forbidding shores of lonely Kerguelen Island while racing along the westerlies of the great southern ocean towards Australia. Clara gets home safely, in time to enroll again at the high school in Saint John for grade twelve; she completes the year with honours with an average mark of 92.27 percent. She went to normal school and taught school for four years, then went on to McGill University as an honours student in biology. After working at Woods Hole Oceanographic Institution and the Huntsman Marine Laboratories, Clara took a Master's degree from McGill and a Ph.D. from the University of Toronto in 1923, subsequently teaching at the latter. Dr. Fritz retired in 1954 as chief of timber pathology at the Forest Products Laboratories in Montreal. Like her younger sister Madeleine, she remained unmarried. She died at the age of eighty-five. Clara's letters from sea suggest a love of sea travel, but never indicate a desire for a sea career. Nevertheless, she did go on to an impressive career in what was still a man's world.

In the Last Windjammers

Sailing ships began to be laid up or sold for use as barges. Of the masters who made the transition to steamships, some took their wives with them, but periods away from home were shorter now. Many an old sea captain, unwilling or unable to make the move, hung on to a sailing command. Often these men had never had a home of their own on shore, their ships being the only permanent address for themselves and their wives. There were no pensions and their major investment, shares in sailing vessels, became worthless as the old ships were sold off for a fraction of their former value.

On a long voyage from Antwerp to San Francisco in the ship *Port Elgin* from 1904 to 1905, Frances Hand suffers what her husband guesses is a lung infection. The captain treats his wife for consumption, but she dies: "My dearly beloved wife passed away after an illness of 34 days," he records. Frances Hand was thirty-seven. Captain Hand preserved his wife's body in spirits with the intention of returning it to her home. There were many cases of either husband or wife dying at sea, worn out by the life and diet, but with no home to go to on land.

One of the most famous of the last big steel windjammers clinging on in the Australian grain trade was *Grace Harwar*. The ship gained a reputation as a killer because, like many ships, a seaman or two were lost in the fight with the South Atlantic below Cape Horn. Under a Captain Hudson, *Grace Harwar* sailed on in 1907 with Mrs. Hudson buried in the cargo. Her husband could not bear to bury his wife at sea, wanting to take her home, somewhere.

In the last days of the square-riggers, women were sometimes keepers of the store budget in the after cabin, watching the food with a sharp eye, hoping to save a little towards a retiring nest-egg. There had long been dishonest captains who cheated on the weights of the standard food rations fed to the crews and pocketed the savings. A second mate who was about to sign on *Terpsichore* in Port Talbot, Wales, in 1910, sat down to his first meal, which was presided over by the captain's wife. He picked up a biscuit and started to butter it. "Turn that biscuit over," shrilled the wife. In about a second, the new mate grasped the message: he was buttering the rougher side of the biscuit, the side with the holes that would absorb more butter. He thought better of signing onto this vessel where the dining was sure to be very light.

When the deep-sea trade faded away for the Canadian and American east coast seamen and owners, the few with the determination to keep plying their trade turned to the coastal trade. For this north-south sailing along the Atlantic coast from Canada to Argentina, the schooner, with its fore-and-aft rig with no square sails and smaller crew, was best because it allowed sailing closer into the variable winds but it also required sailing closer to hostile shores. Large schooners were built and operated from the late nineteenth century into the 1920s, when many of them became tug-towed barges.

Women still sometimes went to sea with their husbands in the schooners, although the incentive was not so great because the voyages were now not so long. Jennie Inness of Yarmouth, Nova Scotia sailed with her husband from 1909, when she married, until World War One, in his large, three-masted "tern" schooners *Success*, *Lavengo*, and *W.N.Zwicker*. The Innesses sailed the coastal runs from Canada and the United States to the West Indies and South America as well as on trips to Madeira and the San Blas Coast of Panama. Jennie describes her life at sea as pleasant, though she enjoys more particularly the time in port with its visits among friends aboard other vessels. A young woman, she enjoys the parties, entertainment, and courtesies that come the way of a visiting captain's wife.

At the outset her husband lays down the rules—stay clear of the galley, don't interfere with the cook, and never give any orders to any of the crew. After the birth of her first child, Jennie goes back to sea with the baby. She describes the food aboard as ample and of good quality, though she says she misses having fresh butter and always welcomes fresh vegetables on arrival in port. For an obviously good sailor, most of the days at sea pass pleasantly with her chores around the cabin and her needlework.

There are bad days, of course. Mrs. Inness' first Christmas at sea, for example, is a gloomy one. There is a heavy gale and the cook falls ill and dies. Heaving-to in the stormy seas on Christmas day, a great sea comes inboard, washing away the casks containing the ship's fresh water supply. There is little thought of a festive dinner and water is strictly rationed as the damaged schooner limps to port. On a later Christmas, all is well and the crew comes aft dressed in fanciful costumes to entertain and give homemade presents to the Innesses' two young daughters.

The two world wars strike the final blows to the square-rigged fleet. Many were sunk by German submarines in World War One as they sailed without convoys. One of the merchant raiders successfully deployed by the German navy was the auxiliary windjammer *Seeadler*, commanded by the famous Count von Luckner. Von Luckner sank a number of sailing ships before having *Seeadler* sunk in turn. Even after this war, in 1924, the ship *Bertha* vanished on a voyage from Jacksonville toward Hamburg with Captain Groth Rodden and his wife Emilie and baby son on board. They are presumed to have struck a drifting mine.

In the twenties and thirties there were still great steel "jammers" sailing the specialized bagged grain trade from South Australia to Europe, usually an annual voyage. These were the ships of the German, French, and Finnish fleets. There were not many women living in these business-like vessels, but a few rare adventurous women made the celebrated voyage around the Horn as apprentices or stewardesses or, occasionally, as passengers.

The private, twenty-ship fleet of Gustav Erikson, based in the Aaland Islands of Finland, was the last line of windjammers. Erikson was a one-man shipping company, and his word was law. Erikson looked after everything, and reportedly stayed in business by penurious ways. Fortunately, he saw to it that his ships were well crafted and his crew reasonably well fed. He bought up cheaply German, French, and British ships that were no longer considered commercially viable. Many of the ships he bought had been sail-training ships with large accommodation for apprentices of the steamship lines. Erikson advertised for passengers to sail around the world: thirty-thousand miles for ten months at ten shillings per day. A few took the voyage, about half of them single women.

Seventeen-year old Ruby de Cloux sailed to Australia early in 1933 with her father, the famous Captain Robert de Cloux, in his big four-masted Erikson barque *Parma*. At Spencer Gulf, where the grain was loaded, Ruby was joined by Betty Jacobson, an American friend, for the return voyage. Both had been to sea as children, and both were daughters of captains. They were signed on as apprentices in *Parma*, but according to the account of a passenger, the well-known author and seafarer Alan Villiers, it does not appear that they did any serious sailoring. The thirty-two-man crew of *Parma* was comprised mostly of young cadets or apprentices of an average age of seventeen. These overworked and underfed apprentices were inclined to take out their resentment by "hating" the girls—from a distance, of course—although they still gave them the flying fish that landed on the deck, a special culinary treat. They were also apparently surprised to find the women did not bring the ship bad luck: their ship made the run home in a quick eighty-three days to win the unofficial "grain race" that year.

Betty Jacobson returned from England to New York and to life on land. Her novel adventure made the newspapers and a clipping found its way to Montreal where it had a galvanizing effect on another young woman: Annette Brock, the nineteen-year-old daughter of a successful Montreal business man and an Englishwoman. Annette's background was upper class, but she was a "tom-boy," determined from an early age to have a career at sea. When she should have been thinking of "coming out" in Montreal society, she was absorbed in yachting, ship modeling, and a correspondence course in navigation. She was acquainted with the sea, having made trips to England in passenger steamships, where she poked her nose into all the workings of the vessel. She was bright and single-minded.

In the thirties, the acceptable way of rising to the top at sea was still to serve an apprenticeship in sail, and Annette Brock was well aware of this. She also knew that openings for men were scarce and for women they were just about closed. They "slammed their doors in sheer horror at the mere mention of such a proposition," she says. On one family trip returning from overseas, Annette meets an English apprentice, Ben Davis, who pursues her with serious intent. She tells him she will look upon him with some favour if he helps her get an apprentice's berth in a square-rigger.

Realizing Erikson's *Parma* was in England and would soon head for Australia again, Annette has Ben call on the captain and the ship's agents to plead her case. The reaction is favourable, but when final confirmation comes from Gustav Erikson, Brock is assigned to another four-master, *L'Avenir*, then at Copenhagen. It is entirely possible that Erikson places her on *L'Avenir* because there will be several women passengers on the voyage and plenty of cabins on this former cadet training vessel. As an apprentice, Brock has to pay a premium of five-hundred dollars for her training (twice that of male apprentices). Erikson noted at the time that *L'Avenir* "was to get an American Miss who wishes to sign on as an apprentice. I don't know if she can work on deck at all, but maybe she will be able to attend the women passengers." He will, at least, get five-hundred dollars back against her food and miniscule wages.

Annette Brock rushes off to Copenhagen with excitement and trepidation to fulfill her dream. There the reception is mixed with some obvious signs of disapproval from many of the officers and crew. The captain, fortunately, is relaxed about the situation. Brock signs the apprentice's indenture, written in Swedish, in which the usual Erikson agreement to guarantee further employment after this voyage is left out. Captain Nils Erikson takes his apprentice aside and asks her if she "want[s] to work," offering her by suggestion the easy way that Gustav Erikson had envisioned. The easy way is not for Annette Brock, however, and she lets him know she wants nothing short of the full apprentice's regime and credit.

The story of Annette Brock's voyage around the world as a full apprentice in a windjammer is a valuable record and fascinating picture of such a voyage and the attitudes of her fellow crew. It is a rare documentation of this greatest of voyages by an amazing woman who did every job the men did and met the challenges and impediments thrown her way head on. The mostly Swedish-Finnish crew were difficult, often threatening and hostile towards a "girl" who had the temerity to invade their world, supposedly depriving a man of a job. Whenever she had difficulty she was advised to go home, wash dishes, and have babies; that, according to men, was her job. Slight of build, she fought hard to keep up with her fellow apprentices in all aspects of the job, proving finally that she could do her share, from chipping rust in the bilges and steering to working the anchor capstan and furling sail aloft in a gale. And she had to learn rudimentary Swedish as she went along. Grudging acceptance came from her fellow sailors, but they were also angered when she gained the confidence of the officers with her ability to help with navigation. There was almost mutiny when the tired officers began going below together for a coffee break, leaving her unofficially, but effectively, in charge as the ship bounded through the southern ocean.

Brock not only gained the crew's unreserved respect by the end of the voyage, but she also won the respect of the half dozen passengers, who included the world class Australian composer and pianist Percy Grainger and his wife Ella. The captain's report must have been good as Brock was offered a berth on another voyage, this time in the barque *Viking*. In correspondence home from Australia, *L'Avenir's* captain, Nils Erikson, says that Gustav Erikson had been wrong in his earlier

Apprentice Annette "Jackie" Brock among her mates, young Finns and Swedes, at sea en route to Australia in the great windjammer L'Avenir in 1934.

assessment of Brock's potential, and comments: "I am pleased with the woman apprentice. She is in full work as the others. She is not any flirt, who mingles with the crew." Brock expressed appreciation for the fairness of his report and for Gustav Erikson's opening of the door of sailing tradition to women.

But what could have been a promising career at sea is stopped when Annette Brock marries her boyfriend, Ben Davis. She had hoped to keep the marriage a secret until she had another year as a seaman in square-sail, but she was betrayed and Gustav Erikson cancelled her appointment to *Viking*. Annette Brock Davis turned to a career of domesticity and art in England, becoming a marine painter of considerable stature and raised a family. Spending World War One in Montreal, she studied with Arthur Lismer. Her husband was invalided out of the merchant marine just as he was to receive his master's papers. Annette always prized her exclusive membership in L'Association Internationale Cap Horniers de St. Malo, attending reunions of shipmates and others who had sailed the Cape Horn voyage.

A handful of the big square-riggers survived into the forties in the grain trade, with adventurous youth striving for an apprentice's berth, or any job, to experience this fast-vanishing adventure. One of the last lucky ones to seek the greatest ocean adventure was an enterprising twenty-three-year-old English woman named Gwynneth Ann Stanley. In 1948, in Port Talbot, Wales, Stanley talked her way into a job as temporary stewardess aboard *Passat* while she was in port.

High out on the royal yard shifting sail aboard L'Avenir *at sea, Annette "Jackie" Brock performs the whole job of a seaman in square-rig sail.*

From this vantage point she pressed for a berth on the forthcoming voyage to Australia. After considerable suspense, word finally came from Gustav Erikson allowing her to sign on as a "mess girl" at five pounds per month. It was a good deal for the ship as she made herself indispensable in the rather slack steward's department. *Passat* sets sail carrying seamen from *Viking* and sails from *Archibald Russell*, both recently laid up permanently, a sign of the dwindling fleet.

In the steward's department, Stanley keeps a detailed journal of ship's life from her perspective in the special position between the after guard officers and the crew in the forecastle. Aside from lively celebrations of Christmas and Finnish Independence Day, it is a largely uneventful voyage of a little over three months out to Spencer Gulf on the south coast of Australia for grain. She notes with tolerance a seaman, "Mossy," who pays her a lot of attention. She dismisses him as suffering from what was known as "Southern Cross Fever," a result of long weeks at sea without female company.

The crew was typical of last days of deep-sea sailing: professional Finnish seamen, failed students from various quarters, and two professional engineers look-

It was high in the rigging of this four-masted windjammer that Jackie Brock proved her mettle as a "seaman" on the stormy route to Australia.

ing for an adventure before settling down. There was also a paying woman passenger. The captain was an old Finn whose moods swung widely according to whether there were favorable or contrary winds. The grain crop of South Australia was traditionally handled in bags, loaded slowly by hand from lighters or long jetties in the shallows of Spencer Gulf, east of Adelaide.

Passat arrives at anchor to find its sister ship *Pamir* anchored nearby. Anne Stanley witnesses the traditional gams between the ships. There is dinner aboard *Passat* with the two captains, the mate of *Pamir*, and his wife. Then a day is spent aboard *Pamir*. There is a lot of drinking when in port, Stanley reports, but never at sea. She likes the look of the country on visits ashore, so she decides to sign off the ship. She sets off, hitchhiking to Adelaide and Melbourne with the seaman "Mossy" for company. The Southern Cross fever must have been catching, for Stanley and Mossy marry and settle down in Australia, raising a family on a houseboat.

As the twentieth century progressed, especially following their participation in work traditionally accorded to men during World War One, women slowly entered the men's world of professional seamanship. Women at sea became a common sight as cooks and stewardesses on coastal and inland vessels, then as mates and skippers of tugs. At first, the only women acquiring formal officer status on ships were the unique "conductresses," who had charge of groups of immigrants travelling on large passenger liners. It was not until the late thirties that the final barrier was broken and a female licensed sea-going master appeared. But the achievement was not easy. One observer noted that female officers and even female captains, especially from the East Bloc, became sufficiently numerous. Many sailors who accepted women as crew working alongside them were disturbed or threatened by women who behaved as though gender were irrelevant, and were irritated by these increasing numbers of professional women at sea.

One who thought her gender irrelevant to her career goals was Myrtle "Molly" Kool of Alma, New Brunswick. Molly helped out on her Dutch father's sixty-four-ton coastal auxiliary schooner during summer vacations, performing all of a sailor's jobs. As soon as she was through high school, she signed on as a seaman, plying the tricky tides of the Bay of Fundy with her father for five years. Seeing no reasonable ceiling to her ambition, Molly pestered reluctant authorities at each stage for the right to take the examinations and eventually to gain her mate's certificate. She studied navigation from a sympathetic instructor, Captain Richard

Pollock, who liked the idea of training a woman as a master mariner. Her fellow students were polite but skeptical seamen.

Continuing opposition from the authorities forced Kool to wait three years for permission to sit the exam for her master's certificate in coastal trade. With the help of an old friend and captain, and following intense grilling by the examining masters at Yarmouth, she got through navigation school. Having passed all the other barriers, the opposition crumbled and the Canada Shipping Act was revised to accept women as shipmasters.

At the age of twenty-three, Molly Kool was a licensed master with a "home trades steam certificate," dated April 1939. She is considered to be the first female master in North America and the second in the world after a Russian, Captain Anna Shehetinina. A Norwegian, Gudrun Trogstad, acquired a master's certificate for small vessels in 1929 after gaining experience in lakes trade and taking courses at the Oslo Seamen's School. Another Canadian woman, Ollie Johnson of Montreal, is reported as having been licensed as a tug skipper for the St Lawrence River and Great Lakes about the same time as Molly Kool.

Captain Molly Kool was the first female licensed master in North America and second in the world with her master's certificate for coastal waters. She operated in the Bay of Fundy and on the coast of Maine.

Molly Kool followed in her father's footsteps, plying the coast with cargoes of lumber and other goods, mainly in the often treacherous Bay of Fundy with its notorious fogs and tides, and in the Gulf of Maine. She was always in sure command, cool, and unflinching. She was tough enough to take up a belaying pin and rout a boarding party of Norwegian seamen who were trying to steal her berth at a wharf in Moncton. She shipwrecked three times, the last leading to romance and marriage. Captain Kool said recently that she had no great sentiment for the sea and she was no feminist, it was just one way to make a living and she enjoyed it.

At the end of the twentieth century and the beginning of the twenty-first, modest numbers of women work in all areas at sea, from the engine room to the bridge, in merchant and naval vessels. Women are no longer the object of fear, suspicion, or superstition with their male crew mates. In the spirit of equality, women are accepted simply as workers. A few women still go to sea simply to have a visit with officer husbands as huge cruise ships, tankers, and container ships move about the seas, seldom visiting a home port. As in other fields, women have won the right to a professional place at sea alongside men or above them. Before that, although little notice was taken of their contributions, their occasional presence softened the harshness of a male preserve and sometimes provided women with the chance to prove themselves equal in ability to the men they sailed with.

Women stow jibsails aboard HMS Rose, *a modern reproduction of an eighteenth-century warship, partaking of the ancient but newly popular character-building art of sailing.*

Glossary

Aft: In the direction toward the stern.

After (or aft): Adjective for the one more toward the stern.

Ballast: Stone or other material placed in the bottom of a vessel, permanently or temporarily, to keep it from capsizing. When there is no cargo a ship sails in ballast.

Barque: Vessel with three or more masts, all square-rigged except the aftermost mast, which is fore and aft rigged.

Beam: Width across the vessel's hull. Beams used for ratio of beam to length.

Boat: A small craft, such as a lifeboat, yacht, tug, or ferry. Ships carried boats named by type as whalers, cutters, pinnaces, and gigs.

Bow: Forward or front end of a vessel.

Brig: Two-masted vessel, both masts square-rigged.

Brigantine: As brig, except only foremast is square-rigged.

Chandler: Merchant dealing in supplies for ships.

Fore: The one more toward the bow, as in foremast.

Foreward: In a direction toward the bow.

Fore and aft rig: Arrangement of sails mounted on booms and gaffs in line with the length of the vessel.

Forecastle (fo'c'sle): Seaman's accommodation. In earlier vessels in fore part of the hull, in later vessels, a house on the main deck foreward.

House: Structure located on main deck usually housing crew, galley, carpenter shop; or raised after-structure.

Insurance classification: Quality of a vessel determined by insurance surveyor on which premiums are based. Usually by the French Bureau Veritas or Lloyds in London. Included a grade and the number of years it would be valid.

Keel: Backbone of a vessel running along the bottom on which a vessel's frames were mounted.

Keelson: Top piece laid on the keel adding structural strength.

Log: Vessel's official book recording events and navigational information.

Masts: Vertical spars on which sails are suspended. Include foremast, mainmast, and, if installed, mizzen and jigger masts.

Master: Master mariner, a qualified captain who has his license or "papers."

Port: Left-hand side of vessel when facing forward.

Poop: After end of a vessel's hull, raised above the main deck line and housing officer and passenger accommodation.

Rigging: System of fixed and running ropes and cables that support the masts and sails. Hence square, fore, and aft rig.

Schooner: A vessel with only fore and aft sail rig and two or more masts.

Ship: In the age of sail this was specifically a vessel with three or more masts, all square-rigged. In modern parlance it is used for any large vessel.

Square rig: Sail arrangement with major sails carried on horizontal spars mounted cross-wise on the masts.

Starboard: Right-hand side of a vessel when facing forward.

Steamer: Steam-powered vessel, in nineteenth century British North America often referred to as a boat regardless of size, and classed as square-rigger because of the auxiliary sails it carried.

Stern: Back or after end of a vessel.

Tack: Direction of vessel angled toward the wind to make headway against it.

Tonnage: Size. Deadweight tonnage is weight of water displaced by the vessel, hence actual weight. Gross tonnage, the type most used here, is a measure of cubic content or capacity, not weight.

Vessel: General term for all craft larger than a boat.

Voyage: Planned trip of a vessel, usually a round trip, possibly including several ports.

Yard: Horizontal spar mounted cross-wise on a mast to carry square sails. Named according to mast and sail supported.

List of Illustrations

MMA–Maritime Museum of the Atlantic
AYCM–Archives of Yarmouth County Musuem
NBM–New Brunswick Museum
PANS–Public Archives of Nova Scotia

37. Kay Ladd and pig in bath. AYCM PH-62-Belmont-42.

38. Hong Kong portrait of Forrest Ladd. AYCM Ph-51-Ladd-2.

39. Kay Ladd with "Pilot." AYCM PH-62 Belmont-20.

40. Captain Frederick Ladd with Captain and Mrs. Lee and daughter Marjorie. AYCM PH-51-Ladd-13.

41. Cora Hilton aboard *Abyssinia*. AYCM.

42. Marion Hilton with her father. AYCM.

43. Marion Hilton and "Fiddle." AYCM.

44. Marion Hilton with binoculars. AYCM.

45. Edna Williams and Marion Hilton in the saloon of *Abyssinia*. AYCM-PH 131-1.

46. Barque *Abyssinia*. ACYM-PH 131.A.

47. *Troop*. Painting by C.K. Miller-NBM.

48. Mrs. and Captain C.W. Salter at the wheel of *Silver Leaf*. MMA-MP400.133.2 Neg. N23, 430.

49. Estelle (Porter) Crosby and husband in the main cabin of *Sokoto*, 1901. AYCM. MMA-MP400.26.1 Neg. N23. 429.

50. Susan Fulton and others aboard *Queen Elizabeth*. Courtesy of Betty and Richard Fulton, Dartmouth.

51. Susan Fulton and companion. Courtesy of Betty and Richard Fulton, Dartmouth.

52. Annette "Jackie" Brock among her mates. Courtesy Gale Natali and Hounslow Press. Photo Jurgen Jurgeson.

53. Annette "Jackie" Brock aboard *L'Avenir*. Courtesy Gale Natali and Houslow Press.

54. *L'Avenir*. Courtesy Gale Natali and Houslow Press.

55. Captain Molly Kool. King's County Record, New Brunswick.

56. Women stow jibsails aboard *HMS Rose*. Photo D. Baird.

Bibliography

The accounts presented here originate in diaries, correspondence, published and unpublished reminiscences, logbooks, and contemporary news reports. Many are taken directly from the originals in public and private collections and some of the shorter ones have been recounted in more than one previously published book.

Introduction
Day Spring
"Epic Story of Day Spring." *Halifax Morning Chronicle*. January 1 (1921).
Pirates and Stowaways
DePauw, Linda Grant. *Seafaring Women*. Boston: Houghton Mifflen, 1982.
Stewardesses
Fingard, Judith. *Jack in Port, Sailor Towns of Eastern Canada*. Toronto: University of Toronto Press, 1982.
Sam Samuels, Packets, Sheffield
Atlantic Crossing. Chicago: Time-Life Books Inc., 1981.
Marco Polo
"The Great Voyage." *The Atlantic Advocate*. July (1961). Fredericton, New Brunswick. (Consisting of the diary of Edwin Bird from National Library of Australia.)
Mary Wallace
Wallace, Mary. *Life in Feejee, Five Years Among the Cannibals, By a Lady*. Boston, Mass.: William Heath, 1851.
Annie Harding Slade
DePauw, Linda Grant. *Seafaring Women*. Boston: Houghton Mifflen, 1982.

Chapter I
Eliza Williams
Williams, Harold, ed. *One Whaling Family*. Boston: Houghton Mifflen, 1964.
Mayhew, Norton, Jernegan, Williams, Lawrence
Rousmaniere, John. *The Luxury Yachts*. Seafarers Series. Alexandria, Virginia: Time-Life Books Inc., 1981.
The Seafarers. Boston: Time-Life Books Inc., 1979.
Mary Coffin
Logbooks, *Athol, Margaret Rait*, and *N.B.Lewis*, 1888-90, Crowell Collection, PANS. Halifax, Nova Scotia.
Doane, Benjamin. *Following the Sea*. Halifax, Nova Scotia: Nimbus-N. S. Museum, 1987.

Chapter II
The Clippers
Lubbock, Basil. *The China Clippers*. Glasgow, Scotland: Brown & Son, 1922.
Albenia McKay, Sarah Low, Matthew Maury, Eleanor Creesy, Cordelia Waterman, Mary Ann Patten
Whipple, A. B. C. *The Challenge*. New York: William Morrow, 1987.
The Clipper Ships. Boston: Time-Life Books Inc., 1980.
Mary Ann Patten
Northrup, Everett H. *Florence Nightingale of the Ocean*. Kingsport, New York: U. S. Merchant Marine Academy, 1959.

Chapter III
Sarah Ann Smith
Captain David Smith's outline of his career. Original at Quaco Museum, St Martins, New Brunswick.
Virginia Slocum
Teller, Walter Magnes. *The Voyages of Josh Slocum.* New Brunswick, New Jersey: Rutgers University Press, 1958.
Emma Spicer
"Emma Spicer's Diaries, 1880-1882." Harold Lister Collection, PANS. Halifax, Nova Scotia.
William. D. Lawrence, Mary Lawrence Ellis
Wallace, Frederick William. *Wooden Ships and Iron Men.* Boston: Charles E. Lauriat, 1937.
Schull, Joseph. The Salt Water Men: Canada's Deep-Sea Sailors. Toronto: MacMillan, 1957.
Abigail Ryerson
Extract of personal log, Nova Scotian (August-September, 1847). Yarmouth, Nova Scotia: Yarmouth County Museum Archives.
Haws Family
Haws, G. A. "The Haws Family and their Seafaring Kin." Dumferline, England: Private Publisher, 1932.

Chapter IV
Annie Cochrane, Lilly Parker, Ida Parker, Bessie Parker
Parker Papers. Robert and Susan Ewing collection of correspondence.
Troop & Son vessels, John Parker Shipyard
Baird, Donal. "Under the Diamond T, Rise and Fall of a Square-Rig Fleet." Unpublished manuscript.

Chapter V
Glorana Fownes
Personal Journal of Glorana Price Fownes. New Brunswick Museum Archives.

Chapter VI
James W. Elwell, **Sara Farrington**
Medcoff, J. C. "Loss of the *James W. Elwell*." Collections of New Brunswick Historical Society, No. 16 (1961).
Feature Ariticle. *Saint John Globe.* October 20, 1890.
Frank N. Thayer and *Criccieth Castle,* **Mrs. Thomas**
Carse, Robert. *Twilight of Sailing Ships.* New York: Galahad Books, 1965.
Alpharetta Fownes
Saint John Globe, November 24, 1890.
"Husband and Child Gone. A Night of Terror on the Ship Lizzie C. Troop." *Saint John Telegraph.* October 18, 1881.
Mrs. Coalfleet
"Yarmouth Record of Shipping, 1881." Yarmouth, Nova Scotia: Yarmouth County Museum Archives.

Chapter VII
Alice Coalfleet
Edited Personal Diary, 1886-92. Courtesy Robert Dimock, Dartmouth, Nova Scotia.

Chapter VIII
Josie and Janie Turner
"Turner Family Papers." Lister Collection. Saint John, New Brunswick: New Brunswick Museum Archives.
Idella and Janie Gullison
Crowell, Clement W. *Novascotiamen.* Halifax, Nova Scotia: Nimbus-Nova Scotia Museum, 1979.

Janie and Beulah Gullison
Perry, Beulah G. "Remembering—Growing up as a Sea Captain's Daughter." *Nova Scotia Historical Review*. 2: 2 (1987).

Ida and Janey Crowe
Crowe, John C. *In the Days of the Windjammers*. Toronto: Ryerson, 1959.

Chapter IX
Amelia Holder
"Sea Voyages and Diary." Personal Diaries of Susan Amelia Holder. Edited by Beth Quigley. Saint John, New Brunswick: New Brunswick Museum Archives.

Chapter X
Helen Grant
Grant, Francis W. *Courage Below, White Wings Above*. Hantsport, Nova Scotia: Lancelot Press, 1979.
Druett, Joan. "The Female Chronicles." Log of *Mystic Seaport*, 40:4 (1989).

Eliza Frame, Navigation
Spicer, Stanley T. *Masters of Sail*. Toronto: Ryerson Press, 1968.

Bessie Hall
Campbell, Catherine H. "Bessie Hall, Master Mariner." *Nova Scotia Historical Review* 7:2 (1987).

Chapter XI
Grace Ladd
"Letters of Grace Ladd." Yarmouth, Nova Scotia: Yarmouth County Museum Archives.

Kathryn Ladd
Prosser, Ingrid. "A Social History of K." Unpublished manuscript. Yarmouth, Nova Scotia: Yarmouth County Museum Archives.

Chapters XIII and XIV
Cora Hilton, Captain Arthur Hilton
Reminiscences, diaries, and letters of Cora and Captain Arthur Hilton. Collected by Marion Hilton. Transcribed by Julie Hilton Marshall. Yarmouth, Nova Scotia: Yarmouth County Museum Archives.

Chapter XV
Clara Fritz
"Letters of Clara Fritz." Saint John, New Brunswick: New Brunswick Museum Archives.

Windjammers
Villiers, A. J. *The War with Cape Horn*. London: Hodder & Stoughton, 1971.
Randier, Jean. *Men and Ships Around Cape Horn*. New York: David McKay and Company Inc., 1966.

Inness and Schooners
Parker, John P. *Sails of the Maritimes: The Story of the Three-and-Four-Masted Cargo Schooners of Atlantic Canada, 1859-1929*. Toronto: McGraw Hill Ryerson, 1960.

Ruby de Cloux
Villiers, Alan John. *Last of the Wind Ships*. New York: William Morrow, 1934.

Annette (Brock) Davis
Davis, Annette Brock. *My Year Before the Mast*. Toronto: Hounslow Press, 1999.

Ann Stanley Moss
Greenhill, Basil and Ann Gifford. *Women Under Sail*. Newton Abbot, England: David & Charles, 1970.

Molly Kool
"Molly Kool." *Halifax Herald*, 10 March (1938). *Atlantic Advocate*, August (1941).
Nelson, Charlene. "A Pioneer." *Kings County Record*, June (1992).

INDEX